*What MORE Would You
Like to Know
About the Church?*

Answers by
Father Kenneth Ryan

Carillon Books

WHAT MORE WOULD YOU LIKE TO KNOW ABOUT THE CHURCH?

A CARILLON BOOK
Carillon Books edition published 1978

ISBN: 0-89310-043-9 — Hardcover
        0-89310-044-7 — Papercover

Library of Congress Catalog Card Number: 78-59318

Printed in the United States of America

CARILLON BOOKS is a division of
Catholic Digest
2115 Summit Avenue
St. Paul, Minnesota 55105
U.S.A.

NIHIL OBSTAT   David A. Dillon
                        Censor Librorum/Deputatus
                        June 12, 1978

IMPRIMATUR   †John R. Roach
                        Archbishop of St. Paul and Minneapolis
                        June 14, 1978

Contents

Foreword

A quick look at the table of contents of this book may not bring any surprises. The general subjects are those which must be covered in any work on Catholic doctrine and practice. If this volume has any claim to distinction it will be in the colloquial questions readers have asked of the Catholic Digest over the last few years. The readers are real persons who have problems in living out their faith, persons with real interest in their Church and the changes which have recently come over it.

If the answers have any validity in these present times it will be because the questions are honest. People who for most of their lives were accustomed to be passive in religious matters have been jolted out of their complacency by the dreadful moral crises of our present society such as abortion, divorce, political and religious anarchy. They seem to be saying they didn't listen so carefully back in the old quiet days when the Church through sermons and encyclicals was quietly and steadily — to the point of boredom for a good many — explaining why the Church was what it was and why it taught what it did.

Now they live in a world where people they know personally favor abortion, abandon sexual morality and make a religion out of trouble-making. It is the time and there is the need for a review of every single issue on which the Church opposes her enemies.

The average reader doesn't ask philosophical questions or name philosophers, he generally asks about something that has happened to him, something he has heard, something that concerned the daily practice of his faith. The answers, on the contrary, cannot always be on such an everyday level. If they are to be adequate they sometimes have to drag in Marx and Marxism and spell out names like Camus, Sartre and Schleiermacher. They have to tell the inquirer more than he cares to know, in the sense that they may require his study, but at all costs they have to give him more than the simple Yes or No which was enough of an answer in the old pre-Vatican II days.

The Sign of the Cross

Beginning prayers and even athletic activities with the Sign of the Cross pretty well identifies the Catholic. Widespread as the Sign is in present-day use, it has declined as a symbol of Christianity since its universal use by the early followers of Christ. Perhaps if people knew more about its origin and development they would use it oftener and more publicly than they are now inclined to do. The western world seems to be moving back toward the pagan state it was in before the coming of the faith and any outward, open profession of that faith in public, such as the Sign of the Cross, is becoming not only rarer but apparently odder. Yet the spoken Sign is the best teaching tool the Church has, a kind of compendium of the basic truths Christians adhere to, the rallying cry most often heard over the centuries. People should ask and learn what it is all about.

THE QUESTION:

I am the mother of three, a grandmother to two, and the wife of a convert. I can still remember that when I was a young child, our father would gather about four or five of his brood of nine together each Sunday night, and we learned to say our prayers in his native tongue. He came to the U.S. from Czechoslovakia as a young boy. He had a great allegiance to his new country, an unusually deep respect for the American flag. But he also wanted his children to share his religious traditions, and we looked forward to this time together.

We were always taught to address our Lord with the Sign of the Cross. Today, it's my way of saying: "God our Father, I would like a few words with You." Can you tell us how the Sign of the Cross originated?

Mary Hall

THE ANSWER:

Like many obvious and commonplace things in the Catholic Church, Mary, the Sign of the Cross has changed over the years. Nevertheless, it has ancient and even divine origin. The words we use, "In the Name of the Father, Son, and Holy Spirit," are a quotation from our Lord, and the cross was his own choice of an instrument for his death and sacrifice.

In the early centuries, the times of persecution, the Sign was an identifying mark of the Christian. Significantly, I think, heretical sects, in breaking away from the Catholic faith, gave up the Sign. What I'm driving at is that even today when you see a boxer or a golfer make the Sign of the Cross before a round or a putt, you may have the opinion that the athlete is acting out of superstition, but even so you can be pretty certain that he was "brought up a Catholic."

You, Mary, certainly do not need to be told what we mean by the "Sign of the Cross", but since many who read this answer will not know exactly what we are talking about, let me specify. The old Baltimore catechism included a question on how to make the Sign. The answer was, "We make the Sign of the Cross by putting the right hand to the forehead, then on the breast, and then to the left and right shoulders, saying, *In the Name of the Father, and of the Son, and of the Holy Ghost, Amen."* Of course, *Ghost* has now been modernized to *Spirit.* At Baptism, Confirmation, and the other Sacraments, and at Mass, the Sign may be made otherwise; a small cross made with the thumb of the priest baptizing or the bishop confirming on the forehead of the recipient, or at Mass a medium-sized cross made by the priest in the air over the gifts of bread and wine and so on.

Now this Baltimore catechism form of the Sign is relatively recent and even local. Other forms have been used and are still used in various countries. Changes have been made since the time of the first Christians. If you want to be thoroughly scholarly about the subject, as Father Herbert Thurston was in his book *Familiar Prayers,* you can go back before the first Christians to Old Testament times. Ezechiel, the prophet, was told by God to "make a T" on the foreheads of the good people of Jerusalem. From the circumstance that a carelessly made *T* could look like a cross and the Cross itself may have been in the shape of a *T,* spiritual writers have seen a foreshadowing of the Sign of the Cross in this passage.

In pre-Christian times slaves often bore a permanent mark of their owners on their foreheads. There were also groups of religious devotees who would mark themselves in the same way to symbolize their devotion to some pagan god or other. So it was only natural for the first Christians to use a sign to identify themselves. Tertullian (A.D. 200) wrote, "whenever we come in or go out, in dressing or in putting on our shoes, at the bath, at the table, at the lighting of the lamps, in going to rest, in sitting down, whatever employment occupies us, we mark our foreheads with the Sign of the Cross." So we know that the rather elaborate and formal Sign of the Baltimore catechism had its beginning in this smaller but much more frequently used Sign on only the forehead. Scores of writers of the first four Christian centuries are as clear as Tertullian in demonstrating the widespread use of the Sign, but perhaps the best testimony of all is in the fact that the infamous emperor, Julian the Apostate, was several times observed making the Sign in moments of peril.

Julian, and others of his time, made the small Sign on his forehead, but when the persecutions were over Christians began to make the Sign more conspicuously.

It is certainly safe to assume that this small sign on the forehead was made, as would be easiest, with the thumb. The first variation of this form, as we learn from legends of the saints, was to make the Sign with one finger. Bishop Donatus "made the Sign of the Cross with his finger in the air and spat on the dragon." Bishop Julian "made the Sign of the Cross with his finger three times over a poisoned chalice, drank it, and came to no harm." A certain servant of God, Martyrius, made the Sign of the Cross with his finger over some loaves of bread which the baker had forgotten to mark with the cross. Though the loaves were in the oven at the time, they came out properly marked. I don't, of course, quote these legends to prove the efficacy of the Sign of the Cross, but only to show that at one time it was ordinarily made with one finger.

It may sound utterly ridiculous that the next step was the use of two fingers, but true Christians did make the Sign of the Cross with two fingers to combat the teachings of certain 7th- and 8th-century heretics. The Monophysites held that there was only one nature in Christ, whereas the Catholic doctrine was that there were in Him both the nature of God and the nature of man. A good many of the true Christians began to use two fingers in making the Sign so as to profess their faith in the Catholic doctrine. There is some evidence that the Monophysites continued the use of the single finger to express their own belief. Finger signs to indicate particular beliefs had been used in earlier times. St. Cecilia, for instance, when disinterred in the catacombs, was found to have three fingers of her right hand extended. This was hailed in legend as testimony to her belief in the doctrine of the Trinity, three Persons in one God.

It was probably the use of the two-finger Sign that led to the making of a larger Cross. If you wanted to profess your belief you would make sure that the number of fingers was evident to anyone watching you and you would use a greater movement than that required to make a small cross on the forehead.

It also is probable that our present large Sign of the Cross had its origin (like the two fingers against the Monophysites) in an effort to express doctrine through a gesture. A Spanish bishop of the 13th century explains that in his time the progress of the right hand in making the Sign of the Cross represented the progress of Christ. He went from heaven (the forehead) to the breast (down to earth), to the right hand of the Father (right shoulder), by way of hell (which would have to be the left shoulder). This bishop's teaching also was used in a perennial controversy as to whether one touched the right or left shoulder first. Understanding the arguments is complicated by the fact that the speaker did not always make clear whether he was blessing himself or blessing some other person or thing. *Right* and *left* would be terms of interchangeable meaning, depending on which of the two persons facing each other was used as the reference.

It sounds like a silly argument, but of course in theological circles nothing is silly or even unimportant. All the Churches of the Eastern rites go from the right shoulder to the left in making the Sign of the Cross.

As to the different ways of making Sign, Mary, I don't know how much up-dating there has been in Spain, but the pre-Vatican II catechisms there prescribed that first one makes a small Sign on the forehead, lips and breast (as we used to do at the beginning of the Gospel at Mass). Then with two fingers (we know why — to confute the Monophysites), the large cross as the Baltimore catechism prescribes except that the hand goes lower than the breast, to the region where the womb would be in a woman, to indicate the coming of Christ to the body of the Blessed Mother Mary. Finally, a little cross is made by crossing the thumb and index finger of the right hand which one then kisses. The words for the first three little crosses are "By the Sign of the Holy Cross, deliver us, O God, from our enemies." The words that go with the large cross are the same as we use. The cathechisms distinguish the three little crosses from the large cross by calling the former 'signing oneself' and the latter, 'blessing onself.'

Since it is basically a form of prayer and devotion, Mary, the Sign of the Cross has not been the subject of much legislation. Such national local variations are permitted and even in the official liturgy of the Church the words accompanying the gestures are not always the same. The Sign evolved from the inconspicuous, almost secret sign of the early persecuted Christians, to the more elaborate procedures of the Spanish and Baltimore catechisms. There was even, in 13th-century Spain, a custom of making the cross from forehead to chin to cheekbone to cheekbone (whether from the left to right or vice versa, no one now knows).

Your father was certainly right, Mary, in handing on to you his reverence for the Sign of the Cross. In its wording, "In the Name of the Father and the Son and the Holy Spirit," it proclaims our belief in the most basic of all doctrines, the Trinity; in its gestures it proclaims our belief in everything the Cross means — Christ is our Brother in suffering, our Redeemer from sin, our Model of patience — as well as our belief that Christ came from heaven to earth, descended to hell, and went back to heaven.

The Sign of the Cross is a profession of faith because it is visible and intelligible. We should use it publicly (say Grace in the restaurant as well as at home) as a witness that we are practicing Catholics. A present threat to the Church is the tendency to fade away as a visible distinct organization (eat meat on Friday like everybody else, go to Mass on Saturday so you can ski or golf on Sunday like everybody else). If the Church is really only an antinomian (that means no regulations, no rules, no laws) religion-debating society we have no need to a symbol such as the Sign of the Cross. If the Church is a visible organization of human beings established by Christ, all experience of human history points to the fact that we need a rallying symbol. The rest of Western Christianity has ceased to use the Sign of the Cross as such a symbol, so its use now will mark you plainly as a Catholic.

Personally, Mary, I believe there is much truth in legends. Constantine, the first Christian Emperor of Rome, according to legend, had a vision of the Cross, complete with an inscription: *In Hoc Signo Vinces* (In this Sign you will conquer). He did conquer and in that Sign. I think we too can conquer under that Sign not only the world, the flesh, and the devil, but maybe gain incidental victories over false ecumenism, situation ethics, secularism, fetus-murderers, and second thoughts in general.

Meat on Friday

Nearly all religious organizations give moral values to observances which do not in themselves have moral value. The Muslim kneels and faces Mecca three times a day, the Catholic at one time could not eat meat on Friday. Now he can, except for Good Friday. It would seem that both Mohammed and the Catholic Church are proclaiming that sin against their decrees is sin against God. The simple searcher after truth has the right to ask whether God honors the sanctions of mere men guiding churches. Are there people in hell now for eating meat on Friday when there is no longer even a law against it? The question only seems to be a joking one, it can be answered.

THE QUESTION:

When I was younger I was taught that it was a mortal sin to eat meat on Fridays, and that if a person died with such a grievous sin on his soul it meant instant Hell.

I don't write this question to make fun but now that the Church has changed the no-meat law, does it seem fair for souls that committed this sin to be damned for something which is perfectly acceptable now?

Dixie Lee Souza

THE ANSWER:

Come to think of it, it doesn't. But I don't want to make fun, either, Dixie. Your question and your conclusion that God and the Church are unfair are logical — but only on your premises, some of which are not written out in full in your letter.

Just to get in the right frame of mind let me start my answer with a story, a true one from my long past youth about premises and logic. Our eighth-grade teaching Sister had explained that on the upcoming All Souls Day, we children could gain some very special indulgences for the Pour Souls in Purgatory. We understood, as I think few grade-school kids would now, what these "plenary indulgences" meant: if you gained the indulgence for one of the Poor Souls, he or she would be released from Purgatory and would enter Heaven. To gain the indulgence Sister told us about, you had to visit a church on the day called the "Commemoration of All Souls", say six *Our Father's*, six *Hail Mary's* and six times "Eternal rest grant unto them O Lord . . ." with its response. The point of this anecdote is that this indulgence was a *Toties Quoties,* which meant that every time you fulfilled the conditions you could gain the indulgence for a additional soul in Purgatory.

We must have had a really wonderful teacher because three of us boy-pupils, just out of school on a beautiful football afternoon went first to the church, said the prayers, though with football distractions, and hurried out. However, once outside, it seemed to occur to all three of us at once that we could get three more people out of Purgatory by going back in and saying the prayers again. We did, and coming out the second time, Wally, the oldest and most serious of our trio, said, "Gee, just think of the poor guy next in line!" Well, we went back in again, but at the third exit, Morrie, the youngest and most unprincipled, showed that he must have been unduly distracted in his prayers by telling us how late we would be for football if we kept on gaining indulgences.

Now, Dixie, there is a connection between that story and your letter. On our own kind of logic, on our own premises, we should have kept going in and out of the church until the *Toties Quoties* expired at midnight. But common sense came to the rescue. Applying more common sense will involve checking out what the Church intended by the *Toties Quoties* and what the Church intended by forbidding meat on Fridays. Checking out these "premises" will change the seemingly logical conclusions.

It was never true that "If you eat meat on Friday, you are *automatically* consigned to hell." Nor was it ever true if someone said the prescribed indulgenced prayers for you you went *automatically* from Purgatory to Heaven. There are so many conditions attached to one's attaining Heaven or being plunged into Hell that listing them in full would require a review of almost all human knowledge, revealed or unrevealed, and certainly all of moral theology and human psychology.

Just for openers, to go to hell for eating meat on Fridays in the old days, would, according to the catechism, require that the eating be done after "sufficient reflection and full consent of the will." To children "sufficient reflection" usually meant only that the eater had not forgotten it was Friday. To the investigative theologian it brings the need of considering whether the eater was subject to the law, was he Catholic, did he live in a country where the law had been promulgated, did his mental state permit him to make responsible decisions, did he live in a place where the law was habitually disregarded, was he well-instructed in his Faith, and so on for pages and pages before a sound, unassailable decision about the sufficiency of the eater's reflection could be honestly made. "Full consent of the will" to the child meant something like deciding to eat the meat "anyway;" the theologian would have to investigate things like the eater's heredity, the extent of his hunger, the possibility of social pressures at a formal dinner, the availability of alternate foods, again so on to the point of seeming absurdity. All this would be a theologian deciding after the fact whether the act of eating meat had been a mortal sin. How many people in history went to all the trouble and THEN ate meat on Friday "anyway" has never been decided. The Church proclaims some persons to be saints in heaven but not even Judas has been formally proclaimed to be in hell.

What the Church does proclaim in making a law like Friday abstinence is that obedience will show a love of God and devotion to the Church. That is the purpose of the law; it is not the purpose of the law to set up a new way of sinning.

But it is still possible to commit mortal sin by disobeying a law of the Church. As we just saw, there are many considerations to be made before a theologian can assert that a sin was even objectively mortal, but you cannot deny that mortal sin is possible, objectively and subjectively, unless you want to deny that man has free will. If you don't believe in that, there is no sense or logic in trying to be good or religious.

Now, if you admit you have free will, you have to realize that the number of ways you can sin is limited only by your imagination. Even a slight insulting gesture, if you formally give it the meaning of "blasphemy" can be a mortal sin. The old example in the theology manuals was that of a man firing a gun toward the sky at God. I doubt that any sane man ever chose this way of turning away from God, but you can't deny the *possibility* of such a mortal sin. You see, all mortal sin is something like the sin of Lucifer, later known as Satan. It's all a matter of pride, prefering your will to that of God. The particular means you choose to express this preference can be murder, adultery, apostasy, firing a gun at God, or just (until

the law was changed) eating meat on Friday. Persons conceivably in Hell for having eaten meat on Friday are not being
kept there unfairly now that the law has been changed because
their act was only one of many they might have chosen to turn
away from God. If they are in hell now it is because they chose
to turn away from God.

I hope, Dixie, I am getting the point across that God and the
Church do not arbitrarily set up a list of "Thou Shalt Not's" or
"Thou Shalt's" and automatically punish those who transgress.
That is not true, persons in hell are there through their own free
will. The Commandments of God are based on the normal
operation of sound reason in human beings; the Precepts of the
Church are based on its desire to have its members show more
love and obedience to the laws of God and his Church than
they do to the abstract rules of ethics that bind all human
persons, in or out of the Church. Neither set of rules was set up
just to see whether you or I would obey them, or so that
punishment could be given us if we did not. The Commandments of God can't be changed, the Precepts of the Church can,
but whatever they are, it is the will and intention of the sinner in
addition to the specifics of the precept (Friday, meat, Sunday,
Mass, Communion once a year, etc.) that bring about the
commission of mortal sin.

To get back to the *Toties Quoties* incident, Dixie, I think
that Morrie, who decided to play football, understood the
Church better than we two older boys. The Pope who granted
that indulgence never intended that the full 24-hour period
should be employed entirely and mechanically in getting souls
out of Purgatory. He did intend to make it possible for
Catholics to gain more than one plenary indulgence in one day,
which was the maximum under the law then prevalent. He
might have been thinking of persons who had several equally
dear deceased parents, relatives or friends. Anyway, it was a
human thought conceived a charity not a spiritual-mathematical
arrangement to bail as many as possible souls out of Purgatory, as we boys (on our mistaken premises) thought it must be.

In bringing this subject of indulgences to my mind, Dixie,

you are in good company. Francis Thompson, the famous Catholic poet writes, "There is no expeditious road / To pack and label men for God / And save them by the barrel-load." Just as the theologians would have to investigate the remote corners of the Friday meat-eater's mind before they could say he committed a mortal sin, so also the theologians explain that indulgences require good "dispositions" on the part of everyone involved. Plenary indulgences require plenary amounts of charity, good will and devotion. There is nothing automatic about them.

Over the years the Church has had such difficulty explaining its doctrine of indulgences that they have officially become a much less prominent part of Catholic devotion than they were in my eighth-grade days. It's too bad in a way, because there is nothing wrong with the doctrine except that so many people misunderstand and misinterpret it.

So, we don't have much talk of indulgences anymore and we can eat all the meat we want on Fridays. The present mind of many Catholic lawmakers and people is evidently that there are better ways than indulgences and Friday abstinence to attain the purposes for which indulgencing and abstaining were instituted in the first place.

Maybe there are, but to be sure we will have to wait for the Final Judgment when we will learn also whether our indulgenced prayers "worked" and what persons chose eating meat on Friday to express their utter disdain for God.

Prayer

The fundamental difference between a religious man and one who is not religious is that the first one, at least at some time in his life, prays, the other never does. If you are intelligent and still do not believe in God, it is, indeed, an exercise in futility to go through the motions as the atheists used to do in foxholes. But, as in so many things about religion, misconceptions about prayer are everywhere. In fact, the first task of Christian missionaries in completely pagan countries is to change the habits of the people from magical practices to true prayer. In civilized countries the task of Christian teachers is much the same, they must convince the sophisticated unbelievers that prayer is more than an exercise of magic. Their purpose should be to get unbelievers then to ask something like, "Well, then, what is prayer if it is not magic?"

THE QUESTION:

I was reared in a Catholic home, attending both Catholic grade and high school. Throughout those years I was always taught God will answer your prayers.

Now I am told by a college professor of psychology that I am wasting my time, as no one is going to hear my prayer. He said he shudders every time he sees the postmark "Pray for Peace." If there is going to be peace in this world, it will come through man, he says.

I would appreciate your opinion of such a statement and would like to know more about prayers and praying.

Bernadine

THE ANSWER:

Your request is sweet and reasonable, Bernadine, but it is only seemingly simple. Prayers range from the baby's "Now I lay me down to sleep" through the printed appeal to "Pray for Peace" to the ecstasies of the saintly mystics.

Explaining prayer completely would involve a complete discussion of the nature of God. What most gave me pause at your letter was remembering how I once tried to explain that there was no past or future in God, only *totum simul* (everything at once) and a slow-thinking, frustrated reader sent me three letters about it, the last cancelling his subscription.

If your professor believes in God but not in prayer it would be something like this absolute unchangeability in God that keeps him from prayer. If he *is* a real atheist, prayer is unreasonable. (Remember the atheist dial-a-prayer? Nobody answers the phone.) If he is an agnostic, a person to whom God has not given the gift of faith, he probably has inadequate ideas of what Christian prayer is.

So I call on your patience, Bernadine, to let me go over what may be familiar ground to you, but unexplored territory for him. Christian prayer, like *sacrifice* in the catechism and *religion* in the theology text-book, comprises adoration, thanksgiving, propitiation and petition. In the more appealing terms of Father Lasance's prayer-book (copyright 1910) at Mass we should "Adore till the Gospel / Give thanks till the bell / Till Communion ask pardon / Then all your wants tell." The good Father wrote before the liturgical revolution, of course, and was out of "sync" with the ceremonies but his verses express very clearly what the Mass and good prayer are all about. People without the gift of faith, possibly including your professor, Bernadine, tend to think of our prayer as being *only* petition.

Petition alone, naked and unashamed, is on a level with superstition. It is what some primitive people engage in with magic spells, curses, hexes, and so on. It is a resort to supernatural force only to get something they want, whether good for themselves or evil for others. It even has overtones of devil worship when the petition is for evil to come upon others.

Devout Christians who used to say sententiously during the last war, "There are no atheists is foxholes," were, on reflection, wrong. A man in a state of fear for his life will wish desperately that it may be saved and call that wish a prayer. But unless his plea has some traces of adoration or love of God, and is in admission of dependence in addition to being a raw petition for safety, it is a completely selfish, self-interested act and cannot be called a prayer or an act of religious faith. His fear is just a reenactment of the animal fear of primitive man for the thunderbolt — it wasn't till primitive man thought of some higher personal force as hurling the thunderbolt, that there was any religion or any act of prayer.

So, Bernadine, if the professor thinks that our prayer is only petition, only a wish, or a reaction like that of the atheist under artillery fire, he is right, on his own premises, in rejecting it in favor of positive action. But as his understanding of true prayer improves, he should stop shuddering when people pray for peace — even through postmarks. It's true that postmark prayers, like chain-letter prayers and Buddhist prayer wheels, can easily be put down as superstitions, but any trace of adoration, thanksgiving and propitiation added to their simple petitions can raise them to the rank of prayer.

Even in the lowest pagan religions adoration has a place in prayer. As the place of adoration becomes greater, the religion becomes higher. In the Judaeo-Christian tradition of prayer, disinterested adoring petitions come first, such as the first three in the Lord's prayer, or the "Blessed be God forever" of the Jewish *beraka*. Good Christians and Jews know, and try to explain to others, that there is more to prayer than asking for benefits.

But even if your professor agrees to all this, Bernadine, his further complaint against prayer might be that he doesn't think it gets results. If this discussion was just part of a debate in which one tried to score points, Christians who pray might say that human efforts in the history of the world so far have not brought the peace he talks about. He has had no answer either. He hopes and apparently believes that human efforts can bring peace but that is about the same cast of mind (hope and belief) that people have when they put "Pray for Peace" on their postmarks.

In such a debate the professor's rebuttal might score the same point against prayer, since it hasn't brought world peace, but he again would be speaking out of a misunderstanding of prayer, this time of its purposes. Is the purpose of prayer to get an answer? Well, Yes. But it is not the only purpose and good prayer is not discontinued because there is no perceptible answer.

The problem of unanswered prayer bothers a lot of people, even some from whom you would not expect such a reaction. One time in the *Catholic Digest* we printed a prayer-poem by one of what were then called the "new-breeders." It seemed devout enough and really up-to-the-minute in its spiritual expression, but one of our more conservative readers found it smacking of heresy on the point of unanswered prayer. I don't remember now just how the poem went, but upon reconsideration, we found it true that the author, under the poetic verbiage, really did take God rather severely to task for not entering into spoken dialogue. We said what we could to the irate reader, mentioning among other things Psalm 88, whose complaint verges on despair and our Lord's words from the cross, "Why has Thou abandoned me?" a quotation from Psalm 21. The psalm-writers were not despairing, but they were complaining that their prayers were not being answered. We have to admit that not all prayers are answered. "Of course not," the nuns used to teach us, "You wouldn't give the lighted match to the baby who cried for it, neither does God answer all your prayers." That is still as good a solution as I have heard, but we are dealing here with a professor who denies that even reasonable prayers can get an answer. I think the most we could get out of him would be a kind of statistical admission to the effect that prayers are at least seemingly answered 50% of the time since, on his premises, the same events would take place whether or not prayers were offered for them to happen.

To get down to the level of high-school debate again, we could say that that percentage is about what we could expect from an all-wise God. If He answered all petitions automatically, few would go on to adding adoration, thanksgiving and pleas for forgiveness to their petitions. If He answered no petitions at all, even petitions would cease and of course there would be no adoration, thanksgiving and pleas for forgiveness. By answering half the time, God keeps our prayers good. So there is another answer as to why some, at least, petitions should go unanswered.

But, of course, as all pious people are by this time bursting to tell me, every true prayer *is* answered, not always to the exact specifications of our petition, but equivalently, with grace. Now what keeps this rather easy answer from being only a tasteless sop to disappointed children who don't get to the circus after all, can probably be understood only by a mature, as opposed to a childish, mind.

I do have to go back to the nature of God, even at the risk of a few subscriptions. He is unchangeable, and if you'll pardon me, unswayable. God does not *foresee* the future, He *sees* it, it is present to him, it is not something yet to come as it is with us. With this thought in mind, it is easier to understand why petition is meaningless until it is joined to acts which are independent of time (the past, the present and the future) for their meaning: adoration, thanksgiving, and plea for forgiveness.

This combination is true prayer; true prayer God always answers. The answer is in the request itself, to adore God is our highest destiny. Prayer is its own answer.

But we are all pretty much like little Willie whose prayers did not get him to the circus. And such abstract considerations about time and eternity do not always convince us of the desirability of prayer. We humans are guided by both reason and emotion and there is a bitterness in unanswered prayer. I'm doing a lot of supposing, but I think that that is why God has put a built-in antidote to the bitterness into prayer itself. It is consoling, as everyone who has truly prayed knows. Reconciliation to the will of God increases with the length of our prayer, and granting of material and even spiritual favors becomes of less importance.

There is even a psychological satisfaction in the recital of prayers. I remember being surprised at this. I was in the seminary in the days of the first stirrings of what is now the liturgical reform and was beginning to get disdainful of such devotions as the Nine First Fridays, the Thirteen Tuesdays and saying the Rosary more than once a day. My first appointment as a priest was in the country and I used to get rides into the city from time to time in parishioners' cars. All these good people insisted on reciting rosary after rosary on the way. I joined in, against my inclinations at first, and was amazed that the "old-fashioned" prayer made me "feel good." It was just psychological, certainly, but then it was God who gave that effect to prayer. Transcendental Meditation and various Buddhist procedures have the same effect, so "feeling good" is not why we should pray. Any "feeling" is just a fringe benefit of prayer not by any means a necessary part of it. The necessary part is expression of the love of God, through adoration, thanksgiving, and pleas for forgiveness. When we truly pray we fulfill God's purpose in creating us, our off-and-on adoration of the Almighty here on earth is the beginning of blissful eternal adoration.

So, Bernadine, I think I will begin putting "Pray for Peace" on all the envelopes of my correspondence and let the professor shudder all he wants.

The Four Eucharistic Prayers

Reforms, whether in Church or State, are always difficult to carry out against the inborn resistance to change that so many of us have. Dieticians tell us that we are likely to carry a preference for foods we have eaten as children all through our lives. No chef ever surpasses the pies "that Mother used to make." The prayers, rites and devotions of our childhood are just as likely to be favored by us over the recommendations for other things proferred us by the liturgical experts. But whatever the explanation for our preferences and prejudices there is no denying of the right to ask why changes are made. Take the question "Why do most priests give up saying the old Roman Canon at Mass, even though it is given first place in dignity in the list of new Liturgical Prayers?"

THE QUESTION:

I attend daily Mass and have been disheartened in the past year by the almost constant use of Eucharistic Prayers #2 and #3 in daily as well as Sunday Mass. In my opinion they compare unfavorably with #1, the Roman Canon. When I questioned the pastor about this he said that #1 was used on feast days.

I attended Sunday Mass in another section of the country today and #1 was used. Is there a ruling on which of the Eucharistic Prayers are to be used? Does it depend upon the decision of the bishop of the diocese or what?

Ava

THE ANSWER:

It depends on the decision of the priest "presiding at the Liturgy," who, if he used those terms instead of "saying Mass," may on Sunday be under the collective thumb of his Liturgical Commitee. If he is, its members decide.

Ordinarily, of course, for daily Mass, the priest makes his own choice. In making the choice he has direction but no absolute rules in the General Instructions to be found in the front of the Sacramentary. The Sacramentary is the book the priest reads from in reciting his part of the Mass. It is one of the two volumes which now make up the Missal, the other being the Lectionary containing the readers' parts.

The norms, as they are called, are found in item numbered 322 of the General Instructions. You can't call them rigid rules because they say only that certain choices are "suitable." They point out in regard to Eucharistic Prayer #1 (Roman Canon) that it has alternate passages for use at special times: on Christmas, Epiphany, Holy Thursday, Easter, Ascension and Pentecost. On these feasts #1 is obviously appropriate but the instruction says it may be used any day. Your pastor, Ava, was only half right in saying it was for feasts. It is not reserved to the great feasts.

Eucharistic Prayer #2, the norms say, is suitable for week days and special circumstances because it can be varied by the use of Prefaces other than the one written into it and has a special formula which can be inserted when the Mass is celebrated for the dead.

Eucharistic Prayer #3 "is suited for Sundays and feasts" and also may be used with the special formula for the dead.

Eucharistic Prayer #4 has an unchangeable Preface which is part of the continuing thought of the rest of the Eucharistic Prayer. It is most "suitable for a congregation which has a comparatively good grasp of Scripture." While there is no prohibition in the norms for such a use, this prayer has no formula for the dead and presumably would be unsuitable in Masses for them.

For better understanding, it might be well before going farther to set forth here just what prayers we are talking about. The Vatican Council of 1962-1965 decided on a revision of the ceremonies and prayers of the Roman Mass as established by the Council of Trent some 400 years before. Changes were made very gradually. I think first the "Last Gospel" was dropped, then gestures were changed. Next the Latin canon prayer was spoken aloud instead of secretly, then spoken in English instead of Latin. When the finished new Missal came out all in English even the "core" prayer, the Roman canon, was changed in places and certain omissions could be made at the option of the celebrant.

In this new Missal three newly composed prayers were included, any of which could be substituted for the Council of Trent canon. These four prayers, now called the Eucharistic Prayers, are what we are concerned with.

Ava, since you express a preference for the old Roman Canon, you are very probably among those who ask why any change in it or prayers alternative to it were necessary or even desirable. Its merits were obvious. It had gone unchanged for 400 years and large parts of it are traceable to the 5th and even

4th century. It was in one language for the whole Roman church and gave the world traveler a sense of the Church's universality when he heard the same words in the great cathedrals of Europe and the tiniest missions in rural China. To those who can look back that far there is simply nothing in the new liturgy to compare with the Roman Canon's high point, the Consecration, when that breathless hush came over the kneeling congregation. All coughing, all shuffling, all creaking of pews and providentially even the crying of babies ceased for a few wonderful moments. That awe of the Almighty and the sense of a new Presence of Christ made people love the old Canon in its old setting. The reason we don't ordinarily have the same awe and sense of Presence with the newer canons is that they lack the force of tradition that produced those emotions.

These considerations in favor of the old Canon, which were entertained by the average good Catholic, were reinforced by what the professional liturgist called the "theology of offering." This means that the old canon in its general tone emphasized the idea of sacrifice. The bread and wine were offered first as a symbol of ourselves. God transformed them through his Spirit to the Body and Blood of Christ. We in the Spirit could be thus united to Christ. Then the Body and Blood were offered. The offering of gifts *before* and *after* the consecration brought out this sacrifice-aspect. The Eucharistic celebration was the offering of and by ourselves, of and by Christ, culminating in union with him at the sacrificial meal, (Communion).

Though these concepts were supported by what later turned out to be possibly just an editorial arrangement of the various old Roman prayers, they were valid. And despite the technical terms required to express them soundly, they got through to the average Catholic, which is very likely why the Roman canon survived the liturgical reform.

I say "survived" because the liturgical reformers had had objections to the Roman canon and wrote the others to take its place. Their first objection was to its lack of literary unity. It is indeed a collection of prayers each cut off and separated by the recurring "through Christ our Lord." It is not apparent why one particular prayer follows another. The thought of one prayer does not often lead into the next, nor does it often derive from the prayer just previous. The *anaphoras* (Eucharistic Prayers) of the Eastern churches do not have this defect and are comparatively logical in the progression of the thought.

The puzzle of the composition of the Roman Canon is age-old. Some 50 years ago, Monsignor William Busch, one of the founders of the Liturgical Movement in this country, diagrammed the Roman Canon showing how each prayer *before* the Consecration was balanced by a prayer *after* the Consecration. The two most obvious balancings were the two lists of saints and the intercessions for the living (before) and the dead (after). His diagram went far beyond those two, however, and he finally had it made up with a tree or vine theme into a stained glass window for his home-town church. When the town built a new church the window was placed in the new library of the St. Paul Seminary. His thesis was that someone sometime back in the early centuries had rearranged a more logically flowing prayer into this systematized balance of shorter prayers. Father Busch had no idea changing it all back; after all, a stained glass window is a testimony of love, not disagreement. His reverence for the old canon was of the kind that was considerably upset even at so small a change as Pope John's insertion of St. Joseph into its first list of saints. The Pope did that, in my view, just to show that the canon could be changed. Everyone but the reformers was finding change unthinkable. Father Busch's protest was also part of the effective opposition when the reformers wanted to leave all reference to the Lord's hands out of the English version of the Roman Canon. Happily, one of the former two references remain.

So, Ava, if you prefer the Roman canon to the others you can find good reason and precedent for doing so. The reformers, of course, had other reasons for having other canons. Among them was the monotony of saying the same prayer everyday. There was something to this argument. I remember our professor of liturgy in the seminary giving us some very practical advice. He told us that occasionally no matter how pious we tried to be we would become so distracted during Mass and so automatic in the performance of routine actions that we might sometimes "come to" and not remember how far we had gone in the Mass ceremony. His suggestion was that we than ask the altar boy whether he had rung the bell. According to the boy's response we would know whether we had said the words of Consecration. I once confusedly turned two pages of the Missal at once and found myself in need of this help. But more recollection rather than new canons would seem to be the answer to the monotony argument and the reformers did have better reasons.

During the high excitement of the 60's there were priests so determined on change that they made up (disobediently) their own Mass prayers. It was partly to satisfy them that the new canons were provided. I think the turning point came at one of the unauthorized but advanced liturgical conferences where the adlibbing priest left out all reference to Christ and the words of institution of the Eucharist so that in no way could he have said a valid Mass. The new canons did put a stop to that sort of thing.

So, Ava, I can certainly sympathize with your preference for Liturgical Prayer #1. I love it, but I am sad to hear you are "disheartened" by the use of other canons.

As a matter of fact they are intelligent and beautiful prayers. They follow in their structure the prayers of the Eastern Churches, which are older even than the ancient Roman Canon, in form if not in actual wording. The earliest Mass prayers followed basically the Jewish order of prayer-thought: exclamation of God's goodness, remembrance of what God had done for the Jews, petitions for further favor and a final hymn of praise. The Lord, at the Last Supper, was observing the Jewish Passover worship which followed the order just given above. This general order of thought is what the writers put into the new canons.

The old Roman canon had the four elements but in a less logical order in the view of the new canon writers. In all three of the new canons the order of elements is as follows: 1. Praise to the Father (first of the Jewish elements). 2. First acclamation by the people (Holy, holy, holy). 3. Invocation of the Holy Spirit. 4. Reenactment of the Lord's Supper (corresponding to the Jewish remembrance of God's benefits to them). 5. Memorial acclamation of the people. 6. Memorial prayer of offering. 7. Invocation of the Holy Spirit. 8. Intercessions (corresponding to the Jewish petitions) for the Church and the dead, offered in the union with the Saints. 9. Final doxology (corresponding to the Jewish final hymn of praise).

The additions to the four Jewish elements are of course specifically Christian in that they present the ideas of the Trinity and the divinity of Christ.

The Roman Canon had more emphasis on the idea of sacrifice but that is present in the new canons also. Eucharistic prayers #3 and #4 have the word *sacrifice* in their texts. Eucharistic prayer #2 speaks of Christ's freely accepted death, of the new convenant and the offering, (after the Consecration) of lifegiving bread and the saving cup. Of course, persons suspicious of the intentions of the prayer-writers might see in the avoidance of the word *sacrifice* too overt an effort to counteract the emphasis on sacrifice found in the Roman Canon, but the terms quoted above certainly express the idea of sacrifice in its traditional terms.

In addition to the elements necessary to Christian prayer and sacrifice each of the new canons has a theme. That of #2 is Christ. In addressing the Eternal Father, the prayer thanks him for what Jesus has done for us. In this is follows the thought of Hippolytus, who wrote the prayer on which #2 is based, at the beginning of the 3rd century.

The theme of #3 is the connection between our sacrifice and the working of the Holy Spirit. The memorial prayer following the consecration and its acclamation speaks of "this holy and living sacrifice," "your Church's offering," and "the Victim whose death has reconciled us to yourself." The "praise" section refers to the work of the Spirit in gathering the people for this sacrifice and the communion invocation pleads that we, nourished by the sacrificial meal, may be filled with the Holy Spirit. The theme of #4 is the Blessed Trinity and the world. It reviews salvation history. It is addressed to the Father, takes up the mystery of the Son, considers the extension of the creative power of the Father and the redeeming power of the Son through the operation of the Holy Spirit.

All the new canons were written with consideration for speech rhythm and unambiguous sound in English as well as with great care in translating from the Latin original. There have been some disputes about the translation (the famous "for all men" to translate the Latin *pro multis,* for instance) but nothing has had to be corrected.

Forgive me, Ava, if I see in your letter a gentle protest against the liturgical reform. There are many people who are against it. I would like to suggest that what has displeased them is not the new texts of the Mass, so much as the experiments in liturgical procedures that came with them. The new texts really don't go any better with bongo drums, hand-clapping hymns and high-decibel guitar playing than did the old Roman canon. To such people, perhaps including you, Ava, I would say figure out exactly what it is you don't like. I doubt very much that anyone can dislike the new canons.

The Mother of God

Paradoxes attract attention. Like jokes which depend on the mental agility of the hearer, they often draw the question, "What's that again?" That God, in Christian theology the first cause for the very existence of everything knowable to man, could in any sense be said to have a mother is a statement thought by many to be not only a paradox but an impossibility. So it has to be shown how this paradox comes to us from God's world of mystery, where truths exist that are beyond our understanding. It must also be shown how mysteries of the faith fit into one another, depend upon one another, support one another so that they form a beautiful totality. So beautiful and so total that if you say "Mary is not the Mother of God," you destroy in yourself all that the Christian should believe of God.

THE QUESTION:

As a recent convert to Catholicism and as one interested in learning more about the traditions of my faith, I would like to know how we can say in the Hail Mary, "Holy Mary, Mother of God?" I know of course that Mary is the mother of Jesus, but I have always thought of God as the Eternal Father.

Marcy Caruthers

THE ANSWER:

The learn-it-by-heart answer for both new and old Catholics, Marcy, is in the Baltimore Catechism. Question 71, in Lesson 7 goes, "Is the Blessed Virgin Mary truly the Mother of God?" The answer is, "The Blessed Virgin is truly the Mother of God, because the same Divine Person who is the Son of God is also the Son of the Blessed Virgin Mary."

That is good logic, but like most reasoning in theological matters, it is convincing only if both the questioner and the answerer understand exactly the same things by the terms used in the reasoning. For instance, and as your letter indicates, even the term, *God*.

"Mother of God" in Catholic theology does not mean "mother of the Blessed Trinity" or "mother of the Godhead." A good many persons outside the Church think it does. I get letters less polite than yours every now and then from people who have heard the Catholic expression "Mother of God" and take rather violent exception to it. Others just think I must be a little slow mentally not to see that Mary is only the mother of Jesus, not the mother of God.

But yours is an intelligent question, Marcy. The great minds of antiquity were intrigued by it. Just about every possible angle of this question was studied at the Council of Ephesus (A.D. 431), which pronounced as a dogma of faith just what the Baltimore Catechism says: Mary is the Mother of God.

Nestorius was the man whose doctrines were condemned. He was the patriarch of Constantinople in the days of the Eastern Emperor Theodosius II. Since he was a man of considerable eloquence, it is not beyond possibility that the need to have something to say brought him to attack that title of Mary.

Even his own patriarchal church was named *The Mother of God Cathedral* so he certainly knew what he was doing. But he said he couldn't see how a son could be older than his mother, nor how God could be spoken of as being a baby.

Doubts of this kind come to anyone rather readily, as they evidently do to some of those who write me letters. It is impossible to give them an acceptable answer, much less change their minds, without going into the horizonless background of mystery.

The Trinity, the Incarnation, and the Redemption are mysteries of our Faith. They are *beyond* our reason (but not *against* our reason). You can't tell Nestorius or his present-day followers how it is that a son can be older than his mother, nor how God can be a baby, unless they are willing to listen when you refer to the fundamental mysteries of the Catholic faith.

The reason the Catholic Church is so uncompromising on "Mother of God" is that an attack on the title is an attack on the divine Christ whom true Christians follow. To begin with, Mary is the mother of Jesus. When you call her the Mother of God, you are saying Jesus is God. Unless you say that Jesus is God, you are denying his adequacy as a redeemer, for only a divine redeemer could pay in full for offenses against the divine dignity of Almighty God. The Redeemer's sacrifice had to have an infinite value.

If Christ's sacrifice was only that of a human person and therefore not infinite, we, who have sinned against God's infinite dignity, are not redeemed. If we are not redeemed there is no meaning or purpose in life, except perhaps pleasure and power, so what are we talking about religion for, anyway?

That's a long, somewhat disjointed, but nevertheless logical progression of thought but you have to go through it if you

want to understand why Catholics call Mary the Mother of
God. It doesn't convince everybody who hears it any more than
it would have convinced Nestorius, because, as I said before,
everybody does not agree on the meaning of the terms used in
the argument.

It would seem that every possible meaning was given to every
term by some sect or other. So the theological water gets just a
little deeper at this point: we have to use the terms used in the
5th-century controversies. The chief terms were *person* and
nature. The Catholic doctrine was and is that in Christ there is
one person but two natures, the human and divine. Your
"person" is who you are; your "nature" is what you are.

That seems plain enough but Nestorius didn't seem to have
the same meaning for *person* as the Fathers of the Council. His
preaching allowed the interpretation that there were two
persons, 1. Jesus, and 2. the Son of God, in Christ. Nestorius
repeatedly denied that he believed there were two persons in
Christ so the kindest thing you can say of him is that he
couldn't express himself properly. But you can't dismiss the
whole affair as a quibble because whatever it was he had in
mind, it made him say that Mary was not the Mother of God.

There were at his time others preaching in Greek saying
Mary was only *Anthropotokos*, mother of the man Jesus.
Nestorius thought he was solving a problem by calling her
Christotokos, Mother of Christ, which was a true enough
expression. But the other half of this compromise was to deny
her the title of *Theotokos*, Mother of God, by which she was so
well revered by the people of Ephesus that they rioted in
celebration of the condemnation of Nestorius.

A little more background of the various heresies may help us
understand Nestorius. Those preachers who called Mary,
Anthropotokos, mother of the man, derived their doctrine
from the Arian heresies of the century previous, condemned at
the council of Nicaea. In simplest terms, they did not believe
that Jesus was God. There was an opposite teaching: Jesus was
not really a man, He was the Son of God in a continuing
miracle appearing on earth disguised as a man.

Then there were all the predictable variations: The nature of the Son of God had taken over the nature of the man Jesus Christ, or, there was only one nature in Jesus Christ, or, there were two persons in Christ, in short, a confusion of the terms *person* and *nature*. Generally when the heretics believed in two natures in Christ it seemed necessary to them to believe in two persons; when they believed in one person in Christ, they found it necessary to restrict nature to one.

The outcome was that the Council of Ephesus declared that there were two "whats" (natures) in Christ, but only one "who" (person). This was the only formula which would explain the Incarnation and Redemption. The Redeemer had to be a God (divine) if his sacrifice was to have sufficient worth; He had to be Man (human) if his payment was to be credited to the account of our human race. It was really incidental that this definition verified Mary's title, *Theotokos,* Mother of God; but unless that was a true title the whole Christian faith crumbled to dust.

Nestorius, followed even in this day by opponents of the Church, thought that this title made Mary a goddess. But go back to what we said about *nature* and *person* and remember that the Church never said Mary had more than one nature. That nature was human. She was the mother of a person who had the two natures, human and divine. She could not be the mother of only a human nature as some of the heretics thought; a mother gives birth to a person, not to something abstract like a "nature." The fact that her offspring had the nature of God does not confer divinity on Mary but it does entitle her to be honored as the Mother of God.

Marcy, I have not gone into, nor will I go into, the part of the controversies which concerned how the two natures are united in Christ. The Council settled that, too, by saying it was a hypostatic union, by which was meant a more than physical and a more than moral union. It was, I suppose you could say, a perfect union, the only one of its kind.

At this point, in the unlikely possibility that any reputable theologians are reading this, their protest will be that I have

over-simplified the matter ridiculously; but I know there also
will be complaints in our Catholic Digest Reader's Poll that
such matters are far too involved for people of simple faith to
bother with.

It is true that Nestorius lived more than 1,500 years ago and
it may seem true that to dig around in the old theological
graveyards lacks relevance to our modern problems, but the
modern problems are the old problems.

A high percentage of anti-Catholic prejudice comes historically from opposition to giving Mary the dignity accorded her
by the Council of Ephesus. A Nestorian bishop was one of the
instigators of the Iconoclastic heresy in the 8th century, which
smashed the images of Mary and the Saints. The cathedrals of
England today have empty niches where once statues of the
Virgin stood. In our own time supposedly Catholic theologians, just like Nestorius, feel a need of having something
different to say. They are expressing second thoughts on the
need to believe in the perpetual virginity of Mary, which for
devout Catholics is guaranteed by her title Mother of God.

The present decrease in popular devotions to Mary has been
brought about by people very much like Nestorius. They, too,
are being so careful about what they can believe that they
finally find themselves criticizing traditional doctrine.

Nestorius, as heretics go, was not such a bad fellow and got
rather rough treatment, all in all. Pope Celestine took the side
of St. Cyril, who was the archrival of Nestorius. Nestorius was
anthematized before the whole council had time to convene
which could be one reason he didn't submit. He was deposed by
a change of mind on the part of the feeble emporor who had
made him patriarch in the first place. After his final defeat in
the council he retired to his old monastery in Antioch but
through the zeal of his enemies he was banished to Egypt. He
was captured there by a band of Nubians and came back with
his arm and a rib broken. He returned to monastic life and
started writing again but thought it better to do so under a
pseudonym, Heraclides, since anything by Nestorius would be
subject to unfair treatment. The lot of the fifth-century heretic

was not a happy one, but maybe the lesson of Nestorius for modern theologians is that it all started when he denied that Mary is the Mother of God.

In theological manuals at the ends of chapters there are sometimes tucked in what are called *scholions,* a few paragraphs on subjects which are related to the treatise but not really necessary to its development. Believe it or not, one can be developed on "5th-Century Heretics and the 20th-Century Abortionists." Present day abortionists when they make any pretense at all to moral considerations, deny that what they advocate is murder because the fetus is not yet a "person." Since the fetus is undeniably the beginning of human life, most pro-abortionists would concede only that it has a human "nature." This is really in line with 5th-century heresy. Unless Mary conceived a person and not just a nature there was no true Incarnation at the moment of her conception of Jesus.

A delay of even an infinitesmal period of time between the conception of Jesus and the Son of God becoming Jesus would destroy the God-Man concept on which the Catholic faith bases its doctrine of the Redemption. Such a delay would mean that one of the heretical variations on the doctrine was the truth.

When the U.S. Supreme Court in its theological wisdom implies that the person begins not at conception but three to six months later it is expressing a form of 5th-century heresy. One variation, heard still in these modern times, was that Jesus realized his divinity at his baptism by John and that it was then that He was named and became the Son of God. But whether the "person" is said to begin three to six months after conception as the abortionists maintain, or 30 years after birth as some old and new heretics believe of Jesus, the heresy is the same.

You can't follow that mixture of pseudo-scientific and theologically erroneous ideas and be as logical as the Catholic doctrine of Redemption by the God-Man. To be logical you have to believe that Mary is the Mother of God. (End of scholion.)

Holy Mary, Mother of God, pray for us.

Face-To-Face Confessions

Calling the Sacrament of Penance "Reconciliation" was occasioned by the changing of the ritual of what is still rather generally known as Confession. The provision in the new ritual for the confessor holding his hands over the head of the person confessing implied that the old screen and confessional were no longer necessary. This change, though it was not made obligatory, shook up a lot of people for whom the whispering and general air of privacy seemed an integral part of the sacrament. People who ordinarily took church procedures as they came were moved to inquire into the history of confession and the the rituals associated with it down the centuries. Most Catholics will find spiritual profit in learning the history, because the history embodies the Church's continuing attitude toward sinners and their forgiveness. That has not changed at all.

THE QUESTION:

I am in my 40's, attended a Catholic high school for four years
and Catholic College for one year.

Because I cannot walk without help it has always been rather
difficult for me to utilize a confessional, but recently it has
become all but impossible.

With the coming of the option for face-to-face Confession, I
am grateful but confused. We were taught not to look at the
priest at all during Confession. Now it appears to be permissi-
ble to look at the priest if the penitent chooses to make his
Confession, say, in a small room.

Please explain if, in the beginning, confessions were heard
face-to-face, and when and why the change came about.

Maureen Reiners

THE ANSWER:

I'm sure you knew it all along, Maureen, but for the benefit
of those just tuning in, there was never any obligation on the
handicapped to use the standard confessional for the Sacrament of Penance. There always was, however, for them the
added handicap of having to make special arrangements of
time and place. For many of them the inconvenience may be
removed by the abandonment of the "box" as we know it. The
inference may made from the 1973 rite for the sacrament now
enjoined in the U.S. The celebrant is to extend one or both
hands *over the head* of the penitent while saying the formula of
absolution. With the customary wall and grill between the
confessor and the penitent this would not be possible.

The new rite does not ban the confessional box but the
official directions clearly envision its absence. Of course, a
good many people would rather use the confessional box than
engage in a face-to-face ceremony. They shouldn't worry.
There are enough of them to ensure that in the foreseeable

future the option of using a grill will be everywhere provided.

The requirement of using the confessional box for routine hearing of confessions dates from St. Charles Borromeo, who made it obligatory in his diocese about the year 1500. Why he did it is not related in the ordinary accounts but his action probably had the same reason as your being taught "not to look at the priest." That is, the spirituality of the time regarded inter-personal factors as distractions, possibly morally dangerous.

It is unlikely that St. Charles ordered the use of confessional boxes to put an aura of gloom, tension, or mystery about the ceremony; it is more likely that in an age when the noble families guarded their daughters with duennas and chaperones it seemed only proper etiquette to provide complete privacy for the confession of their sins. In many European churches confessionals are so built that men may kneel directly in front of the priest with no screen intervening, while the women use the standard booth for confession.

At any rate the confessional box seemed such a good idea that its use spread throughout the Church. Since 1918 a fixed grating between confessor and penitent (not a whole confessional) has been required by Canon 909 of the code of Canon Law, though the second paragraph allows the confessions of men to be heard without it.

The official dropping of the law requiring a grating will come, if and when it does come, most probably with the completion of the revision of the code now in process.

Your request, Maureen, for an explanation of whether "in the beginning" confessions were face-to-face, takes us back further in history than St. Charles Borromeo and into the deeper reasons for now calling the rite not "confession" which suggests privacy, but "reconcilation," which suggests a public ceremony.

It seems that the procedure used for the sacrament up to now came from the Celtic, that is to say Scotch and Irish, monks of the 6th and 7th centuries. They apparently didn't like the practice of public penance, which in many jurisdictions was very strict. Some sins in some places could never be forgiven according to the bishops of the places. In other dioceses forgiveness for certain sins could be obtained only on one's deathbed. Penances for grave and public sin in many places routinely lasted for 20 or more years.

In a reaction to this severity the Celtic monks practiced secret confession to each other. Contemplative monks still have a kind of non-sacramental open confession and accusation, to and of each other, of faults committed in observance of their rule of life. It may be that the custom of private confession of deliberate sin against the law of God began with an observance of this kind. At any rate, the priests among the monks (not all were priests) began to exercise the power of the keys and to forgive sins after each confession, in reaction to the severities of the public reconciliation procedures.

Some lay people took up the practice of confessing their sins to one another in imitation of the monk's confession of faults. There was the story told in medieval times of the wife who nearly broke her husband's heart with her confession to him of her infidelity. He properly, though with much effort, forgave her and in turn confessed his own infidelity only to be beaten over the head with a broomstick. The story probably sounded more humorous in the male chauvinist confines of the medieval monastery than it does to us, but there is some kind of a moral there about the values of sacramental secrecy in matters pertaining to sin.

I don't suppose anyone could furnish the details of how the replacement came about, but eventually the verbal confession of sins was made only to priests and privately. My personal guess would be that it was because the public ceremonies of reconciliation concerned only sinners guilty of public apostasy, murder, or adultery, and that people who committed lesser or more private sins also felt the need of individual assurance of forgiveness. Thus the practice of secret person-to-person confession was assimilated into the ritual of the sacrament.

In those early times there was no possibility of Rome decreeing, as it can now with modern communications, that on such and such a date the ritual would be changed. It was certainly a gradual change and it was motivated by the *sensus fidelium,* a kind of general agreement prevading the whole Church.

St. Augustine (400 A.D.) pleaded that the grave sins not publicly known be forgiven through a rite of private penance. Pope Gregory the Great promoted Augustine's teachings. Saints Ambrose and Jerome, though they were confuting the rigoristic Novatians and were not speaking of the Celtic monks, defended the practice of priests privately exercising the power of the keys, customarily exercised in their time only by the bishop in public ceremony.

As to whether confessions during this time, to get back to your precise question, Maureen, were face-to-face or through a grill or curtain — who knows? The logical presumption would be that such use would depend on how much privacy was desired. Probably the use of screens increased up to the time of St. Charles Borromeo, who certainly was not introducing anything newfangled when he prescribed the use of the confessional box. He received no opposition.

We saw that instead of *Confession* the name *Reconcilation* is now preferred for the rite of the Sacrament of Penance. (The name of the Sacrament of Penance has not been changed, only the name of its ritual.) *Confession* would not be an accurate name for the rite in the early centuries either, since the sins forgiven publicly were already known to the public and there was no need to confess them in the public ritual itself. Probably, before anyone took part in the public ceremony, he made arrangements with the bishop and established his need for absolution by a confession of sin ahead of time. But the public ceremony then would be a reconciliation rather than a confession.

You see, Maureen, we are used to combining the four parts of the sacrament into one. The parts are contrition, confession, an act of penance (satisfaction), and absolution. In the earliest days of the Church the absolution in the public ceremony always came after the other three, often years later, only then completing the reconciliation of the sinner with the Church. In later times, including our own, the act of penance, usually the recitation of specified prayers (five *Our Father's* or ten Hail Mary's), was the last of the four parts to be performed.

The 1973 rite allows even the confession of sins to be the last of the four parts under certain conditions. Soldiers, for instance, who may at any moment be called to battle, may be absolved upon expression of sorrow and may defer the confession part of the sacrament. In mission teritories the visiting priest who has no time to hear many confessions may give general absolution upon hearing the penitents recite an act of contrition. The deferring at such ceremonies of spoken confession of sins is perhaps the source of the mistaken idea that the Church may do away with the confession of specific sins, whether face-to-face or through a grill. But all the Church has done is allow one of the four parts of the sacrament to come last in certain specified cases.

Involved here is the circumstance that Christ, in giving the Apostles power to forgive sins, spoke also of "retaining" sins. The Apostles evidently would have to make a judgment in individual cases as to whether the penitent was worthy, through his contrition and promise of penance-works, of being forgiven. No judgment could be made if the Apostles heard no personal statements of contrition and promise of amendment.

Accordingly, the new rite requires that those who receive absolution in a general ceremony (soldiers, mission parishio-ers, etc.) must confess mortal sins specifically later whenever they can possibly do so. The precept of *confession,* once a year for those who have committed mortal sin, is still in force even though absolution has been obtained. And presumably the confessor can declare that the sacrament was unworthily received, should the deferred confession reveal defects in intentions or resolution.

Though by this time it may not seem so, Maureen, all this has something to do with your question about face-to-face confession and looking at the priest. Others will find much greater trouble than you say you will in giving up the privacy and secrecy of identity afforded by the confessional box. The new rite includes a part-way, built-in solution. The changes in the rite for the Sacrament of Penance were made to rescue the sacrament from becoming only a kind of private devotion rather than a public reconciliation with God. Strictly speaking, persons with only venial sins do not need reconciliation with God; they have not turned all the way away from Him.

Accordingly, the instructions for the new rite of Penance include directions for a penitential celebration which is not a conferring of the sacrament, but a set of ceremonies proposed in the hope of restoring to the people of today something of the fervor the early Christians must have had in submitting to the public reconciliations. The ceremonies are compounded of prayers and readings from Scripture and I think it is fair to say they are intended to replace the "confessions of devotion" popular until very recent times, in which the penitent had no grievous sins, only venial sins or only already-forgiven mortal sins, to tell. It has always been the doctrine of the church that venial sins could be forgiven by any good works and prayers, so there is no break here with the past.

For those not in mortal sin, actual graces corresponding to those received though sacramental confession of venial sins can be gained by attendance at the new penitential celebrations. For the handicapped, like yourself, Maureen, who formerly had to make special appointments with the priest because they could not use the customary confessional, attendance at such a ceremony can be as comforting as, and far more convenient than, using the confessional box, and incidentally the whole question of grating vs. face-to-face disappears.

Another way of understanding the new penitential celebrations would be to see them as efforts by the Church to keep alive the spirit of contrition while deferring all four of the parts of the Sacrament of Penance till the time when mortal sin makes reconciliation necessary.

PRIVATE REVELATION

People who claim to have had visions and seen messengers from the other world have always been with us. They get scorn, indifference or fanatical followings in about equal measure. Since the Christian faith is itself based on revelations from on high in the person of Christ and since the scriptures are filled with narratives of God's messengers speaking to living human beings, questions arise for people who believe in the supernatural. Who can they believe? What must they believe? The world of science for the most part devotes itself to explaining on natural grounds things that seem to many people unquestionably supernatural. What does the intelligent Christian do to solve such dilemmas?

THE QUESTION:

I've found your question and answer section helpful when I try to explain Catholicism to non-Catholic friends. It also helps my husband and me get over what seem to be new hurdles being set up in the Catholic Church. Don is a convert to Catholicism, baptized a month before our first child was born. We have three "natural children, 8, 6 and 3, and a foster child, age 2. (She is our third foster child.) I was born and reared a Catholic.

Among my best memories of the parochial school are the stories the nuns used to tell us about the saints. After 15 years, these still haunt me, particulary the "letter" story where Mary gave the three children a letter which was not supposed to be opened until 1960. (Two of the childred died but the third and oldest became a nun.) I vaguely remember that the Pope at that time decided *not* to read it. Why? Exactly what is the mystery behind this letter? I am curious! Maybe you can shed a little light on the matter.

Mrs. Kathy Ishmael

THE ANSWER:

The latest I heard is that the letter was deposited in the Vatican archives after having been given to the Pope by the Bishop of Leiria, who got it from the surviving child, Lucy. I hadn't heard that the Pope had not read it, and am just as curious as you are about what was in it. It is generally known as the third secret of Fatima, the first two having been disclosed in the published writings of Lucy. If it really is a dictation from the Blessed Mother herself it is probably just an exhortation to pray more and do more good in the world. That content would disappoint persons who are looking for specific revelations from on high about such things as the end of the world, the final battle with Communism, or imminent natural and political catastrophes. Offhand I would say that if it had any predictions of that nature in it, there would be doubt that it really came from the Blessed Mother and that is the reason the Pope (who must then have read it) buried it in the archives.

Now for the benefit of those who have just tuned in, I must give some further background. In presenting it I have the choice of repeatedly saying "Lucy said ... " and giving you the impression that I don't believe what she said, or I can relate it all in historical form with flat statements that the "Blessed Virgin appeared and spoke to Lucy" and give you the impression that I am a firm believer. Just now I don't want to give you either of these impressions so read the following with both my reservations in mind.

In the spring of 1916 three children, Lucy Santos, nine years old and her cousins, Jacinto and Francisco Marto, aged six and eight, were living in Aljustrel, a small village near Fatima, Portugal. Their usual occupation was to watch over the sheep owned by their families. During that year they had three visions of an angel, who taught them a prayer to say and at his last visit gave them Holy Communion. A glorious Lady appeared to them May 13, 1917, and told them she would return on th 13th of each month until October. Lucy, against the agreement the children had made among themselves, did not keep quiet and told the family. She was not believed. But on the festival of the local patron, St. Anthony, June 13, the children went off to keep their appointment with the Lady. As they recited the Rosary, there was a flash of lightning and the Lady appeared again. The small crowd of curious people who had followed them saw the lightning and could see that the children were in ecstasy but could not see the Lady.

July 13, there were 5,000 people there, when the Lady appeared to the children. August 13, the children were kidnapped and put in jail by the mayor of Fatima at the instigation of Portugal's anticlerical government. They were soon released, with their story unchanged by his threats and August 19 the Lady appeared to them at a different place, Valhinos, where there was no crowd.

September 13, 30,000 people assembled at Cova da Iria, where the first apparitions had occurred. The Lady appeared to the children and promised them a great miracle for October 13.

October 13, 70,000 were there and at noon the lightning flashed and the children saw both Christ and Mary in their vision. No one else saw anything until the clouds parted, the sun shone brightly, changed colors and appeared to all to be spinning and plunging to earth.

In the course of the visions, the Blessed Virgin gave the children special prayers to say, said that the younger children would die soon but that Lucy must live to spread devotion to the Immaculate Heart of Mary, requested a daily Rosary and prayers for peace, foretold the World War of 1939-45 and the rise of atheistic Communism, told the children they would suffer and asked that a chapel be built at Cova da Iria.

Francisco died in 1919, Jacinta in 1920. The content of the visions we know only from still-living (Sept. 1978) Lucy but there were thousands of witnesses to the fact that the children were ecstatic, that the lightning flashes preceded the ecstasies and that the crowd of 70,000 reacted in terror to the appearance of the sun.

Now the Fatima devotion arose from these events. Like that of countless other shrines of the Blessed Virgin, (Lourdes, Guadaloupe), it is based on a "private" revelation. In Catholicism, this expression means that God spoke either directly or through an appearance of the Blessed Virgin or an angel to some person or persons with specific instructions to announce his will in some particular matter — a church is to be erected in a designated place or certain forms of prayer and devotions are to be proclaimed. The person receiving the instruction is seldom one having any authority in the Church and the guidance he or she gets must not be confused with the guidance the Holy Spirit gives the Pope and councils in dogmatic matters.

This "private" revelation does not have the importance of God's "public" revelation which began with his speaking to

Adam, continued through the Jewish religion and its true prophets, culminated in the Incarnation of the Son of God and his preaching and example here on earth, and ceased with the death of the last of his Apostles. This cut-off date is essential to an understanding of the difference between public and private revelation.

The cut-off date means that you do not *have* to accept the claims of anyone after that date to the effect that he or she has a direct line of communication with God.

So your husband, Don, when he joined the Church, would not have had to express belief in the Fatima story as a condition of joining. It is only a "private" revelation and need not be accepted as the Bible and the teaching of Christ must be. Christ gave his own authority to his Church, so that now the Church passes final judgment on all such revelations. The trouble with some of the believers in private revelations is that they insist that their doctrine is an integral part of the Church's teaching and must be accepted. That is not true and it's a good thing because thousands of mutually contradicting visionaries have one idea in common — that people must believe them because their words are the words of God.

You can find all the classic examples of deranged and self-deluded visionaries in Ronald Knox's book *Enthusiasm.* He points out that a good many of them end up identifying themselves with God, claiming his divinity for themselves.

The cut-off date we mentioned protects us against most of the present day claimants to such special lines of communication with God. If a doctrine wasn't contained in the deposit of faith made before the death of the last living Apostle of the Lord we need pay no attention to it. Men of great minds, like Cardinal Newman, have shown in what sense we can accept development of doctrines within the deposit of faith and the discovery of deeper meanings and modern applications. But anyone proposing doctrines contrary to those in the deposit of faith is by definition in error no matter how strongly he felt the inspiration of the divine within himself or what visions he saw. So the Church, as we said, does often pass judgment of the claims of person who have, or think they have, received private revelations.

Now here is the point of everything I have to say. This judgment of the Church is based on the outward results of the publication of the revelations. In the case of Fatima, Lourdes and Guadaloupe the results have been a flood of grace. Acts of charity, worship and prayer have multiplied in what has been itself a statistical miracle. You don't have to believe in them, but promised miracles have come off on schedule, things like the *creation* of bone tissue have occurred and spiritual miracles of conscience, resignation and conversion are beyond estimate. The Church approves private revelations which have such results by establishing liturgical feasts, approving indulgenced prayers and by Papal blessings or Papal visits to the shrines. What would be the final approval, the requirement of belief in the original visionary, is never given, because all this happened after the death of the last living Apostle of the Lord.

So, as I said, your husband Don was certainly not required to express a belief in Fatima upon joining the Church. But I hope he believed in it and that he still does believe in it. Such belief can do him nothing but good.

You say, Mrs. Ishmael, that you get help from this department in explaining your faith. Well, Catholics must exercise caution in our presentation of the devotions arising out of a private revelation. Persons coming into contact with some of the surface manifestations of Catholic devotions, if they have had no good explanation offered them, must certainly be bewildered by such images as the Sacred Heart of Jesus and the Immaculate Heart of Mary, the story of the spinning sun, miraculous recoveries from fatal illnesses and so on. They should not be left to believe that such things are the principal content or basis of Catholic faith or that one must begin by accepting them if one is to become a Catholic.

For the more intellectual non-Catholics most of the private-revelation devotions are barriers to union with us. Their tendency is to dismiss the spinning multi-colored sun as an atmospheric disturbance, the ecstasies of the children as psychological abnormalities, the crowd reaction as mass hysteria. The possibility that in particular instances such phenomena are only natural, not special interventions in nature on the part of God, is one reason why the Church does not require belief in them as a condition of remaining a Catholic.

But the basic reason that the Church sometimes approves of private revelations and devotions and in general promotes those which produce spiritual good is that she believes in the supernatural, in the existence of more than the material world. If you take the supernatural angels out of the Old and New Testaments as some of the avant-garde interpreters of the Scripture are proposing, you don't have much left of the story of man's salvation. If you explain away fulfilled prophecies of the future as coincidences and the miracles of Christ as mass hallucinations you are left in the world of the philosophers Camus and Sartre with no answers to any of the fundamental human questions and a revulsion against your own existence.

So the choice is between explaining away the marvels of private revelation as natural occurrences and seeing in at least some of them the hand of God himself. The Church turns toward the Almighty for whom all things are possible. There are reputable theologians who acknowledge the existence of true miracles even at Mohammedan shrines, though they add that such wonders are done not in testimony to the truth of the Mohammedan religion but only in proof of the transcendance of God. On the other hand, our Lord specifically made his miracles testimonies to the truth of his doctrine. "If you believe not me, believe my works."

Still, the general thrust of most Church legislation is against the private visionary and any person feeling special inspira-tions can expect having a hard time with Church authorities if he brings them to the general public. I remember once our magazine was interested in publicizing the story of a private visionary, but we dutifully and ahead of time sent the galleys of what we planned to our bishop. He came personally to our office and smilingly drew blue pencil lines lengthwise through each galley. Technically, what we had set up was a flat statement that the Blessed Virgin had appeared in our own area. The bishop told us we could only say that the visionary "said, claimed or averred" that the Blessed Virgin Mary had appeared. But apart from this technicality, I'm sure the bishop was following the usual extreme caution of the Church in regard to private revelations. "By their fruits you shall know them," he quoted, and added that at the time there was no fruit by which to judge. To assuage our disappointment, he told us that he had under confidential consideration the cases of several visionaries with far more intriguing "revelations" than the one we were promoting. As it turned out, none of these cases produced fruits like those of Fatima, Lourdes or Guadaloupe, so the bishop was right.

You also said, Mrs. Ishmael, that this department sometimes helped you over some of the hurdles in the modern church. Well, in these days of *aggiornamento* there is little danger to the average Catholic from persons claiming private revelations. Visionaries are out of style. The modern hurdle corresponding to that of the visionaries comes up now in theological studies of "on-going" revelation, a way of thinking that would eliminate the cut-off date, the death of the last Apostle. The revelation that God made to Adam, the Jews and the world in the time of our Lord, is now thought of as continuing past the cut-off date.

So far, none of the theologians involved have claimed any special revelation for themselves, but they do redefine *revelation* as being the "on-going" or continuing action of God by which He makes himself known to the individual person. They seem to me to be making no distinction between private and public revelation. It is certainly true that men, one by one, come to the knowledge of God within their individual minds, but this is accomplished now through what we called public revelation and the ordinary learning processes of the human mind, not through private illuminations resembling what we called private revelation. At any rate this is only speculative theology which contradicts the documents of the Council of

Trent and both Vatican Councils, all of which speak of the "deposit of faith" and none of which speak of this "on-going" revelation.

None of this may seem to have any application to you, Mrs. Ishmael — but you spoke of your children (and foster children). Should they come home from school or catechism class with strange doctrines or teachings that seem to you to be in contradiction to what you were taught as being in the deposit of faith, do not hesitate to correct them. It just might be that the CCD teacher or even "Sister" has been reading books written by some one with a perverted idea of "revelation." Just jump the hurdle.

Meanwhile, I'm still wondering with you about what *was* in that letter. If I ever find out, I will try to let you know.

Jehovah's (and Other) Witnesses

Prosyletizing is the activity of persuading someone with different religious beliefs to change to yur own beliefs. It must not be called "converting" because that term should be reserved for those coming from no religion to the Christian religion or from a life of sin to a life of struggle against sin. Because a person possessing any religious beliefs has ordinarily done considerable thinking and even arguing about them, he may find it annoying to be asked to change them. Also, in argumentation between denominations and sects, points of difference tend to be more specialized, of a more technical nature, than those between the unbeliever and the Christian, which is a source of further irritation to the person being proselytized. Sound ecumenism seeks out things on which to agree, proselytism stirs up the muddy waters of controversy. When grabbed by the lapel and shouted at, the good Catholic has the right to ask "How am I to deal with these people?"

THE QUESTION:

Upon graduating from high school in June, I began my
college career this summer. Being only 17 years old, I was
rather unsuspecting when members of various religious organizations began talking to me. I made several friends, but after a
while, these members of the so-called "non-denominational"
groups began to attack Catholicism.

In the course of a few weeks, I heard that the Catholic Mass
and the idea of confession were wrong. Besides criticizing the
hierarchy, some even claimed that Catholics "worship" the
Pope. They continued by saying that since it was not ever
mentioned in the Bible, praying to saints or to the Virgin was
not only wrong but sinful. Some said that Catholics believe
that only members of their faith can go to heaven. On the other
hand, some said that Catholics have lost God's grace because
they have deviated from his word in the Bible. These are only a
few examples. For me the trial continues every day as more
people say untrue things because of their lack of knowledge of
Catholicism.

I would like to know how a Catholic can deal with such
situations. I try my best to explain the real beliefs of Catholics,
yet few if any are willing to change their opinions. What kind
of answers should I give?

                                                    Jack Levic

THE ANSWER:

Keep on giving what you know to be the right answers, Jack.
Proclaim your belief. Your problem was faced by the Lord
himself and he spoke a parable about it. "A sower went out to
sow his seed ... " You remember the rest — only a small
percentage of the seed fell on good ground, most of it never
grew or took root. You are really the sower, though it is evident
that you are regarded as good ground by what might be called
your competition.

Christ founded a missionary Church and as true members

we are bound to spread its doctrines, but we live in a world that
seems indifferent to the doctrines and even bent on distorting
them, or stamping them out. You are not alone with your
difficulties. We could take here a brief look at other Catholic
sowers.

The feistiest approach to the immediate problem of being
surrounded by counter-missionaries is made by the Catholic
Evidence Guild of England. Its most famous alumnus is the
great controversialist, F.J. Sheed, who is still writing marvelous new books on the old perennial themes and showing
those who will see always fresher insights.

Members of this organization take advantage of the Hyde
Park tradition in London that anyone can speak his mind on
anything there. Speakers on soap boxes spend more time
answering hecklers than in straight lecturing. But they spend a
lot of time preparing before being allowed to speak and their
satisfaction comes from outwitting the opposition as much as
from proselytizing members of it. Their report in general is
much like yours, Jack, the number of converts made by
overpowering hecklers with logic is small, chiefly because the
hecklers don't understand logic.

The Jesuits, in counter-Reformation times, took an approach opposite to that of the soap box. Their missionary
activity was so vast that it is perhaps unwise to generalize but
they went after persons in power rather than the man in the
street. Amusing and thrilling stories and legends of their
disguises in the royal courts of Europe where they exerted
political influence are in all the chronicles. Their ingenious
methods of getting important attention, like Father Ricci's
present of a ticking clock to the Emperor of China, are further
testimony to their zeal. Their methods brought political help to
the Church but, no more than the soap box, did they conquer
the world for the faith.

The most successful missionary method was the plain
approach of the Apostles of the Lord and of those men who are
now national patrons like Patrick, Boniface, Cyril and
Methodius. The original Apostles had the advantage of

preaching a doctrine obviously superior to the decaying
polytheism of the pagan world; the national saints came from
cultures superior to those of the barbarous tribes to which they
preached.

You might say, Jack, that the Church has used the method
most feasible in each historical period. When the world had
great unexplored territories her missionaries went forth with
the basic good news of the coming of the Son of God. In
political times political methods were necessary for her
survival. In these later sad times Catholics have to go one on
one with Jehovah Witnesses on the front porch.

It's no great admission to say that the average Catholic is
unprepared for slam-bang debate with the type of zealot you
see so much of today. He is unprepared because he has never
been given the commission nor the obligation to teach specific
doctrine. The reason, of course, is that the Catholic Church
constitutionally is composed of the *Ecclesia docens* and the *Ecclesia docibilis,* the teaching Church and the learning Church.
This division began when Christ told the Apostles, not the sum
total of his followers, to go forth and teach all nations. Since
that time there has been a teaching authority in the Church.
Paul, certainly the greatest of Christian preachers more or less
bragged about how he had "withstood Peter to his face" but it
was only in a disciplinary, not a doctrinal, matter. The greater
point was his admission that Peter out-ranked him. The whole
concept was that Christians should learn the truth from those
who learned it from Christ. The "teaching Church" was
recognized by friend and foe alike through the Christian
centuries and reached its high point in the days of Pope Pius
XII. He regularily gave "allocutions" to his audiences, who
came from all classes of society: atomic physicists, street
cleaners, midwives, railroad employees. Each audience got
definitive direction for its state of life from the ultimate
Catholic authority. There never has been much encouragement from the teaching Church for Catholics in the other part
of the Church to get into the intellectual wars with non-
believers.

All in all, this policy has had very good results for the unity of the Church and its preservation. The history of the sects which have broken away from the Church is one of breaking up into smaller and smaller divisions, despite periodic attempts at reunions and amalgamations.

The efforts of the Church to preserve her doctrines have included such things as the education of priests in special schools (seminaries), censorship of books written by priests *(imprimatur, nihil obstat)* and requiring special permissions (faculties) for priests preaching outside their home dioceses. All this was because she had learned from the experience of the heretical sects that the unlearned person in the average world population had no more trouble attracting an audience or a readership than a highly educated scholar would have — but the possibility of error was thousands of times greater. It was true that any leader of men who had no knowledge of the past was bound to repeat mistakes made many times before.

So your real problem, Jack, is not how to change your answers but how to reconcile yourself to the attacks of the proselytizers. Sometimes you will simply have to break off discussions, not in an admission of defeat, but because the average zealots will not follow the guidelines of reasonable controversy. Never argue about points of fact. When they tell you Catholics worship the Pope and you say you are a Catholic and do not worship the Pope, that wins that argument. They have to start then by saying some Catholics worship the Pope or that they still believe that all Catholics worship the Pope, none of which settles any arguments about what the true teaching of the Catholic Church is.

Isolated texts of Scripture are the chief stock in trade of the hecklers. When their interpretations are strictly literal there are weird results, as in the case of the snake handling sects in the South, based on Mark, Chapter 16, Verse 18. Their further presumption is that the Bible is the only rule of faith (though it doesn't itself say so anywhere). The reason that Catholics in general were never educated to argue to ultimate truth from isolated texts of Scripture is that Scripture is too complicated in its manuscript sources, languages, translations and literary forms for that to be done except by scholars with proper authority. The Christian faith did very well for several centuries before any definite list (canon) of inspired Scriptures was set up as a rule of faith additional to the traditions handed down by word of mouth. The letters of Paul, now acknowledged as inspired Scripture, were written not to the pagan world but to churches of established Christians. He, because of his vision of the risen Christ and closeness to the other Apostles, was accepted as a member of the *Ecclesia docens.* Christians learned what their faith should be from those who had heard it from Christ.

As time went on it became necessary for the new Scriptures to be interpreted by persons who knew enough about them to be authoritative. Necessarily there were arguments for and against their interpretations. But all this is quite different from solving a personal problem by opening the Bible at random, closing your eyes and sticking a pin into a page to find the text that will solve the problem. There are those who do such things. Private interpretation, in other words.

A typical instance of this kind of Bible interpretation is the "brethren of the Lord" text. It seems perfectly obvious to the private interpreters that this text is a decisive proof that Christ had blood brothers, Mary was not a virgin and that consequently the Catholic Church is in error. What they have to disregard to arrive at these conclusions I tried to present in another article in this book. There is more to Sacred Scripture that the verbatim quoting of texts for the sake of argument. Modern Scripture scholars often speak rather slightingly of "proof texts" meaning that the text itself is only the starting point for the proof of any doctrine. It has to be considered in relation to the language in which it was originally written, the literary form in which it was included, the viewpoint of its human author and so on and on before anyone can say he knows its exact and complete meaning.

So Jack, maybe there is not much you can do in confuting the real Bible-thumpers. On top of everything else what they want to quarrel with you about is only usually a minor point in a far deeper difference. The Jehovah Witness that throws the "brethren of the Lord" text at you is not even a Christian, does not believe that Jesus is God so that even if by some miracle of grace you did convince him that Jesus had no blood brothers, his beliefs about the Blessed Mother and the divinity of Christ would not be corrected. The only "argument" that would convert such people would be one we have not yet mentioned. At one time in history, Christian kings, notably Charlemagne (800 A.D.), upon conquering a barbarous tribe would submit its members of forcible Baptism and instruction. Of course, the Lord never recommended this method, and the Church lost countless thousands to the Mohammedan missionary conquerors in other areas of the world in the same century. But over the long haul the method had some success. Once-pagan Europe still claims the name Christian and once-Christian North Africa and the Near East are now Muslim territories. But both Christian and Muslim religious leaders, if not the conquering generals, must have known that conversion by force, even by force of argument, was not what religion was really about. The good follower of Christ teaches as Christ taught. He proclaims the faith and leaves conversion to it up to the free will of the hearer and the grace of God. He does not try to convert anyone by force, he grabs no one by the coat lapels and shouts in his face.

We have been running a continuing feature in the *Catholic Digest* for more than 30 years now which invariably is highest in our reader popularity poll, despite its old fashioned variance from the present vogue of ecumenism. The Open Door is devoted to first hand stories of conversions to the Catholic faith. Its ever-recurring lesson is that people are brought into the Church by the good example of Catholics. I don't remember one instance of anyone being brought into the Church by force of argument. We have had many stories of conversions by real intellectuals who worked out their own religious problems but certainly none that I remember of any party to a debate saying finally "You win. I'll become a Catholic."

So it seems to me, Jack, that you are on the proper track now. You may not realize it, but if you are now patiently explaining the facts of Catholic belief and practice to those who knowingly or unknowingly misrepresent them you are giving them what they need most. You are already doing just about all you can be expected to do.

The Brethren of the Lord

There are some statements in Scripture which not only allow more than one literal interpretation but which provoke the sharpest and most unending of controversies. Somehow the arguments which seem so inescapable to one side seem plainly fallacious to the other and all that ever happens is that the same old arguments are used again and again without converting anyone to the other side. In the field of religion one might expect that if the subject was one which involved opinion or theory but it is more surprising to meet it in the matter of points of fact, like "Did Jesus have blood brothers and sisters?"

THE QUESTION:

I am 43 years old, a school teacher, married. I have taught
Confraternity of Christian Doctrine classes for a number of
years and have a Master's degree from a Catholic university.
My wife (who is a Protestant) is thinking about joining the
Catholic faith. But a question has come up which we both
would like answered.

She and a number of neighborhood women belong to a
nonsectarian Bible study group. The book they are now using
is *James' Belief in Action* by Keith Brooks, published by the
Moody Bible Institute of Chicago, copyright 1962.

It states that Jesus had brothers and sisters. It gives very
convincing evidence with several quotes from the Bible:
Galatians, chapter 1, verse 19; Matthew c. 13, v. 55; Mark c. 6,
v. 3 (Luke c. 8, v. 19, we found ourselves.)

We have three different translations of the Bible including
the traditional Catholic one and they all read the same. It
appears to us that Mary had other children after Jesus.

Now if I remember correctly I was always taught that Jesus
had no brothers or sisters. My wife, who has studied religion
quite a bit, cannot recall ever running across this before in her
church.

Even if you don't want to put your answer in the *Catholic
Digest*, please take time to write and give us an answer.

Leland Schmit

THE ANSWER:

The answer is that Jesus had no brothers or sisters and we
have put it into the *Catholic Digest* in this department twice
before.

But of course I don't want to start out that brusquely nor
question your sincerity and interest in asking your question,
Mr. Schmit. It is a constantly recurring problem to people who
are taking the Church's advice to read the Bible, and the subject
should be investigated as often as necessary.

I have not read the Keith Brooks book and don't know how ecumenical it is, but the "Brothers of the Lord" has been a staple of anti-Catholic pamphleteering since the invention of printing. I imagine that every Catholic apologist has had occasion to make rebuttals, but the point is that neither party to the controversy has given in to the other.

The core of the difficulty is, as you point out, that various translations of the Bible into English speak plainly, openly and even frequently of the "brethren of the Lord." Some of the recent versions say "brothers" instead of "brethren," whether out of a desire to modernize the language or take the anti-Catholic side in the controversy, I can't say.

"Brethren" is not much used in modern speech, though occasionally very formal sermons still begin with "My Dear Brethren." It connotation is not "brothers and sisters with the same parents as the speaker" but "a group united" for some purpose, ordinarily a religious purpose. At times, of course, such a group could be incidentally blood brothers.

The Catholic contention that "brethren of the Lord" means only relatives is allowable because the Semitic languages have no single word which would mean "persons having the same parents," with the meaning "kinfolk" excluded. Hebrew for instance, uses *aho* whether a relative is meant or a blood brother. If you wanted to say "relative" and "brother" in Hebrew as spoken in the time of our Lord you would have to use the same word for both. The word would be subject to the same double meaning that *brother* and *brethren* have in English.

I have the Book of Genesis in Hebrew in my library and have managed to puzzle out that word, *aho* in Genesis, chapter 14, verse 14, and chapter 29, verse 12.

The Torah, A Modern Commentary, published by the Union of American Hebrew Congregations, translates *aho* as "kinsman" in both places. The Rheims-Douay (Catholic) version has "brother" even though one person referred to was Lot, the son of Aran, while Abram (the "brother") was the son of Thare. The Revised Standard Version (Protestant and

Catholic) translates *aho* as "kinsman" in both places. The New American Bible translates it as "nephew" in chapter 14 and as "relative" in chapter 29.

Of course, we don't have Hebrew manuscripts of those parts of the New Testament which may have been first written in Hebrew, so we can't show that *aho* was the word translated into Greek as *adelphoi* and into Latin as *fratres*. But in both these languages the words have both the literal and figurative meaning just as *aho* has in Hebrew. That is to say, they can mean "children of the same parents" or "kinfolk."

What all this boils down to is that it cannot be proven that the word *brethren* must be taken in the literal sense, since in all Biblical languages it can have also the figurative sense of "members of a group." Now, I did not say that this double meaning of a word proves the Catholic contention. It only shows that we may possibly be right.

Staying for the present just with Scripture, our next step would be to inquire into who these brothers and sisters might be. The list is in the text you gave the numbers for, Mr. Schmit. Matthew, chapter 13, verse 55: "Are not his brethren James and Joseph and Simon and Judas? And are not all his sisters with us?"

The female relatives are not mentioned again anywhere in the Scriptures. That leaves James, Simon, Joseph and Judas. All four of these could have been members of the same family, a family quite distinct from that of Jesus, Mary and Joseph. It takes considerable supposition and accomodation in the spelling of names to set up the theory, but the result is certainly within the range of possibilities.

The father of this family would be Alphaeus, named specifically as the father of James. Joseph (spelled Jose in the Standard Revised Version of Mark) is called by both Matthew and Mark a brother of James. Judas (if he is, as most scholars think, the author of the Epistle of Jude) calls himself the brother of James. If these persons were blood brothers of Jesus Himself, it seems odd to have them identified as brothers of a lesser person.

For Simon, we have to reach a little further, but Hegesippus, (A.D. 150) though spelling the name Simeon, calls Simon the son of Clopas. Clopas could be Alphaeus and thus the father of all four. *Clopas, Cleopas* and *Alphaeus* are all spellings in Greek of the Semitic name *Halphai*. It's a fine point but the *H* in our English spelling of the name represents a guttural sound, something like clearing your throat, which doesn't exist as a language sound in Greek, Latin or English. Try sort of clearing your throat while you say "Cleopas" and then "Alpheus" and you will see how the *could* be the same name. These considerations could make James, Joseph, Simon and Jude all sons of the same father and even sons of the same father and mother.

In Luke, chapter 8, verse 19, which you found for yourself, there is reference to the mother and brethren of Jesus. This verse, along with all the other verses using the term *brethren,* is given a footnote in the Revised Standard Version, to the effect that the Greek word translated by "brethren" was used for varying degrees of blood relationship. It could mean cousins or kinfolk, as in the other cases.

Lest I leave myself open to misunderstanding, Mr. Schmit, let me repeat here that I do not maintain that what I have said so far *proves* that the "brothers" were only kinsfolk. It does indicate that they *could have been* only relatives, that we do not *have* to say that Jesus had blood brothers and sisters.

Next question: Why does the Catholic Church take so strong a position on the meaning of what is admitted to be an equivocal term, *brethren?*

It is because the person who says the Lord had blood brothers denies by that statement the perpetual virginity of Mary. Such a person denies her the name by which she has been called in the Church from earliest times, Blessed Virgin.

There is no record of anyone even thinking that Jesus had blood brothers until the time of St. Jerome, the great scholar of Hebrew and Aramaic and translator of the Bible. St. Jerome (using that word *aho*) refuted the statement of one Helvidius that the "brethren of the Lord" were children of Mary.

Nobody had said anything like that before because these same brethren were prominent in the Church in Jerusalem. James was its first bishop and Simon its second (according to Hegesippus writing in the second century). Joseph we don't know more about, but professional scholars of Scripture believe that Judas was the author of the Epistle of Jude, certainly a prominent man. It seems impossible to Catholics that if these persons were children of Mary any tradition that she was perpetually a virgin should spring up. Catholics think the tradition was easily established because nobody claimed or was even thought to be a blood brother of Jesus.

The birth of Christ from a virgin is proven by the dialogue between Mary and the angel at the time of the Annunciation, that she had no other children follows from her great dignity (pardon my interjecting at this point that it is this dignity that the anti-Catholics want to destroy.)

That Almighty God would use the virgin body of Mary for the incarnation of his only Son and then allow it to be used for the procreation of mere human creatures is unthinkable to Catholics. Could Jesus be God's only Son but not Mary's only son? It seems evident to Catholics that only those who deny the divinity of Christ or those who unthinkingly discount that divinity could believe that Mary had other children.

The Scriptures offer us a far more homely argument, the kind you could use in confuting Jehovah Witnesses who invade your front porch. Luke, chapter 2, verse 41 reads, "Now his parents went every year to Jerusalem at the feast of the Passover." They lived in Nazareth, 75 crow-flight miles from Jerusalem. The year Jesus was 12 and sat among the teachers in the Temple would be — on the real-brothers theory — a year in which Mary had at least seven younger children to care for. Even if they could travel in a caravan no compassionate mother would subject her toddlers to that yearly expedition. Your front-porch disputants might then say she could have had baby sitters in Nazareth but I doubt that they could back up that statement with sound research.

Another difficulty you could put to them would be to show

you in the Scriptures a text in which Mary, the mother of Jesus, is spoken of as the mother of anyone else. They won't be able to do that, they have only the ambiguous "brethren of the Lord" expression for their side of the argument.

And then of course our Lord from the cross committed Mary to the care of the Apostle John. If He had blood brothers, why would He give her into the care of someone outside the family? There is another argument to be found in the Greek version of the same scene at the Cross. Jesus, if you take the Greek word for word, says, "Behold *the* son of thine." Had there been several sons in the same family and had John been one of them the words would have been spoken without any *the,* which in translation would come to "Behold *a* son of thine." From the way the Lord spoke the ordinary inference would be He was substituting a single son for a single son.

So it is this chain of Scriptural considerations along with the ancient tradition expressed by the great majority of the Fathers of the Church that makes Catholics deny that Jesus had blood brothers. The tradition was so strong that St. Jerome was thrown into one of his famous explosions or argumentative fury by the notion of Helvidius. The idea did not pop up again until the 19th century as part of the rationalist treatment of the Bible and the denial of the divinity of Christ, in the assertion that He was the only one of the sons of Joseph, the carpenter.

A further reason for the strong stand of the Church is that, like every one of her doctrines, the perpetual virginity of Mary fits into a grand and perfect pattern of truth and mystery. If you assert that Jesus had blood brothers, you certainly imply that He was the son of two human parents and that He came into the world with no attendant circumstances like birth from a virgin which would attest to his divinity. You can pursue this thought until you destroy all Catholic belief. Logic will force you to say that a man born of two human parents could not be the divine victim required for the redemption of mankind.

One could go on and on, but in short, if you insist that Jesus had blood brothers you raise more theological problems than you solve Scriptural difficulties.

That is all the "brethren of the Lord" question is, a difficulty. Even though it takes scholarly ingenuity to explain it "away" satisfactorily, it is worth the effort of following the arguments so that a serenity of belief in the whole sum of Catholic dogma can be preserved.

Being Saved

All deep theological questions eventually filter down from the professors who thought them up to the people who have only ordinary education in religious matters. When this happens the deep questions are usually reduced to slogans and rallying cries which stir up as much opposition as they attract support. In the interest of ecumenism, an inquiry in the other direction, so to speak, from the slogan to the underlying doctrine, can sometimes do away with the frictions between Christians with apparently different beliefs. Often, as in the case of "being saved", it turns out that the real difference is in the meaning the different parties attach to a term and once this difference is understood, resentments and conflicts will not occur as often.

THE QUESTION:

I was reared in a large Catholic family. I had seven sisters and two brothers. My mother has always been very religious. She lost her beloved sister last year. Aunt Eva had a daughter who changed from Catholic to Baptist, which hurt Aunt Eva very much at the time, though she learned to accept it. But her daughter would not let her alone and just before Aunt Eva died, the daughter made her profess out loud "Jesus is Lord!" and then proclaimed her as "saved." This was very upsetting for my mother as she loved her sister very much. She wants to know what the Church has to say on being "saved."

Mrs. Jeanie Dargle

THE ANSWER:

Just to stick to the facts of your letter, Jeanie, I don't see how saying "Jesus is Lord" could hurt your aunt in any way. Of course, what worries your mother is the possibility that even so pious a statement could be a formula for renouncing the Catholic faith. But again I don't see how your aunt could think of it in that way nor why you or your mother should worry about what happened.

Your direct question is "What has the Church to say on 'being saved'?" Plenty. All Christians have heaven — eternal life in God — as their goal. Catholics would give the meaning "arrival in heaven" to the expression "being saved." Other Christians give it meanings which vary from sect to sect, but some, like your cousin, believe that there is a moment in the earthly life of the human person (not every human person) when he is "saved." This saving is accomplished by accepting Christ as a personal savior, by an irrevocable commitment to the Christian faith and by attaining a feeling of certainty of getting into heaven. There is nothing against good religion in any of these actions from the viewpoint of Catholic theology, except in those cases where *feeling* certain of being saved is made a theological condition for final arrival in heaven.

It was this feeling that your cousin had in mind. We can presume her good faith, so that she in her own way was acting like you or I might in baptizing an abandoned dying baby, even though its parents might be Muslim, Jewish or pagan. She believed that the *feeling* of certainty of getting to heaven was lacking in your aunt and that the profession that "Jesus is Lord" would give your aunt that feeling. Your cousin thought your aunt had to feel saved *before* she died.

Needless to say, this is not Catholic thinking. Rather surprising to say, the idea of once-and-for-all "being saved" was popular among the early Christians. They thought that to sin after Baptism was almost inconceivable. The great Emperor Constantine, for instance, delayed his own Baptism because he did not think he could live up to the ideal. But as a result of the sad cases of the *lapsi*, the baptized Christians who had apostatized under the pressures of the Roman persecutions, provision was made for readmission of sinners to the Church through public penance. Practical experience made the early Christians give up any idea they might have had that Baptism alone (even when it includes the ideas of personal acceptance of Christ, complete commitment to faith in Christ, and the "feeling" of being saved) assured salvation. For the present-day "backslid Baptists" or "burned out" Pentecostal sectarians I do not know what is done within their own religious communities, though surely they are committed to the mercy of God. The Catholic sense of down-to-earth practicality in spiritual matters seems to have started with the Lord who forgave sins himself and gave his Apostles the power to forgive them even when committed by the baptized.

A further source for the concept of being saved forever by a sudden enthusiastic conversion to Christ can be found in the lives of such saints as Paul of Tarsus and Francis of Assisi. Both had religious experiences so intense that they did indeed seem to be thereafter sure of salvation. And the original Apostles of the Lord, though we don't have extensive scriptural details, followed him immediately and without debate. We can guess from the way one told another of their finding of the Christ that they very likely did experience bursts of enthusiasm as did Paul and Francis. But the point here would have to be that this type of "being saved", if indeed they all felt it, did not in the case of Judas save then and there and forever the Apostle who betrayed Christ.

The Catholic believes that being saved is a matter of using one's reason, that emotion can be present but is not necessary. When confronted with Francis and Paul the Catholic teacher of this point is something like the rabbi told of in the Talmud. He was arguing in a group in which he was outvoted nine to one, but which needed a unanimous vote for its purposes. Unable to sway him, the nine said, "Let's do it this way. We will say to this wall, 'Remove yourself.' If the wall stays there we will vote with you. If it departs you must vote with us." Without waiting for his answer they said "Begone" to the wall and it moved away and way lost to sight. But the lone rabbi said, "That was a miracle, it was not an argument." The Catholic Church looks with joy upon the real glory of sudden conversions to Christ, but cannot set them up as the sole means of salvation. There is too much danger that such conversions are only psychological reactions to something or other. Unless the human reason enters into the decision, the grace of God is working in an out-of-the-ordinary way.

We must also consider that "being saved" on the psychological plane works in reverse. Apostasy can bring the same human joy that emotional conversion to Christianity brings. Will Durant, the popular historian, told in his early book *Transition* how good he felt when he *gave up* Christianity. Without going into things too deeply, it would certainly seem fair to say this was an emotional reaction because he had come to look upon Christianity only as a set of depressing moral axioms. "Priests in their gowns were making their rounds / and binding with briars / my joys and desires" was the way William Blake expressed the same experience. The Catholic Church discounts "feeling saved" because both converting to Christ and forsaking him can cause a feeling of relief from emotional tension.

Of course, it is not as simple as all that in the works of the Protestant theologians who first elaborated "feeling" as the basis of all religion. Friedrich Schleiermacher (1768-1834), though I doubt your cousin ever heard of him, probably furnished the theological background which made her want to give your aunt the "feeling" of being saved. In the psychology of his time the human mind had the "faculties" of knowledge, action and feeling. Schleiermacher (who was defending, not attacking, religion) found the basis of religion in the third faculty, feeling. I suppose that in his scheme of things Catholic theology would find the basis of religion in knowledge obtained through God's revelation and in action in the sense that the God-Man worked our redemption. But Schleiermacher was not disputing the Catholic Church directly on this point. He saw as his chief opponents the atheistic scoffers at religion and the fatalistic Deists of his time who thought of the world as an inexorable clock wound up by a remote and uncaring God, for whom they didn't care much either. He didn't even try to argue the truth of any particular doctrine with them, his only attempt was to convince them that religion came out of a faculty of the human spirit itself and was an element of manhood. This is not a position that the Catholic theologian would strive violently to disprove, but in the course of time Schleiermacher's thought did give rise to the attitudes of people like your cousin for whom "feeling" became not only the source of true religion but even the criterion by which they could know whether they were among the elect, sure of being saved.

Being sure here and now in this life that one is forever saved brings with it a fanatical enthusiasm to share the certainty with others. Your standard Catholic rarely has this approach because he has been taught to work out his salvation slowly in fear and trembling. For him being saved is a life-time project, not a matter of almost momentary duration. For him it is a matter of receiving sacraments, learning dogmas and following laws. He may, and really should have, some religious emotion in his life but in the cold dry tomes of his theology enthusiasm is

not necessary for salvation. On top of this he knows that he has
no right to salvation, God owes him nothing no matter what his
merit (though he believes that God in his infinite justice and
mercy and love will be fair with him, forgive him and treat him
as an adopted son). Of being saved he will never be sure until he
is judged at his death. St. John of the Cross, the great mystic,
even taught (mistakenly) that one of the torments of Purgatory
is in not being sure even there of being saved. His was never the
majority opinion of Catholic theologians but it shows how far
a faithful Catholic can get from the notion that it is possible to
be saved forever at a moment in his present life. Speaking of St.
John of the Cross, there is a certain parallel between this mystic
seeking God in the dark night and the ordinary Catholic
plodding through his daily affairs. St. John's marvelous poem,
Dark Night, Stanzas of the Soul, ends with the soul's ecstasy
and oblivion at the touch of God, but in his commentary on the
poem the saint covers only the first three stanzas all of which
deal with the trials and troubles of the soul. It would seem that
he deliberately stopped before he came to the "happy" part of
the poem. Life on earth (his own included persecution,
imprisonment, beatings and illness as well as the honors of
office) was darkness and pain in pursuit of union with God.
Occasional raptures were of short duration and losing them his
soul went again into agony. This was the willingly accepted
life-experience of one of the Church's most self-expressive
saints, a far cry from the serene assurance of eternal happiness
that some people derive from Schleiermacher's doctrine that
all religion stems from feeling.

The Catholic religion stems from the use of reason. It is
reasonable that there is a good God, that this God has revealed
himself to his creatures, that he had the good purpose of
bringing his creatures to eternal happiness with himself, that
He provided the means of attaining that happiness. The
Catholic can reason to the certainty of his own salvation — *if*
he perseveres till death, *if* God grants him the grace and so on.
Your aunt, Jeanie, as a life-long Catholic knew all this and in
knowing it knew already that "Jesus is Lord." She may possibly

also have been acquainted with the words of Jesus, "Not everyone who says to me 'Lord! Lord!' shall enter the kingdom of heaven." He was not forbidding people to call him "Lord" but he was saying it was not a magic password for entry into the kingdom. Those who did the will of his Father were as sure as anyone could rightly be that they would enter the kingdom.

When we ponder our chances of being saved and what degree of certainty we may allow ourselves we must consider that God is infinite both in his mercy and in his justice. Our human minds have trouble in reconciling them. If we dwell only on his justice we are likely to fall into the frame of mind of the early American colonial parsons who drove their congregations into hysterical panic with sermons on hell-fire. If we dwell only on his mercy we are likely to end up with such beliefs as that we can be certain of being saved because we feel that way. The reasoning Catholic believes he will be judged and then punished or rewarded by God at his death. He takes a kind of middle position between mercy and justice. Very few present-day Christians think of God only in terms of justice and hell-fire, but there are many at the other extreme who think that in his mercy He will grant a total amnesty to everyone. This latter kind of thinking accounts, among those who believe in God, for the present crisis in all fields of morality: abortion, artificial birth control, drug use and we might as well include airplane hi-jacking and terrorism. An exclusive dwelling on the mercy of God will allow me to think I am already irrevocably saved and also to sing *Alleluias* instead of *Misereres* no matter whose funeral I am attending.

When I started answering your letter, Jeanie, I never dreamed it would lead me into so much abstract thought, undoubtedly hard to follow. But I know it all ties in because I have often reflected on how I once acted pretty much like your cousin in my days as a public-hospital chaplain.

There was a patient there just short of 70 of whose approaching death I was warned by the nurses and doctor. His family, all devout Catholics apparently, called me about giving him the last sacraments. The difficulty was, they said, that cousin in my days as a public-hospital chaplain.

There was a patient there just short of 70 of whose approaching death I was warned by the nurses and doctor. His family, all devout Catholics apparently, called me about giving him the last sacraments. The difficulty was, they said, that many years before he had quarreled with their pastor and not only never darkened the door of the church again but carried on a kind of organized opposition to anything the pastor undertook.

The poor man received me politely enough but evidently regarded reception of the sacraments as final defeat in his almost life-time battle with his pastor. He said No.

It just happened that the week before I had been asked by the head nurse to give a talk to the nurses on whether to let the dying know they were dying. I told the nurses that it was in my experience seldom necessary, since most patients had a sharper sense of their condition than even the doctor, but that as a Catholic priest I followed a rule. If the patient had been receiving Communion I suggested what we then called Extreme Unction or the Last Rites with emphasis on its possible curative power. In short, I didn't think I or the nurses should upset the patients with bad news.

Each time I went back to see my patient, he was weaker in body but stronger in his opposition to giving in to the pastor, as he thought of it. The day I was sure he was going to die, however, I, like your cousin, could not let him alone. I told him finally and bluntly it was his last chance. He was going to die, perhaps this very day. I will never forget the look in his eyes nor what he said, "Father, how can you say that to me?" But it worked. He said he was sorry for all his sins and I brought him Viaticum and anointed him. The family were all jubilant, the pastor just a touch disgruntled at having to give Christian burial to the chief enemy of the local Church, and the man, I trust, is in heaven, "saved."

So, as I began saying, Jeanie, your cousin and I had different ideas about what "being saved" meant but we both, according to our lights, were trying to get a soul into heaven. I'm sure that's where your aunt is now.

Marriage Annulments and Laicization of Priests

One of the most disturbing, if not discouraging, developments in the Church in very recent times is the increase in the number of priests and sisters leaving the religious life. There may be some consolation in reflecting that the defections were even more numerous in the time of Luther but that the Church eventually recovered. In the meantime a good many lay people are finding many puzzling aspects in the general situation. Does it mean the Church is changing its doctrines? Are all the sacraments, especially Matrimony, undergoing revision in the obligations they impose? Has the Church been all wrong in the past? Well, things are changing but a closer look will show that the changes are only in practices which are by their nature changeable, not in the eternal verities the Church proposes.

THE QUESTION:

I have been a Catholic all my life and have been happily married for 30 years. But one question, often asked me by younger people, still stumps me. I am submitting the question as follows.

Until recently, Roman Catholic priests were never laicized and allowed to marry. Now many have left the priesthood, married and still remain in good standing with the Church — in spite of the text, "Thou art a priest forever according to the order of Melchisedek."

Yet validly married people have never been allowed to remarry and still continue to receive the sacraments. Both Ordination and Matrimony are sacraments. Why can one sacrament be set aside and not the other?

Mrs. Louis Kuhry

THE ANSWER:

The immediate but technical answer to your objection, Mrs. Kuhry, is that different sacraments have different effects. Validly married persons have entered into a life-time contract which can be changed neither at the will of either party separately nor both parties together. Remarriage is allowed to one party only at the death of the other, or upon church court action proving that there was no valid contract in the first place. A true sacramental marriage is never "set aside."

In the case of laicization of a priest, there is no contract existing which would involve the rights of another human person. It is one-sided action on the part of the Church. In the text of Canon law it is spoken of as a penalty or a degradation rather than any kind of privilege or favor. The sacrament of Holy Orders is not withdrawn, obliterated or nullified. The sacrament is not "set aside." The sacerdotal character ("the indelible mark on the soul" of the Baltimore Catechism) remains, only the obligation of recital of the Divine Office and the obligation of celibacy are removed. Once a laicized priest is validly married he is just as married as anyone else.

The obligations of a priest (celibacy, the Divine Office) are of ecclesiastical origin and can be abrogated by the Church; the obligation not to remarry in the lifetime of the spouse is of divine Christian origin and *cannot* be abrogated by the Church. Variations on your question have been coming in right along, Mrs. Kuhry, but yours touches on more points of general misunderstanding than most of the others. To answer it with more than an explanantion of technicalities consideration must be given to recent trends in the Church.

Most of the correspondents object as you do that married people, in the present run of Church rulings, are not being treated as "fairly" as persons in religion. One of them, for instance, asked how a nun, "a bride of Christ" could be released from vows, while the brides of mere men could not be.

To get all this straight in our minds, we have to begin with the idea that the Church is always reluctant to grant laicizations and annulments, even though their recent proliferation would make it seem otherwise. In nearly all cases a request for either laicization or annulment means that someone has failed in living up to previous voluntary commitments.

A seminary-trained priest forsaking his ministry is a man who has spent four to seven years on his decision to become a priest, for the most part getting discouragement and warnings rather than cheers and encouragement from his superiors. It's a grim topic for many seminarians. In the old days the decision was made by the reception of the sub-diaconate order, now abolished, which carried with it the obligation of celibacy. The poor men who were really having trouble with their decision right up to the final day were always given the same frivolous advice by their more determined fellow students: "If you are going to faint at the last moment, be sure and fall backwards. If you fall forward they will make you a sub-deacon." The joke is out of key with the seriousness of the subject but it does show that few students indeed breezed thoughtlessly through the years preceeding their priesthood. The Church expects priests to give at least as much consideration to leaving as they did to entering the priesthood. Contrary to your statement, laicization was always possible; as you imply, it was an extremely rare procedure. In the rules of some religious societies (not in Canon Law) laicization was a formal ceremony with such rites as the scraping of the fingertips that had touched the Host.

People proceeding to marriage do not take the same length of time for deliberation, as a matter of fact, some of them are even annoyed by state laws requiring five days between license and marriage, but for the most part the marriage is a public, deliberate act with the same legal standing as a signed contract.

Here's the point of what I am trying to say just now. The Church must take these commitments at their face value. The whole social order would be demolished to the point of anarchy if solemn promises such as those proferred in Holy Orders and Matrimony are treated as passing whims. Because they are "only" religious promises some people do reduce them to that level. The Church does not think of itself as passing out favors when it grants laicizations or annulments. It is rather only making legally necessary adjustments to the personal histories of the people involved.

A point you make in your letter, Mrs. Kuhry, is that both Matrimony and Holy Orders are sacraments and that therefore people who have received one or the other should be treated with equal consideration. Basically you are right, but here again, I think, the popular misconception lies in regarding these two sacraments only from the point of view that their reception entails obligation. A sacrament is a channel of grace, a means by which the very life of God (grace) comes to us. Human reaction to this profound truth has, in the case of Holy Orders, caused the Church to impose celibacy and the recitation of the Divine Office. In the case of Matrimony, the obligation not to marry anyone else arises not from the Church but from the life-time contract entered into by the participants. Matrimony is indeed a sacrament just as Holy Orders is a sacrament but the obligations are in each case different and of different origins, the Church in the case of Holy Orders, and Christ himself in the case of Matrimony.

From other letters on your subject, Mrs. Kuhry, I learn that some disaffected Catholics regard Church annulments of defective marriage contracts simply as an expedient way to allow divorce. The whole procedure, such persons say, is a mere shuffling of words. To them I can only say that even now, when annulments are becoming greater in number, they are being granted on the same principle, defect in the contract. Canon Law specifically mentions only force and fear as possibly nullifying elements in the contract. In the U.S. this type of contract has been known as a "shot-gun" marriage. Such marriages are rare so the reason for the present increase in the annulment ratio must be found elsewhere. I'm not a party to any tribunal proceedings but it's a good guess that most of the annulments are being declared because of provable psychological inability on the part of one or both parties to enter so solemn a contract as the Catholic Sacrament of Matrimony: one man, one woman, "Till death do us part." As everyone who has any part in the ecclesiastical courts knows, the danger here is in getting so lenient that annulments are declared on grounds which would, if applied, also annul a large percentage of happy marriages.

The popular misconception about the reason for the increase in laicizations and plain forsaking of the priesthood is that the persons concerned want to get married. It can't be denied that nearly all do get married but the real reason, unperceived often by the forsakers themselves, is that they have accepted the latest pseudo-theological fads to the effect that the priest is essentially a social worker, not even a "glorifed" social worker, and that there is no distinction between the sacred and the secular. It fits in with the idea that there is no such thing as "sacred space," i.e., no need for churches or special places of sacrifice — say Mass in the recreation room if you must have Mass. Specifically, the contention is that there is no "indelible mark on the soul" for the man in Holy Orders. If you grant that, incidentally, neither has the baptized Christian any distinguishing mark on his soul, and men are all the same, none bear any dignifying marks from God or anyone else. This gets you into pure secularism, which, unless you are very careful, takes you back into the worlds of Hitler, Stalin, and Attila the Hun.

So the Church, Mrs. Kuhry, while it does take from laicized priests power to solemnize the sacraments licitly, and while it does remove the obligations of celibacy and the recital of the Church's official prayer, does not remove, or even declare faded, the mark on the soul. Your quotation "Thou art a priest *forever* according to the order of Melchisedek," is very apt and appropriate though it is not the foundation of the Church's teaching on the irrevocability of the priesthood. The psalm in which it occurs (Ps. 110) was quoted by our Lord in his argument with the doctor of the law (Matthew chap. 12). It is a poem about the Messiah and the key word requiring emphasis is in the verse you quote, "forever." Melchisedek was priest and king who offered God bread and wine. He was the foretype of our Lord, in whom the same qualities and actions are found, and whose priesthood is "forever." For uncounted decades this, the fourth verse of Psalm 110, was printed on nearly every priest's remembrance-of-ordination card to underline the companion thought that ordination did indeed mark the very soul. This same idea of permanence of the Messianic priesthood seems to have been well learned by the Jews of our Lord's own time for when He told the multitude (John, chapter 12) that He would be "lifted up", that is crucified, they objected that He, then, could not be the Christ who abides "forever."

Apart from this emphasis on the permanence of the priesthood the verse you quote mentions Melchisedek as a foretype of Christ because the "order" of their priesthood was not that of Aaron, brother of Moses, and neither belonged to the Jewish priestly tribe of Levi.

Just to reassure myself and you, Mrs. Kuhry, that I haven't been simply talking random points on the general subject of your letter, let me sum up.

Marriage annulments and laicizations are occuring much oftener now than in the days of Pius XII but each case is given individual consideration. There has been no change in the principles on which the procedures are based, no changes in rules although interpretations of the law and weight given to evidence are obviously much more in favor of the petitioners than in the days before the Vatican II council. Certainly there has been no change in the attitude of the Church to the effect that in marriage annulments and laicizations she is making a humanly necessary legal response to human failure in living up to previously voluntary commitments. The Church in her own mind has no sense at all of granting favors in these instances, much less of bestowing privileges on those of the clerical state to the prejudice of those of the married state.

When Your Children Leave the Church

One of the greatest trials God can allow faithful Catholics to endure is to see a beloved son or daughter give up the faith the parents tried so hard to instill. It is a great trial because the temptation that comes with it is to ignore certain of the teachings of that very faith themselves. The dilemma is dreadful. It would seem that parent must either condone a state of continuing grievous sin in the offspring or put him or her out of their lives. Of course, neither alternative is Christian. When parents ask what to do in such cases they are really asking what the guiding principles of their Christian faith are. Knowing what the principles are will help in proportion to the depth of faith the parent has.

THE QUESTION:

We have two children, neither of whom now practices the Catholic faith. Both claim their religion was chosen for them by us, their parents, when they were baptized. They feel they have no committment to a promise made by others.

Both married non-Catholics in non-Catholic churches, one with a priest in attendance and one without. The older one had the priest only because my wife said she wouldn't attend unless the marriage was in keeping with the rules of the Catholic Church. The other refused point-blank to have a priest at the ceremony. We attended after deep soul-searching but are still filled with guilt and sorrow. This son and his wife even refuse to forgive us for asking him not to enter a marriage invalid in the eyes of Church.

What should a parent do, faced with a child who intends to marry outside the faith he was reared in? Should parents stop expecting church attendance and leave it up to the child's choice? Help us, Father. Help others facing this heartbreak.

I am not signing my name. Our family has had too much grief. We don't need publicity.

THE ANSWER:

Your experiences must certainly be the hardest of your life. Your questions are certainly among the hardest to answer sympathetically. Almost anything said in answer will sound like a platitude. Pray. Hope. Wait. Platitudes offer the coldest comfort of all, but neverthless platitudes are distillations of universal human experience. I'll say what I can.

The response of parents to situations like yours can be of either extreme: they may say, "Never darken my door again" in the fashion of old melodrama or they may, in view of all the modern social pressures, actively defend their beloved children and give up their own convictions.

I can only offer another platitude: don't do either of these things. In itself this advice is not very practical. It is difficult to maintain any social relationships without giving tacit approval. Yet that is what you must do. I'm no expert at imparting social advice, but there is a comparison possible here between what your treatment of your fallen-away children should be now and what it should have been in their baby days had they contracted a communicable, probably fatal disease. Your love and care for them would certainly not be diminished by the disease yet there would have been precautions about kisses and cuddling in your conduct toward them until they had recovered. The disease would have been a physical evil; the abandonment of their faith is a moral evil. Evil of any kind is the basic philosophical problem of this, God's world. We must protect ourselves from moral evil as we would protect ourselves from a physical plague.

So with that much understood, friends, let's take up the points of you letter.

Your children claim you imposed your religion on them. Well, if you did, you were following the evident will of God. The Catholic Church was founded by our Lord as a missionary church, that is, its function was to be the bringing of persons to the knowledge of God, to save their souls. To profess membership in this Church and not to make the missionary effort to impart a knowledge of God to your own children would be completely irrational. I don't need to tell you your children are wrong in holding this effort against you. They have the same obligation to accept the evident will of God as you had. Their mistake is the same one Adam made, rejecting the supernatural gifts of God in the hope of finding something better.

Their particular form of self excuse, that they were baptized in infancy and not given a choice, probably seems an up-to-date style of thinking to them but it is the chief tenet of many old heresies. The anabaptists, for instance, believed in baptizing again (*ana* is Greek for *again*) everyone who had been baptized in infancy — on the same grounds, that the infants had not been given a free choice. The answer is that your children are not now making a choice so much as rejecting a gift. The choice is only that of all sin, choosing an apparent natural good instead of a certain, supernatural good.

It sounds like good common sense to say that you should give each child his own free choice in religious matters, but really it is like throwing him into deep water and giving him the choice of "sink or swim." All good parents have eventually to send their children out into the treacherous sea of life but the wiser ones will have given the children a few swimming lessons. Should the child then reject the lessons and prefer to find out what drowning feels like, the parent will feel natural grief, but not the infinitely worse grief of being responsible for the loss of the child's supernatural eternal life. So you were right in having your children baptized and taught the Catholic faith. You were right in protesting their marriages.

I know that for someone in your intensely human, emotional situation, the disaffection of your children, human comfort does not come from a sense of being right yourself. It might come from advice to jump in the lake with them and take your chances on drowning yourself, but it would certainly not be good advice. The uncertainty you now feel is just the struggle to keep your own heads above water.

You say you are still filled with guilt for having attended the ceremony that took you son out of the Church. You should feel no guilt since you gave the "swimming" lessons in due time and attended the ceremony to show the love the young people denied you.

I know also that such somewhat childish analogies may be as tiresome as platitudes, though they may have just as much truth in them. So we could turn now to another possible source of consolation, though it, too, must be qualified. It is to reflect on the conceivable excuses your children may have had for their conduct.

The first would almost certainly be "We were (or are) in love." This argument wins universal and instant sympathy but we should closely examine just what validity it has. The power of romantic love is such that it can cause kings to abdicate, soldiers to commit treason, spouses to murder their present partners and, as we know too well, Catholics to give up their faith. This kind of love of course is the psychological driving force God implanted in us to ensure the propagation of the human species. It excuses derelictions of duty, treasons, murders and apostasies if it has completely taken away free will. It does not always take it away. As Christ preached his religion, the whole moral struggle is to make free will prevail over such powerful psychological forces. Our Lord didn't put his doctrine in such academic terms, but He did say such things as "If your right eye causes you to sin, pluck it out and throw it away." Romantic love certainly brings the strongest temptations and a person has less free will when he is "in love" than at any other time of life. Yet Christ insisted, in such terms as plucking out eyes and cutting off right hands, that all temptations must be resisted.

Low-level, amateur theologians tend to overlook this attitude of the Lord and to proclaim that love excuses all — always. They confuse romantic love with Christian love. If your children have been taken in by this error you may find some excuse for them in the lessening of their free will and of their understanding of what they are doing through exposure to false teaching.

The false teaching is not only contaminating the doctrine of Christ but pretty well pervades our present civilization. When you add to it the influence of Communism, secularism and liberalism (to say nothing of hippie anti-nomianism) the wonder is that the Church survives at all. It does, of course, survive by the grace of God, a circumstance that should be in our thoughts, especially when we need comfort in the face of family members leaving the Church. The teaching of the non-Christian world is that marriage is only a one-sided temporary agreement. When 90% of your friends and acquaintances (including the person with whom you are in love) believe that about marriage, the Christian ideal makes its appeal only to those willing to follow Christ in his self-sacrifice.

The prevalence of divorce and co-habitation (as opposed to

marriage) in our present culture has made Christian ideals seem so unattainable that the trend in recent Church marriage legislation is in the direction of liberalization. Whether this will be for good or ill remains to be seen; the state of our future Christian society will undoubtedly depend more on the efforts of the Church to infuse young people with her ideals than upon her legislation. Yet, I think a good many young Catholics caught up in a marriage problem, have the balance tipped for them in the wrong direction by such things as not requiring marriages of Catholics to be in Catholic churches. Your children may well have decided that the Church wasn't being as "strict" anymore and that future relaxation of law would be in their favor. That would be another darkening of their understanding, if that can bring you any consolation.

The ordinary reaction of people outside the Church when they get involved in planning a marriage to a Catholic is one of annoyance that the Church should intrude in any way. Even though the time is unfortunately past when the outsiders could be induced to do such things as sign promises that the offspring would be reared as Catholics, they still necessarily find out that the Church regards marriage as a matter to be governed by her laws. The Catholic, if not the non-Catholic, should know that the laws of the Church are all supportive of the Biblical ten Commandments. Catholics must go to Sunday (or Saturday) Mass to ensure that the First Commandment to adore God will be suitably obeyed; Catholics must obey the marriage laws of the Church so that the Commandment against adultery will be obeyed — civil legislation on marriage opposes adultery only for the duration of a marriage, it does not oppose those successive marriages which are, by the definition of Christ himself (Gospel of Luke, chapter 16, verse 18) adulteries.

The Catholic can all too readily catch this infection too, the idea that marriage is none of the Church's business. If he does, the Catholic doctrine, that marriage is a holy sacrament designed to lead its partners to God, is banished from his mind. Whether or not any excuses can be found in any of these present-day obstacles to Christian marriage is of course in the individual's conscience and the judgment is God's. That is why you must not cut yourself off from your apostate children. Through the Church, though, God has put into human power the judgment of external conduct and misconduct. That is why, to use the perhaps over-vigorous figure of speech, you must treat your children as though they were victims of a plague you didn't want to catch.

Dear friends, I began by admitting I had little hope of bringing you real consolation, I could offer only platitudes. So out again with the old platitudes: wait, hope, pray. But don't dismiss them just because they are platitudes. Accept them as the highest wisdom of God's creation. Your present suffering is part of creation's problem of evil. Patient waiting, cheerful hope and honest prayer are the nearest solutions we have to that problem.

Infant Baptism

The ideas of heretics and schismatics have a way of recurring in the Church. Even though in the near or remote past a group has been condemned and put out of the Church, years later another group will arrive at the same erroneous ideas independently and propose them again for adoption by the universal Church. Infant Baptism has been practised from the beginning by the Church but recurrently the idea of postponing the Sacrament comes up from people who think conditions have changed or that there are new reasons for changing the old customs. Quite often the new reasons have a certain plausibility, even validity, but they must be weighed in the balance with the old traditional reasons and rejected if found wanting.

THE QUESTION:

I am 35 years old and the mother of four children, ages three months, three years, four years, 10 years. How the church has changed in regard to the Sacrament of Baptism since our oldest son was baptized! Being born and raised a Catholic, I was always taught that a baby should be baptized as soon as possible after birth. I remember feeling a little weak as we stood in the church during the Baptism of our oldest son just two days after coming home from the hospital. Now, at our parish, we have Baptisms only once a month. The instruction given sponsors and parents beforehand is a good idea but the Church seems to be de-emphasizing infant Baptism.

When I asked at the instructions about babies dying unbaptized I was told that perhaps at the moment of death an infant is given enough knowledge to choose God freely, that perhaps the desire of the parents for the Baptism of the child is sufficient.

Please help to clarify these things for me.

Patricia Welch

THE ANSWER:

Just for a flash answer, Patricia, I would guess that the priests (or the liturgical committee) in your parish are really trying to emphasize Baptism and in the process seem to be de-emphasizing infant Baptism. I think the delay is only incidental; probably Baptism is solemnized only once a month because the accumulation of babies to be baptized makes it a more easily publicized event.

But your concern for soon-as-possible Baptism echoes one of the Canons in the Church's Code of Canon Law, number 770, which says babies are to be baptized *quamprimum*, a Latin word which literally means "as soon as possible." But often in context it can be taken to mean "as soon as conveniently possible." Canon 770, read with its accompanying canons, can be taken in the latter sense, since they forbid such undue haste as baptizing babies still in the womb as long as there is reasonable hope that they will be born and can be solemnly baptized in church. Canon 770 has never been oficially taken to mean that there must be any extraordinary haste in administering Baptism to a normal and healthy baby. At most there should be that "deliberate speed" that the poet Francis Thompson and the U.S. Supreme Court talk about. No undue haste, no undue delay.

Pope Paul, at this writing, has just told a general audience that he wished to reaffirm the tradition of infant Baptism in the Church. In a very general way he may have been troubled by the same thing as you, Patricia. I don't mean about a few weeks delay for the Baptism of healthy babies, but about a de-emphasis of infant Baptism.

There is in Latin America, Spain, Portugal and Italy a movement which has that tendency. These are countries that at one time were almost solidly Catholic but in more recent times have been in danger of being taken over from within by a communistic element that is essentially anti-religious. Members of the movement say that being baptized and called a Catholic became so much a matter of routine in those countries that Baptism and Catholicism came to have too little meaning for the average person. What they want to do immediately is set up some kind of teaching program for Catholics and have suggested that in the future Baptism should not be given routinely to infants but that everyone should wait for Baptism until he or she is old enough to understand and be instructed in its full meaning. They have in mind some kind of reinstatement of the ancient catechumen system. The Pope was in favor of all possible catechumenal instruction but not in favor of doing away with infant Baptism, which he called a "holy custom."

So both his statement and your question, Patricia, lead into a discussion of the historical controversies on infant Baptism. People were not always as concerned about it as were the writers of Canon 770. In the early ages of the Church, there

were certainly more adults than infants receiving Baptism at
the usual ceremony, because the whole Roman world was
turning Christian.

Frequent, repeated confession and absolution of sins had
not yet become part of Christian life, so some converts delayed
their sin-absolving Baptisms even to their death beds to avoid
the penitential disciplines and to insure themselves against
relapse into sin.

Of course, the Church never promoted so unwise a procedure, unwise in the view of the possibilty of sudden death and
subsequent loss of salvation. "He that believeth *and is
baptized"* the Scriptures said, "shall be saved." The great
emperor Constantine deferred his Baptism and, so to speak,
got away with it. But another emperor, Valentinian II, did not.
He died a catechumen, unbaptized. St. Ambrose preached a
funeral oration over him, but this is the only known case in all
antiquity where even this much approval was given to anyone
who deferred Baptism.

Tertullian, who had other heretical opinions, thought that
Baptism should be regularly deferred until the child reached
the use of reason. St. Gregory Nazianzen thought it should be
deferred until the child was able to talk and answer the
responses. But neither of these men denied the validity of infant
(the word means "not yet able to talk") Baptism and neither
had any great following in this matter. The overwhelming
majority of Christians believed in baptizing babies. *Quamprimum.*

Their reasons were primarily scriptural. Luke's Gospel,
chapter 18, verse 15 reads: "Now they were bringing even
infants to him that he might touch them; and when the disciples
saw it, they rebuked them. But Jesus called them to him,
saying, 'Let the children come to me and do not hinder them for
to such belongs the kingdom of God.' "

Now of course this text does not say that the Lord baptized
any babies then and there but we know the lesson his followers
took from his words. There are references to whole "house-
holds" being baptized in the Acts of the Apostles and in St.

Paul's letter to the Corinthians. In no case does it say the "whole household except the babies."

The present suggestions by the leaders of the neo-catechumenal movement that Baptism be deferred were anticipated by several of the heretical medieval sects (the Cathari and Anabaptists). They and the Waldenses, some of whom survive unto this day, taught that the Baptism of infants was not only inadvisable but invalid. I don't have any documents at hand but I'm sure more than one modern sect believes the same thing.

What made the Holy Father speak out at the mere suggestion, let alone the teaching, that babies should not be baptized is the form of our Lord's invitation of Baptism. It is universal. He makes no exceptions for babies.

Heretics who do not believe that Baptism is valid until the one baptized has the use of reason appeal to one of the same texts Catholics use for the necessity of Baptism. It is Mark, chapter 16, verse 16: *"He that believeth and is baptized shall be saved."* They underline the first half of the text. They maintain that no one can believe without the use of reason and that babies do not have its use.

Again we have to appeal to the context. The verse goes on to say that he who believeth not shall be condemned. Our conclusion is that the Lord was talking about persons who deliberately refused the gift of faith, not specifically about the baptizing of infants. The text is still valid in our use of it as a proof for the necessity of Baptism. The argument would run that Christ declared the universal necessity of Baptism, even for babies since he made no specific exceptions, and that he would not be so unreasonable as to require faith of babies.

But of course, Patricia, the ordinary Christians don't get involved in "proof-text" arguments about infant Baptism, for them it is enough that they believe that Baptism by water is a certain, outwardly visible sign that the invitation of Christ has been answered. Relying on Baptism of desire, martyrdom for Christ, or such other substitutes as the faith of the parents or extraordinary action by God while putting off Baptism by water seems unreasonable in so important a matter and the custom from the beginnings of Christianity has been to baptize infants.

Those persons in the neo-catechumenal movement who suggest having only adult Baptisms argue that eventually the quality of Catholicism from the standpoint of conviction and zeal would be much improved. They do not regard the loss of merely nominal Catholics as important. There is some appeal in their suggestion just as there is in that of the heretics who deny the validity of any Baptism received without a full understanding of its meaning. But overall, Catholics tend to follow the thinking found in the old, not very funny joke about deathbed repentance being fire insurance. Baptism, too, is a kind of insurance and to wait too long in putting it into effect is to invite spiritual disaster.

All levity aside, Patricia, I'm sure your concern for timely Baptism of your children came ultimately from your knowledge that Baptism is the beginning of the life of grace. The very life of God is infused into the human soul with that first influx of sanctifying grace. It is the beginning of eternal life in God. No mother with these thoughts in mind and love for her newborn infant welling up in her heart would think of withholding Baptism and would find it hard to delay (even for a month) its bestowal on her child.

"Lead us Not into Temptation"

The prayers you learned at your mother's knee seem forever after perfect. That there should be any mistake in their expression, their theological thought or accuracy comes a shock to anyone who recites them lovingly and routinely. Yet most of our learned-by-heart prayers are full of words from the Bible and the Bible, these latter years, has been under so many scholarly microscopes that there seems to be a new translation or a revision appearing every publishing season. The revisions do not attack any of the standard Biblical teachings but they do often change the terms by which those teachings are expressed. They lead to questions like "Could God or would God ever be Himself the source of a temptation to do something that would offend Him?"

THE QUESTION:

I am 84, a retired vice-president treasurer of one of the large
electric equipment manufacturers, father of four (one an
Ursuline nun), with ten grandchildren.

I understand that there was some discussion of meaningless
prayer at the Eucharistic Congress in Philadelphia. Frankly I
cannot understand why the Church has people saying "Lead us
not into temptation" in the *Our Father* — The Lord's Prayer. I
believe that God loves people and I cannot conceive of God
leading people into temptation. I raised this question with
several people and got only these answers: 1. The phrase is a
bad translation. 2. We say this petition because it was always
said. 3. We do not mean what we say, we are really asking not
to be tempted beyond our ability to resist.

My knowledge of foreign languages is zero and I know very
little of early Church history and I would like to know who
wrote the Lord's prayer, when it was written, in what language
and whether the meaning is the same when it is translated into
Latin, French, Spanish, Russian and so on.

I never say "Lead us not into temptation." Instead I say,
"Help us to overcome our temptations," or "Shield us from
temptation."

Eugene C. Doeker

THE ANSWER:

You do well, Mr. Doeker. Some years ago *Catholic Digest*
carried an article from a book by Jean Daujat which called the
usual translation of this petition "flagrant nonsense." We can
still go along with him with something of a chuckle, because
our present Catholic version of the prayer in our English
liturgy came to us from Henry VIII of England, the one with
the tendency to chop off the heads of his wives. He held the title
Defender of the Faith from the Pope but did not interfere in
liturgical matters until he had broken with Rome. With
Thomas Cromwell and a Bishop Hinsley he produced in 1541 a

manual of prayers which he commanded to be taught to the people by every parson, vicar and curate in England. His version (and spelling) went, "And let us not be led into temptacyon. But delyver us from evyll. Amen." In 1549 "let us not be led" was changed to "lead us not" in the (Anglican) Prayer Book of Edward VI.

The first answer you got was correct as far as it went and the "Lead us not into temptation" phrase which bothers you seems to be the result of faulty translation. Just whose fault, I don't know. Bluff King Hal (Henry VIII) was responsible only for continuing in English what was already present in the Latin and Greek.

The implication that God would influence us in the direction of evil results from the combination of the ideas "lead" and "temptation." One can arrive at a better theology by changing one or the other of these terms. We can say, as you do, "Shield us from" instead of "lead us not into," retaining the word *temptation.* Or, we can say something like "Lead us not to a testing," meaning we don't want our merits to be judged (at least not right away). In this case we could keep the word *lead* but would change the other term *temptation.* It makes rather a long story even to issue guesses on which translators in the long history of Bible versions made the mistakes of combining *lead* and *temptation.*

It turns out that the word "eisenegkes" *(lead)* is part of an irregular Greek verb *(fero)* which, being a root or basic verb, has more than three columns of meanings and citations in the Greek lexicon. Its meaning is shaded and even changed by the words in the sentence. When you say in Greek, "The road carries traffic" and "The road leads to Athens", you can use the same verb, *fero* for both "carries" and "leads."

When Henry's version "And let us not be led into temptacyon" was changed under Edward to "Lead us not into temptation" it was a question of the translators making a choice between two acceptable adaptations of a Greek verb. But, if they were going to use "lead", they should at the same time have changed the word *temptation* to *test,* since the Greek could have had that meaning. As follows, if you're still with me.

The Greek text has the word *peirasmon* for which the definitive Liddell-and-Scott lexicon gives the English equivalent as *temptation*. But the lexicon also refers to the verb from which the noun *peirasmon* comes, *peirazo,* as having the meaning "bring to trial." And there is a word very like it, *peirasis,* found in classical Greek, which meant a "testing". When Matthew's Gospel was first put into Greek it is possible that *peirasmon* (temptation) was used instead of *peirasis* (test) only because the Jewish text of the Old Testament in Greek had used the newer word in various places. On this supposition, the "Lead us not into temptation" phrase should have come out "Lead us not to the test."

There is the further possibility that Henry's *temptacyon* meant "test" to him, not what the word *temptation* means to us in its modern usage, since words change their meanings with the passage of time. Or, Henry might have taken the Greek word to have a 16th-century Christian meaning which it never had to the early Christians. You have to remember that the ancients did not have Christian concepts and consequently had no words with Christian meanings. The Christian and theological meaning of temptation is: the presence to the mind of the possibility of acting or even thinking in opposition to the will of God for the sake of material gain or pleasure. I really doubt that the ancient languages had a word for this complicated concept. The chances are that both those who translated the earliest versions and Henry VIII read a new meaning into an old word.

To get on with our theme, Mr. Doeker, we might consider why we Catholics are using an admittedly mistaken Anglican-church version of the Lord's prayer. Well, in mediaeval England down to the time of the Reformation the people knew only the Latin form of the prayer, though they spoke in English when not praying. All through the centuries since the time of the Roman Empire, Latin had remained the language not only of the Church but also of the law and the government. It was an upward step in education for the peasant to learn his prayers by heart in Latin. There were many translations into English differing from one another in books of devotion, but no official exclusive text in English until Henry's edict.

When the Catholics came back into power under Queen Mary, no particular effort was made to continue the practice of saying prayers in Latin and the version of the Lord's Prayer learned by so many Englishmen under the enforcement of Henry VIII, and as up-dated under Edward VI, was generally accepted by the Catholics. It was a faithful translation of their Latin and the point about God leading people into temptation had not yet arisen. Only a few Catholic books and catechisms used any other version and after the time of Laurence Vaux's catechism (1568) all widely known Catholic publications used the Anglican form of the prayer. Incidentally, Mr. Doeker, one of these variations dated 1506 reads ". . . and suffer us not to be temtyd" which is pretty close to your change "Shield us from temptation."

In response to your query about who wrote the Lord's Prayer, it was first spoken by our Lord in his native Aramaic. His exact words are forever lost, though our knowledge of what he said comes from the Scriptures. He is quoted in the Gospel of St. Matthew in chapter 6, verses 9-13. Irenaeus (200 A.D.) testifies that Matthew preached to the people who spoke our Lord's language in their own tongue and wrote his Gospel for them. Origen in 233 A.D. said Matthew wrote it in Hebrew characters. But we do not have any of his manuscripts. We have only manuscripts in a Greek translation dating from the fourth and fifth Christian centuries, no first-hand stenographic transcript of our Lord's discourse.

With this background, Mr. Doeker, you can understand how versions can differ. The *Our Father* as it is translated in the *New American Bible* reads "Subject us not to the testing" while the new *Order of the Mass* reads "Lead us not into temptation." The scholars working on the new version of the Bible saw the same difficulty you did and changed the translation; the bishops in charge of the new *Order of the Mass* for this country saw the difficulty but decided not to change.

Their reasons are not hard to find. Everyone (even the scholar, I'm sure), has a reluctance to change a prayer he knows by heart. It is associated with all the spiritual experiences of his life. No amount of scholarly explanation of the change affects this emotional attitude. I remember that official changes were made in the liturgical chants for Holy Week while I was in the seminary but our maestro kept on with the old tunes for several years. When the rite of Holy Week was revised in the early 60's, Carinal Spellman asked Rome for a delay in his diocese. Today there is a bishop with considerable following defying the Pope on the matter of giving up the Latin Mass.

All these were, or are, only emotional reactions to changes but they do explain why the second answer you got to your inquiries was that we say "Lead us not into temptation" because it was "always" said. A good enough reason, if your emotions are strong enough.

Your third answer, "We don't mean what we say", follows naturally from the second. Let's put it this way. Your problem arose because of the difficulties (poor translators, lost manuscripts) in keeping written records, even those as important as the Bible, from being changed. An added difficulty is the change in the meaning of words that are preserved as they were in the original manuscripts. The only solution in the case of prayers might well be the third answer you got, "We do not mean what we say." But we can go on saying it if we at the same time know what it should be. This is not as ridiculous as it might sound at first hearing. There is a sect of the Hindus that refuses to have any Scriptures. They say that the only way to hand down the same doctrine from generation to generation is to explain it vocally and be sure it is understood. The hearer can do the same thing 50 years later even though the words in his language have changed some of their meanings and even though he is speaking an entirely different language. The difficulties of lost manuscripts, mistranslations and variations in texts disappear. Personally, I would hate to have anything like this procedure in the field of medicine or law, where the content of knowledge is beyond the capacity of one mind, but maybe for so short a prayer as the *Our Father* the system would work: keep the wording we have, but explain it to every new listener. "Faith cometh by *hearing.*" St. Paul observed, even though he was writing a letter at the time for people to read.

All in all, Mr. Doeker, I would be in favor of keeping the old, learned-by-heart form of the Lord's Prayer. There are other phrases in it that are not perfect in expression. "Our Father who art in heaven," for instance. God is everywhere, not only in heaven. We use heaven because its direction in our minds is upward. "Upward" has connotations of superiority because we men, as opposed to animals, can look upward. *Anthropos,* Greek for *man,* is the upward-looking one. The psychologist Jung says that this concept got into the collective unconscious of man so that he thinks of God as being physically above him.

"Daily bread" means more than "bread every day." It means enough for now. In an affirmation of confidence in God's Providence we make no reference to the future.

"Hallowed" is no longer in use in English except by a few poets and in the expression "Halloween." It has suffered perhaps the most vulgar perversion of any word in English. To hallow meant to make or keep holy, a hallow was a saint, Halloween was the eve of All Saints day. But in the last century the spirits of the departed were thought of as being comically malicious, putting carriages on church steeples and pushing over outhouses. Nowadays little children pretend to be goblins and cry "Tricks or treats" on Halloween. But we still say "Hallowed by thy name."

The point of running on like this, Mr. Doeker, is just to show that revisions of the *Our Father*, like the revisions of the Bible, could be endless. They should be made, as scholars are now making them in the interest of truth and knowledge, but it is impossible to keep all ordinary Catholics up on the needed revisions from year to year, let alone from day to day. Once a version is established, even though it came from the Anglican church, it has advantages for public use that outweigh the need for scholarly knowledge on the part of the public.

Now for private recitation, the changes a person like yourself may make, Mr. Doeker, favor devotion and the quality of prayer. When ordinary caution against exaggeration or misemphasis of doctrine is exercised, it can be a very fine thing to put the official prayers "into your own words." But in public recitation it might be better to follow the words which untold millions of other Catholics use.

. For myself, even the thought of Henry VIII, sitting around in his doublet and hose, quaffing possets of sack and throwing chicken bones over his shoulder a la Charles Laughton, yet originating the version of the *Our Father* we Catholics use, does not deter me from using it. Nor does the fact deter me that some words are badly translated, nor that I am saying it that way because it was "always" said that way, nor that I do not mean exactly what the words I use mean (the three answers given you by your consultants). The *Our Father* as we now have it in the Mass is familiar, comforting, reassuring and all the things a learned-by-heart prayer can be. The far more important consideration is that the distortions are of minor importance when we reflect that the prayer is the Lord's own, lovely and beautiful and obviously beyond the power of mere men to put into His exact words.

The Harrowing of Hell

The descent of Christ into hell in the time between his death on the Cross and his Resurrection has often been represented in Christian art. It is called the "harrowing" of hell in the now archaic sense of plundering or pillaging, which in this case would in turn mean the releasing of souls from the prison to which they were committed until their redemption by the Savior. "He descended into hell" is a phrase in a prayer we say often by heart without too much sharp thought about what it exactly means. Yet it has not only a deep meaning which should be often meditated but is an integral part of the pattern of Christian belief — to deny it is to do away with the doctrine of the Communion of Saints. The question about why it does not appear in the Profession of Faith in the new Liturgy should be answered.

THE QUESTION:

I am 67, a retired school teacher with 20 years experience and at one time I was a teacher in our parish Confraternity of Christian Doctrine program. I am still involved in Church affairs, an avid reader of the Bible and its religious and historical background, and of things Catholic in general. Members of my family think I know all the answers (which God knows I don't).

A few days ago my sister asked me about something we recite at Mass. Before the changes were made we used to say the entire Creed at Mass, one of the articles was "He descended into hell." In the present *Profession of Faith* this article is omitted. She asked me, "Does this mean that the Church doesn't believe anymore that our Lord descended into hell, and that we should stop believing in it?"

I explained to her the different meanings of *hell* and that once the Church has defined or taught a certain dogma it will always remain true, that truth cannot change. Should any such dogma be attacked or denied the Church would re-emphasize it. This didn't entirely satisfy her. What is your explanation?

J.T.

Your letter upset me, J.T. On reading it I immediately sought out a copy of the booklet the people are supposed to read from at Mass and sure enough the *Profession of Faith* did not contain the "descended into hell" phrase. But before deciding that the liturgical reformers had gone entirely heretical I remembered (by dint of reciting it to myself in Latin) that the Nicene Creed never did have that phrase in it. Neither does it have the phrase about believing in the "communion of saints." What you and I were thinking of was the Apostles Creed, usually known by heart by Catholics. Priests learned it from saying it in their office and lay people from reciting it in the Rosary. Both phrases are there.

The present *Profession of Faith* is a translation of the Nicene Creed as it was said at Mass when all Masses were in Latin. In those good old days there was little occasion for out-loud recitation of the Nicene Creed by the people. Ordinarily, and I think even in some of the first vernacular Mass booklets, the Apostles Creed was used for recitation because everyone knew it so well. Maybe you and your sister used one of those.

So there has not been any schismatic influence at work on the Creed in the new Mass, it's just a matter of organizing our memories and adjusting them to the new forms. There is no question of adjusting our old faith, which, as you say, expressed unchangeable thruths.

But this consideration may only give rise to another question about the differences in Creeds within the same true Church. Why isn't "descended into hell" in the Nicene Creed?

Well, the Apostles Creed is so ancient that throughout the Middle Ages it was commonly believed that each Apostle of the Lord on Pentecost Day contributed one article of faith to the Creed. Later scholarly investigations show that it had its origin in the very early ages of the Church as a declaration of belief made by new Christians at their Baptism. Such a declaration could never be more than a summary of the important dogmas of the faith and summaries, of course, differed from place to place. It is known that the phrase you asked about, "He descended into hell," was inserted at the city of Aquileia about the year 400. The Apostles Creed at Rome about 400 A.D. did not have it and neither did it have "Creator of heaven and earth" after "Father Almighty," nor the word *Catholic* in "Holy Catholic Church," nor the phrase "communion of saints." There were other differences from place to place in expressions of the same thought such as "crucified under Pontius Pilate" instead of "suffered under Pontius Pilate." Still other small departures and additions from and to the Roman form of the Creed occurred in other places but eventually, about 700 A.D., Rome itself adopted the additions and what we recite as the Apostles Creed is just about what it was in Rome at that time.

In view of all this it is not surprising that the Nicene Creed, formulated at the Council of Nicaea in 325 A.D. should have a form different from the apostles Creed. As you told your sister, J.T., the Church does shift her emphasis on her dogmas according to what is being denied at the time. At Nicaea, for instance, the big problem was Arius who denied the full divinity of Christ and consequently was in error about the Holy Ghost and the whole concept of the Trinity. Accordingly, the Nicene Creed presents some eight ideas about the Holy Spirit whereas the Apostles Creed, in existence for many years before these Arian difficulties came up, said only "I believe in the Holy Ghost." By the year 700 Arius was just a memory; there was no need for the Apostles Creed to reproduce the fuller expression of belief in the Holy Spirit found in the Nicene Creed. In the same way, no one at Nicaea was opposing belief in Christ's descent into hell, so it didn't occur to the Fathers of that council to include that article of faith.

The Scriptural foundation for Catholic belief in the descent is in the First Epistle of St. Peter, chapter 3, verse 18. "For Christ... being put to death in the flesh but made alive in the spirit... went and preached to the spirits in prison... who formerly did not obey when God's patience waited in the days of Noah." There are also references to Christ's stay in the nether world in the books of Matthew, Romans, and Acts.

It is the province of theologians to clarify and to work out the theoretical and practical implications of statements of Scripture and the descent into hell has been so treated.

Augustine interpreted the phrase to mean that Christ, even before coming down to earth, preached in the spirit to the people in the days of Noah. Clement of Alexandria and Origen thought this descent was some kind of a final effort on the part of the Lord to save sinners. The writer Rufinus, from whom we know about the insertion of the phrase at Aquileia, thought it meant only that Christ really died. But the interpretation of Irenaeus, that Christ went to the nether world to announce the Redemption to the souls of the good people detained there, prevailed, is the present teaching of the Church and the one you and I learned in the Baltimore catechism, J.T.

As a dogma, the descent into hell does not excite the interest of us moderns as it did that of the earlier Christians. Among the Christian writings which enjoyed great popularity was the *Gospel of Nicodemus*. While its title presumes equality with the Gospels of Matthew, Mark, Luke and John, it was not true Scripture, being only an editorial combination of a book called *The Acts of Pilate* with another, *The Descent into Hell*. But it does tell us a great deal about the interests of the early Christian scholars. The whole second half of what purported to be a "gospel" was devoted to Christ's descent into hell. Standing alone, the dogma seems to have only lesser importance even now but in those early days when Christian enthusiasm was considerably higher than now, the faithful seem to have had a greater understanding of how one Christian dogma grows from another and in turn provides foundation for still another.

The people who compiled the *Gospel of Nicodemus* saw Christ's descent into hell as an integral part of the pattern of Redemption. If indeed, the world has been waiting since the fall of Adam for the Redeemer; if indeed, there was no one in heaven till He had redeemed the world; if indeed, the souls of the good people who knew and loved the true God were waiting at the verge of hell near the gate of heaven, it must have been the Redeemer himself who came to tell them their waiting was over. And to devote half of the Gospel story to this event did not seem out of proportion to enthusiastic Christians.

There is significance in the circumstance that where the phrase "descended into hell" was not included in the baptismal or Apostle's Creed the phrase "communion of saints" was also omitted. The glorious concept that the Church extends and continues "membership" beyond the grave into heaven, purgatory and limbo made Baptism an initiation to the supernatural world, quite unlike any admission to a merely human society. The true Scriptures told the early Christians that the Lord after his death brought the good news of Redemption even to the souls of the dead so this Church which they had joined must be a communion of saints. This conclusion was important enough to include in their profession of faith, which we call the Apostles Creed.

All the dogmas in every creed of the Church are inter-dependent in the same way that "He descended into hell" and "I believe in the communion of saints" are. To take another example, you can't deny the divinity of Christ without changing your belief in the Holy Spirit, as Arius had to. So you, J.T., were rightly concerned, in fact had the same concern as the early Christians, when it seemed to you that the Creed was being tampered with. Thank God, it wasn't and I hope that what I could tell you about so seemingly "irrelevant" a phrase as "He descended into hell" will demonstrate the great unity and consistency of the doctrine of the Church.

Immortality

We live in a culture which has at least the traditions of Christianity. Religious people in our culture often go for most of their lives without ever questioning or giving a second thought to the reasons why they believe one thing or another. Then some day they have the sensation not of deja vu but of jamais vu, suddenly some belief they have always lived with strikes them as strange. Sometimes they just feel helpless, but the more curious will investigate for themselves or at least ask the question. Such as, "Will I really live again after I die?"

THE QUESTION:

There is one tenet of Catholic doctrine that I am having difficulty understanding. It is "I believe in the resurrection of the body."

With the admonition, "Dust thou art and unto dust thou shalt return," upon the placing the ashes on the forehead on Ash Wednesday and with the Church's approval now of cremation, I'm wondering what form the body will be in. I've always felt it would be a spiritual body.

At 75 years old I can remember most of the catechism proofs of our religion. This is the only teaching about which I would like to know more, especially how and when it was revealed. Of course if "resurrection of the body" refers to Christ's resurrection or his miracles of raising persons from the dead, there is no doubt or question in my mind. But if it means my own physical body I would like to know its source in revelation.

Roy J. Cutcher

THE ANSWER:

You are right, Mr. Cutcher, about our personal resurrection being in "a spiritual body" (that's what St. Paul says) and I share your apprehension about ashes in general. But Ash Wednesday was instituted to remind us to do penance before our turning to dust makes it too late to do any good, not to deny the resurrection of the body. Cremation has been reluctantly allowed now for strictly practical reasons, not because the Church has changed her doctrine on the resurrection of the human body.

So any answer I can make to your question will be more or less an expansion of that term "spiritual *body.*"

Now, belief in the immortality of the human *soul,* like belief in the existence of God, pervades all human cultures. Anthropologists write books about it when they find a wild tribe that seems not to have the concept. Ordinarily, it turns out that the wild tribe had the concept after all, that the anthropologists misunderstood something or other.

Several Oriental religions have the concept of the soul passing from a dead body to a new living body. Reincarnations of this kind in these religions can be from animal to human or human to animal, and can be rewards or punishments for conduct in the life just lived.

The ancient Greeks and Romans, to judge from their poets, Homer and Vergil, believed in a shadowy future existence in gloomy surroundings very like the Jewish Old Testament *sheol.*

There were Greek philosophers who thought of the soul as being freed to a higher life at death, liberated from imprisonment in the body. A certain flavor, let us say, of this idea, creeps from time to time into some forms of Catholic devotions. So be careful, Mr. Cutcher. To think of yourself as being only a soul or spirit after your death would not be in line with Catholic doctrine. We believe in the immortality of the soul and the resurrection of the body.

The sources of this doctrine are in the words of Christ. In the Gospel of Matthew, chapter 22, verse 23, the Saducees, who did not believe in the resurrection, tried to ridicule the doctrine with their example of the seven brothers who, one after the other, married the same woman. Whose wife would she be in the resurrection? The Lord more or less dismissed this question as a quibble and silenced the unbelievers with ". . . have you not read what was said to you by God, 'I am the God of Abraham, and the God of Isaac, and the God of Jacob?' He is not God of the dead but of the living." Everybody present got the point that the patriarchs to be "living" must have survived death. God said "I *am* the God . . ." not "I *was* the God . . ." of the patriarchs when they were on earth, before they vanished in death.

Then there is the narrative of the last judgment, related by the Lord, which is to take place after the universal resurrection of all men. All nations are to be gathered before the Son of

Man who is to separate them person by person into the good
and the bad as a shepherd separates sheep from goats. Such a
procedure presupposes a resurrection of bodies. This passage is
in the same Gospel, Matthew, chapter 25, verse 31.

Apart from what our Lord said we have in Scripture the
denunciation by St. Paul of those who, even though they called
themselves Christians, did not accept the idea of rising from the
dead. This in in the 15th chapter of Paul's first epistle to the
Corinthians, starting with verse 12. Just as our Lord dismissed
the wife of the seven brothers as of little importance to the
greater question of resurrection, Paul does not exactly go into
detail about the specifics of the risen body. But this passage is
an argument for belief in the resurrection of the body and the
most memorable declaration of that belief in the whole Bible.
Read it.

Paul's next most famous statement on the subject is
undoubtedly familiar to you from its having been one of the
Epistles in the old Requiem Mass and being among the
optional readings in the new Mass of Christian Burial. It is in
the 4th chapter (beginning verse 13) of his first epistle to the
Thessalonians. It ends ". . . so we shall always be with the Lord.
Therefore comfort one another with these words."

If at this point you interject, Mr. Cutcher, that you want to
know what Scripture says about the risen *body* of the ordinary
human being, the plain fact is that there is no academic
treatment of the subject in the Scriptures. The presumption in
all the texts is that, in the resurrection, we will be ourselves.
You will be you. You are body and soul. The Catholic teaching
is that both body and soul are incomplete substances, that the
person "you" can not be reconstituted after death with only one
or the other of these incomplete substances. This is where
Catholic teaching parts company with the belief of primitive
tribes that only the soul survives, with the belief of the
Saducees that only the soul goes to Sheol, with the belief of the
Greeks and Romans that only something like a shadow of the
person survives death, and the belief of the various reincarnationists that the soul transmigrates from perished body to new

body. Resurrection of the body is part of the Christian revelation, not to be confused with belief in immortality of the soul.

The Greek philosophers, of all the pre-Christians, did the most thinking on the subject of immortality. They ruled out the resurrection of the body when they said that man is composed of two intrinsically alien substances, the completely perishable body and the imperishable soul. The Bible never speaks of man as being this Greek addition of two things; it speaks always of man as an undivided unity. There is no word in Scripture denoting the body as separated from the soul, and in the vast majority of instances when the soul is mentioned it is thought of as being in union with a body.

This is where you could interrupt again, Mr. Cutcher, to say that none of this answers your question about what your body will be like in the resurrection. If you will pardon my saying so, your question, far from being original, is one that has intrigued theologians from the beginning of Christianity. I suppose the first new converts didn't think about scientific difficulties; in their enthusiasm for their new faith, they probably conceived themselves as being somehow able to keep the identical materials of the body in which they were then walking the earth forever with Christ in heaven. There are still some sects (called "millenarian") which have ideas of this kind.

St. Augustine, when he wrote his book, *The City of God,* (see the 22nd chapter) departed from this spontaneous assumption when he assured those with defective bodies that all would be put right in the resurrection. His meditation on the text, "The hairs of your head are numbered," brought him to write that people gone bald would have glorious new hair in the resurrected body. St. Thomas centuries later pointed out how reasonable it was that there should be no weak infants or decrepit old people in the resurrection. All should have the perfect age of Christ at his death, 33 years, full human maturity without the deteriorations of age.

St. Thomas continues the thought of Augustine when he goes on to point out other qualities of the risen body which would be incompatible with having exactly the same kind of body as a person living on earth. For instance, the risen body of the just man will not be capable of suffering. It will shine like the sun according to our Lord (Matthew, chapter 13, verse 43) and according to St. Paul (I Corinthians, chapter 15, verses 41 and 42.) It will move without effort wherever the soul pleases (St. Augustine, St. Jerome) and be in all other ways completely subject to the soul, not afflicting the spiritual substance with bad impulses or emotions as it does in the present life.

This common teaching of Catholic theologians about the resurrection of the body is founded on logical interpretations of the rather scanty details of the revealed Scriptures. But the glorification of the body should not lead us to think that it will be an entirely new body, a belief which would make reincarnationists of us in the Oriental sense. The official teaching is that our risen body will be substantially the same as we have in life on earth.

One scriptural basis for the "substantially the same" doctrine is from St. Paul. He says, evidently meaning by "this" his own body, "*This* corruption shall put on incorruption ..." But perhaps it would be better to go back to that argument our Lord had the with Sadducees. As we quoted him before, it might really be hard to see the force of what He said as a declaration of the resurrection of the body since he spoke of patriarchs who at the time were not resurrected. Could it be that He was speaking only of some kind of spiritual survival on the part of the patriarchs? No. The argument was about the ultimate resurrection of the body, and all parties to the argument understood that in the Biblical sense we spoke about, the reconstitution of the person. The Greek idea of survival, of the soul only, did not enter their minds. They were ordinary men, not Greek philosophers. Resurrection to them meant that their *bodies* would rise from the dead. The whole point is that the Lord went along with this, did not tell them their concepts were wrong. In effect we have our Lord's word for the substantial sameness of the risen body with the earthly body.

By the time of our Lord, the Jewish religion had advanced

beyond the gloominess of *Sheol.* Among the Jews that concept had been contemporaneous with the pagan Homer and Vergil.

In opposition to the Sadducees, pious Jews found the doctrine of the resurrection in their Scriptures. Isaiah had said that the suffering Servant would be exalted after his death (chapters 52 and 53). The psalm beginning "The Lord is my shepherd" ended with "I shall dwell in the house of the Lord *forever.*" The prayer of David in Psalm 16 ends "... when I awake, I shall be satisfied when beholding thy form." Daniel had proclaimed the last judgment, "And many of those who sleep in the dust of the earth shall awake, some to everlasting life and some to shame and everlasting contempt." The Maccabean martyrs, one after the other, cried out not only their belief in their own resurrection to glory but in the resurrection of their tormentors to eternal shame. (Maccabees, chapters 7 and 14.)

Among the apochrypha, or pseudo-scriptures of the Jews, the Book of Henoch had a vivid description of a general resurrection and most of these popular works contained accounts of it. And from the way Martha spoke to our Lord when He reminded her that Lazarus would rise again, it would seem evident that the ordinary Jewish people believed in the resurrection. She is almost petulant, "I know that he will rise again on the last day," as though she didn't need Jesus to tell her that. She wanted Lazarus restored to life then and there.

That was the background against which Jesus confounded the Sadducees. You must have remarked, Mr. Cutcher, that neither the Scriptures nor our Lord in the Scriptures specify very much about what the risen body will be like. We know two things for certain, 1. we will not be pure spirits for eternity, 2. our bodies will not be exactly as they are in this life. Theologians have worked out other considerations which we must accept as logical and in accord with the spirit of the Scriptures. But if we let our imaginations go to work on "what it must be like in heaven" we end up with haloed people in long robes sitting on clouds and playing harps. This sort of cartooning leads to disbelief rather than faith. It is the kind of thing that made the novelist H. G. Wells, who thought that that was what we thought of heaven, complain that "people dream of eternity who don't know what to do with themselves on a Sunday afternoon."

And St. Paul warns us against using our imaginations, "The eye hath not seen, nor hath the ear heard, nor hath it entered into the heart of man, what things God has prepared for those that love Him."

After thinking it all over, Mr. Cutcher, I see that your subtle relating of the body to ashes and saying you believed in a "*spiritual* body" after death had a great deal of merit. No matter how glorified our bodies may be, and how important it is to realize that we will be ourselves in the resurrection, the Beatific Vision of God that we hope to enjoy will make any possible pleasure we may find in physical bodies after the Last Judgment really inconsequential. That Vision is unimaginable.

Through Adam's sin our bodies must be reduced temporarily to ashes but we will again and always be ourselves. Gerard Manly Hopkins said it this way:

> In a flash, at a trumpet crash,
> I am all at once what Christ is
>   since he was what I am, and
> This Jack, joke, poor potsherd,
>   patch, matchwood, immortal diamond,
> Is immortal diamond.

Pagans and Hell Fire

The present "intellectual" fashion in matters of religion is to understand, in a very deep way indeed, that God, if He exists, loves all his creatures, that it doesn't matter how, or whether, we approach him in worship, that one religion (or philosophy of religion) is as good as the next one. In such an atmosphere, Christians who have been reared strictly in the tenets of only one denomination, are forced to ask whether their own way is the only one to salvation. Their dilemma is that to say God will save only them is to deny the nature of God as they themselves teach it, and to say that one religion is as good as another is to ignore the teaching of God's Son who certainly did not say or imply that it didn't matter how or whether you worship God. Catholics even believe that He founded only one Church and in past years used the expression "outside the Church there is no salvation" to reaffirm their belief.

THE QUESTION:

I am often thought to be a strict Baptist. I don't drink or
smoke and lead a more Christian life than many I know.
However, I am not a Christian and to my knowledge, my
beliefs are not associated with any established Church. I do,
though, tend to lean toward Christianity over the many other
religions.

The biggest unanswered question I have is: Do the many
people — good people — whose faith goes to another God or
not to God at all go to hell? I ask you because my boyfriend is
Catholic and wants strongly for me to join his Church.

Debra Idema

THE ANSWER:

The answer, Debra, is No. But I have to add "at least not
automatically" and also that I think it would be a good thing
for you to become a Catholic. God would have to give you faith
and you would have to ask for it but really no blame and no
credit would be yours in any event. Should God give you faith
and you then reject it you could be blamed; should you only
pretend to have faith you could be blamed; but there is no fault,
much less consignment to hell, in not being the recipient of the
gift of faith from God. He has his own designs and purposes
which we do not always understand.

But there are things which we do understand, and that is why
I said that should God give you the gift of faith, you should
become a Catholic. You present a profound question in very
personal terms. I don't know anything about your boyfriend,
and may be wrong in saying this, but I think his reason for
wanting you to join the Church is to reinforce the possibility of
future happiness in marriage. I don't think it likely that he has
dwelt on the problems of ecumenism, proselytism, sectarian-
ism and so on which your plain simple question brings up. I

don't think he needs to, but you should have at least a light once-over review of why the Church wants you to become a Catholic and the deeper reasons, perhaps subconscious, of your boyfriend in asking you to join.

Catholic seminarians studying to be priests find in their manuals of theology a tract explaining what the Church is, where it came from, why it is organized as it is and so on. The grand conclusion of this tract is a chapter entitled "Outside the Church There Is No Salvation." Now this statement, in that form, undoubtedly was passed on through many minds, Catholic, Protestant and non-Christian, before you heard it, Debra, but I am sure it is the ultimate source of your question to this department. I think there is a wrong emphasis in the expression because when you read the chapter of which it is the title, you find that the chapter is an explanation of how non-members of the Church are or can be saved, rather than an argument to the effect that they should not be saved. A more accurate title for the chapter would be "Salvation Outside the Church" which doesn't sound at all argumentative and would be just as accurate as far as the material in the chapter is concerned.

One of the points there is that only a person who knows the Church to be the true Church, has the gift of faith, and remains outside the Church, has any culpability as far as non-membership goes. Such a person could conceivably go to hell, since the refusal to join would be what is known as a "grave matter," but to be excluded from salvation he would have to know what he was doing and do it with perfect freedom of the will.

There are also in the chapter various explanations of how persons of good will, who would join if they knew about the requirement, already belong to the Church in what we might call their own way. If they are good people morally they could be outwardly (but ignorantly) enemies of the formal Church organization and still in their own way be members. It is said there also that God could give special graces to savages who have never heard of the Church, or who, having heard of it, would find it beyond their understanding. In any event, we cannot by any human law or regulation limit the action of Almighty God in granting his salvation.

What we can do is try to discover and pass on to others the ordinary way set up by God for us to follow in attaining salvation. We Catholics believe that way is the Catholic Church. It makes sense to us that since the Son of God (as we believe) came down from heaven, became man, and died for our sins to save us from eternal separation from God, He would entrust his message to some kind of human organization and would preserve and continue to proclaim it after He had gone back to heaven. It would also seem logical that in his almighty power He would give this organization or church the assistance it needed in carrying out his purposes. This assistance would include a guarantee of truth in the doctrine taught. Counter doctrines would then be false and only in some special provision by God (an extraordinary not an ordinary provision) could false doctrine lead to God's salvation.

Another way of saying the same thing might be to remark that although there is an infinite number of ways by which God could bring people to salvation, as far as we can tell from his revelation to us, the Catholic Church is the primary way and it would seem to be God's will that everyone to whom He grants the grace should be or should become a member of the Church.

In this connection, it also seems logical to Catholics that Christ founded only one Church. Nobody, as a matter of fact, argues that He established more than one Church. The points of difference with outsiders are are on the nature of the Church or whether there was a historical founding of a visible organization. The prayers of Christ in the New Testament are for unity of his followers, not that there be compromises or negotiated peace between factions. Truth is one. When there are two parties, one saying No and one saying Yes, and they both agree on saying Maybe, no absolute commitment to truth is left. Black is black and white is white, but gray is neither. It is this background of thought in his teachers, if not expressly in himself, that makes your boyfriend, Debra, ask you to join the Church.

You see, the whole career of Christ on earth was that of a missionary — He wanted people to join Him in his way of worshipping the Father. He sent out the 72 disciples during his human lifetime and after his resurrection from the dead he sent the Apostles into the whole world. When your boyfriend asks you to join he is only following the example of Christ.

It is the enthusiasm generated by this example of Christ that has led to the stark statement that outside the Church there is no salvation. As we saw a few paragraphs back, Debra, that statement properly explained and understood is true and valid. However, expressed without full explanation it has been sometimes used in a kind of pious fraud to induce people to join the Church. By pious fraud I mean something like what my grandmother did to me. To this day I cannot without great uneasiness wear my rubbers or overshoes indoors. My grandmother, whether she believed it or not herself and I don't think she did believe it, told me I would get weak eyes if I wore my rubbers indoors. If she was misrepresenting, her excuse would be that I was learning good manners. The same kind of pious fraud led to some Catholics saying no one but themselves would get to heaven and to the overreaction the religious world is now experiencing.

The fashion now is pretty much to abandon missionary effort, to "feel" that it doesn't make much difference what church you belong to, and in general to spend more time trying to understand the other side's position than to persuade anyone of the truth of your own position. The result has been the proliferation of jokes like the one about the Protestant upon his arrival in heaven being shown around by St. Peter. They went everywhere except for a district walled off with no entrances. When the Protestant asked about it St. Peter told him that that district was for Catholics and that no others should enter, "because they think they are the only ones up here." I was told that so many times by jovial fellow-Christians that I eventually had trouble maintaining the fixed smile I reserve for such occasions.

In such an atmosphere the question, "Why try to convert anybody?" comes readily. But the mere fact that others besides Catholics can get into heaven, does not cancel out Christ's evident purpose to found a missionary Church, nor does it cancel out the fact that opposite beliefs cannot be both correct, nor that so far as we can learn from history and be persuaded by logic Christ founded only one Church. To Catholics it is evident that God showed the world a kind of main road to salvation, but didn't destroy all other roads. They say, "Why take the back roads to town when there is a freeway to travel on?"

So, Debra, you certainly should not join the Catholic Church on the grounds that you will otherwise go to hell. I do not recommend that you join only because your boyfriend wants you to in the hope of a more secure marriage. But you should pray God for faith and if he grants it join the Church. Your reasons should be that you are seeking truth and are not content with "maybe" instead of Yes or No; that the evident will of God expressed through the missionary activities of Christ is your membership in the organization Christ founded, and that you see that He founded only one Church, which must therefore be the ordinary way of salvation, preferable to, and easier than, other ways that God has provided.

The result of your joining, Debra, will not be an exclusive right to salvation; your salvation like that of everyone will depend on God's judgment of you. You will, however, therafter have a right to, and, in God's grace the reality of, a wonderful sense of security in the face of whatever troubles this life brings you, a sense of certainty of final solution of whatever doubts and puzzles come into your life. That is the here-on-earth happiness that comes to the totally believing, right reasoning, God-contented Catholic.

Evolution

People who are religious do well to resist ideas which militate against religion. But they really should make every effort to determine whether the idea to be opposed is in itself scientific or religious. Every scientific idea, of course, has religious implications and every religious idea can be related to something or other in "science", but basically an idea such as "evolution" is either religious or scientific. The trouble, as a matter of fact, is that many people have religious ideas which are based not on sound religion but on erroneous science. When a conflict between sound science and erroneous science erupts, their religious world is disturbed and it should not be. Certainly in the mind of God there is no conflict between religion and science, there is only a combined effort of religion and science to discover the ways of God. That still leaves room for argument between them but allays all fear that either will destroy the other.

THE QUESTION:

I've always believed that when God created everything, He
created the earth and He created Adam and Eve as its first man
and woman. I can't understand the prehistoric caveman and
dinosaur bit. Would you please fill me in so when I speak I will
know what I am talking about?

I am 51 years old, father of three, work as a research
assistant, am a convert since marriage in 1952. My parents
were non-church-attending Protestants. I belong to the Holy
Name Society and am past Grand Knight of our local Knights
of Columbus council, but I must confess the Catholic Digest is
passed on to us by my sister-in-law.

Harrison Jorgensen

THE ANSWER:

Harrison, let me say I especially like your phrase "the
prehistoric caveman and the dinosaur bit." It is a pretty
accurate summary of what comes to mind when that well worn
word *evolution* is mentioned. In the popular mind, the theory
taught that men had descended from monkeys; the scholars
held out for a common ancestor for men and apes.

In my youth we often used to have what are now called rap
sessions on Evolution (it always rated a capital letter in our
school work). The play-it-safers (there is *no* Evolution) were in
numbers equal to the take-a-chancers (*maybe* there is Evolution). Only the really opinionated insisted that there positively
was Evolution. Nowadays it is all the other way around. To
hold forth publicly that you don't believe in Evolution is likely
to make you a figure of fun.

Then, as now, the religious pro-evolutionists said that God
would not deceive us by putting so many evidences of evolution
into his creation, had He created the world in six short days;
the anti-evolutionists pointed to the omnipotence of God (He

could have done it all easily in six days just as the Bible says, had He wanted to). Furthermore, He wouldn't allow the Bible to deceive us.

Despite the new theories on how to interpret the Bible, such anti-evolutionists have by no means disappeared. A surprising statistic appeared recently in the newspapers, based on a reputable national poll-taking: 46% of the Protestants in the U.S. believe that the Bible is to be taken "literally, word for word." The poll did not ask specifically about Evolution but anyone taking the Bible literally would say creation took God six days, not the immeasurable eons required by Evolution.

The same poll showed that 31% of Catholics took the Bible literally. I suppose that at the time of the first appearance of the theory of evolution nearly all Catholics opposed it. I say "nearly" because even St. Augustine (400 A.D.) taught that God in his creation implanted "seminal forces" by which Augustine meant about the same thing as does the modern scientist who speaks of "evolutionary forces."

More Catholic, as well as Protestant, opposition to the theory was stirred up by the 19th-century anti-religionists who hailed Evolution as the final refutation of all religion, as the discovery of a force that could take the place of the Jewish and Christian God.

In our modern world of oh-so-polite scepticism, we perhaps do not appreciate the shock Charles Darwin's theory must have been to Christians who had never had occasion to doubt or even discuss the literal truth of the Creation story. The best expression of this shock in English literature is in Matthew Arnold's poem, *Dover Beach,* from which beach the "sea of Faith" recedes like an ebbing tide and leaves him on a "darkling plain ... where ignorant armies clash by night." I'll return to this statement later; it's enough to say here that apparently Darwin and his contemporary scientists destroyed the fragile religious faith Arnold had.

The pre-Darwin faith of Arnold is best illustrated by the research of the Anglican Bishop Ussher, (died 1656 A.D.) who on the basis of Biblical data and then known secular history figured out that Adam was created in 4004 B.C. I'm not sure whether it was the bishop or those who ridiculed him who added that it was March 9th, at 9 A.M. His kind of faith persisted even in the face of the growing acceptance of Evolution. The edition of the Bible I and my classmates used in the seminary was printed in 1912. The editors provided as a note on the Old Testament an outline of dates beginning with Adam (year 1) which extended to Joseph, the foster father of Jesus (year 3934). If Joseph was 70 when Jesus was born we get Ussher's date for Adam, 4004 B.C.

The story according to the now expanded theory of Evolution runs a bit longer. I, of course, don't know enough about it to explain competently, but I remember reading that 20 billion years ago all matter in the universe was one big ball which exploded into the expanding universe we now inhabit. Some time in the future, I think the theory goes, all matter will come crashing back into a big ball and explode again, with the process repeating itself *ad infinitum*. Speaking just for myself, I see no reason either for accepting or rejecting this theory, I feel just like the lady at the tea-party who solemnly announced to Thomas Carlyle, "I accept the universe." "Gad, woman," he replied, "you had better."

The idea of Darwin (died 1882) that the various kinds of animals found in the world (including man) developed from lower species through the survival of the fittest specimens was immediately acclaimed by the anti-religionists but not by the scientific community. In fact, it was only after a renewed (about 1910) interest in the work of the Catholic monk, Mendel (died 1884) that scientists could understand how there could be an *origin* of species, if there were already species there to select from. Mendel's work on genetics showed how a species of plants could endure through many ages and still have some offspring that were different from itself.

In this connection, in 1952 fishermen caught a live, supposedly extinct, coelacanth, a creature also found in four million-year-old fossil form. Had it been caught by Darwin during his voyage on the *Beagle* and had he been able to compare it with its fossils it might have given him pause. (The Darwinian phrase "The origin of species by a process of natural selection" implied an inevitable change in every species.)

Without the work of Mendel people who believe in the six-day Creation would be justified in taking a live coelacanth as a proof of it, since there was no evident evolution of this species.

But Harrison, it seems to me that if we are to talk about Evolution at all, we have to start further back than prehistoric man or even the dinosaurs. Charles Darwin, Abbot Mendel, prehistoric man, and the dinosaurs, as items, pertain only to the evolution of *life*. There was an evolution of *matter* before the earth existed. That big ball of exploding energy was dreamed up and given some plausibility by another Catholic priest, Canon Lemaitre. And since his time a third priest, Teilhard de Chardin, has come along with the added thought of Evolution in the spiritual realm. Now it is true that philosophers call Teilhard a scientist, and the scientists call him a poet and that not all of the poets understand his figures of speech. However, he has with his concept of the "noosphere" and "Christ as the Omega point" enlarged the sweep of Evolution.

Since all three of these Catholic priests, Mendel, Lemaitre, and Teilhard, died in communion with the Church and yet promoted Evolution (vital, material, and spiritual, respectively), I guess we can accept their idea of the universe by saying that our assent to it depends on how great a God we believe in. The Catholic position is that He is infinite.

The evolution of matter from that big ball of energy and the grandiose and sublime dream of Teilhard about the spiritual evolution of mankind have not been proven and may perhaps be unprovable. As far as the evolution of life here on earth goes, recent research within the living cell has found mechanisms which satisfy most scientists as to the reality of Evolution.

Again, it is too complicated a subject for me to handle competently, but the researchers tell us that the living cell is made up of DNA and RNA acids and proteins. Avery discovered in 1955 that the genes, the parts of the cell that governed heredity, were made up of DNA (deoxyribonucleic acid to give it its right name) which appeared as a very large molecule in chain form. Watson and Clark in 1953 showed that the chain was made up of intertwined strands. They called this the double helix and for them, if not for the general reading public, the mystery of the replication *and* variation of a gene in a cell (the origin of species) was solved, and they had direct proof of Evolution.

Darwin had only indirect proofs: fossil records, the development of the human embryo (it progresses through the ascending stages of the lower forms of life), and the symmetrical classification of the known living and extinct species. With the dissemination of the Watson and Clark findings Evolution attained the same scientific standing as, say, Newton's law of motion.

So, Harrison, unless you want to take the Fundamentalist position (creation in six days) I don't suppose you can deny Evolution. There are still some difficulties in accepting it. For instance: Is Man still evolving?

Rene Dubos, the microbiologist, answers that by saying man will not evolve anymore, since he has reached the stage where he can control his environment. Prehuman hominids and prehistoric man, to survive, had to adapt to the environment. For instance, the prepeople in the tropics came to have dark protective skin. But the modern Eskimo will not grow a fur coat such as an animal would ordinarily develop if it lived in the Arctic regions long enough for adaptation to occur. The modern Eskimo controls his environment with his heated igloo and fur clothing and doesn't need to adapt bodily to the cold. Man has everywhere passed the stage where there is any evolutionary pressure on him to adapt his physical body to environment.

Another difficulty is the question about whether the preman hominid passed over the line to true humanity in more than one place on earth. Even in the earliest days of the Evolution controversy religious people found consolation in the fact that God could have changed a single animal into a man by giving the animal a human soul. It was a rather repulsive idea but was a possible solution and tied in with the "slime of the earth" phrase in the Bible. Now the scientists insist that it wasn't just one man (whom we could identify with Adam) who started the whole human race but various groups of evolving hominids in various parts of the world. This statement would seem to contradict the Biblical teaching that there was a first man, Adam, who sinned as the head of the whole human race. Christ, in Catholic teaching, redeemed humanity as the second Adam, as the new head of the whole human race.

Now for heaven's sake, Harrison, don't let me give you the impression that the scientific proofs that we have to accept, if we follow the ordinary human processes of our God-given reason, could destroy my belief in the Bible. Advances in our understanding of the Bible have always kept pace with anything irreligious scientists could prove in opposition to its literal teaching. In this business of the human race having more than one ancestor, it is true that the Papal encyclical *Humani Generis* comes out against polygenism, as the multiple ancestor theory is called. It is also true, as F.J. Sheed has pointed out, that the first draft of the encyclical said "it is clear that it (polygenism) cannot be reconciled" with Biblical teaching. The revised and final published encyclical said "it is not clear that it can be reconciled," opening the door, so to speak, just an inch or two. Eventually, and that may be only in heaven, when scholars attain complete scientific knowledge and our understanding of the Bible is perfect, there will be no conflict of science and religion. In the meanwhile, Matthew Arnold's ignorant armies will continue to clash by night.

There is no point in anyone with the Catholic faith being afraid of a scientific discovery. My memory goes back to a Father Jeremiah Harrington, dead these fifty years, who was my first dean of discipline in the seminary. He made a point of giving us new seminarians impromptu lessons in the great truths of both philosophy and theology. Once he and I were walking back to the residence together from the class building and were climbing the concrete entrance steps. It had recently rained and there on the top step was a group of some 20 or 30 earthworms. "Now, Kenneth," he said, "I wonder how those worms got way up here." Sensing a lesson coming on, I prevaricated and said I wondered too. "Maybe they were washed off the roof," he went on. My facial expression at this made him continue. "Don't think I am crazy. That is the way great scientists think and make discoveries. But all they ever do is remove the difficulty one stage. The next scientist will have to figure out how they got on the roof." He was right. I have often thought of him as new discoveries were announced. Each new and better radio telescope brought new mysteries, as well as new information. Black holes in space. Anti-matter. Discoveries of new particles within the atom seemed only to lead to the theoretical need for other particles, not to telling us of the ultimate composition of matter.

So, science can indeed only remove the difficulty one stage. For it, there will always be problems brought on by the solving of problems. But the problem science cannot remove even its usual one stage is, "Why is there *anything?*" which is at once the most foolish and incisive question man can ask.

Science calls the question completely foolish and unanswerable; religion calls it incisive and finds the answer in an uncreated creating God whose motives are his own goodness and, though we shouldn't speak in such terms of him, his desire to share his infinite happiness with us his creatures.

Harrison, don't worry about prehistoric man and the dinosaurs. Science is doing a wonderful job in telling us from where and what they came. Scientists go back stage by stage to that great big ball of fire, exploding and contracting, "the systole and diastole of the cosmic heart," someone called it. But where did the heart come from? Religion and faith will tell us it was from God, who, as every first-grade catechism scholar knows, "always was and always will be."

Wealth of the Church

Whether the Catholic Church has unnecessary wealth and what should be done with whatever wealth it has are questions which bother all the adversaries of the Church and a good many of the persons within it. They wonder whether the Church should not follow the evangelical counsel to sell what it has and give the proceeds to the poor. That this should be done seems self-evident to a good many people especially, I suppose, the poor themselves. Yet this specific way of helping the poor has not been the first choice of the Church over the ages and the reasons why it has not always been the first choice should be gone into, since the "treasures of the Vatican" and the stone towers and domes of splendid cathedrals really can be stumbling stones for those outside the church.

THE QUESTION:

At Mass this morning there was a second collection and the thought came to me that I should write to your "What would you like to know about the Church?" department and ask this question:

Why, in the face of famine, poverty, and the oppressed and depressed people we have on this earth, doesn't the Catholic Church with its vast wealth and treasures, cash them all in (above necessities for simple operation) and do its best to feed the world and take care of everyone we can? After all, Jesus' words in Luke Ch. 10, v. 3-12 are specific. I have tried to rationalize by saying that the wealth of the Church consists of gifts more or less "given to God" but after a while these words sound empty.

                                                Clara Gadzinski

THE ANSWER:

Just to keep everybody up with us, Clara, let me say that the passage in Luke 10 describes our Lord's sending out of the 72 disciples as missionaries. Verse 4 reads, "Carry no purse, no bag, no sandals ...." It certainly is specific.

It would be wonderful if every Christian could be as self-sacrificing as our Lord told the disciples to be. Many Christians have been. The desert hermits of the early Christian centuries, the mendicant Orders of the Middle Ages, and people like Dorothy Day in our own time have, all in all, succeeded in their personal efforts to use the goods of the world selflessly.

But we shouldn't be too surprised when the theologians tell us that voluntary poverty is a counsel of the Lord rather than a requirement for being a Christian. You can be a much better Christian by following the counsel but because of the practical difficulties teachers of ascetical theology have never insisted on a vow of poverty for all Christians nor the Church as a whole.

You may well object at this point, Clara, that you were not even suggesting that all members of the Church take a vow of poverty. But if you are suggesting anything less than that, it would seem to me that you are only recommending that the Church do something that it is already undertaking, that is, the relief of the poverty-stricken. From the days when St. Paul reproved his Christians for not obeying his admonition to share their food at the *agape*, through all the Middle Ages of faith when there were so many Religious societies devoted to poor relief and so many saints like St. Francis who gave away all they owned, down to the relatively modern saints of social service like Don Bosco, the main thrust of Christian endeavor has been the help of the distressed. On this I don't see how there can be disagreement.

Your letter implies from its use of terms like "vast wealth" that the Church has resources which are not being properly used; more vividly, that people are starving while the Church keeps enormous sums in investments simply for the sake of increasing the amount of money on hand. This is a picture often drawn by the enemies of the Church. It is simply not true of the Church as a whole. One cannot deny that there are instances where it is true. Recently there have been several scandals here in the U.S. in the mismanagement of funds. But to say such things are typical of the Church's management of money is as false as saying Church money has never been mishandled.

So I suppose, Clara, that your thought really was that the Church should do much more than it has been doing for charity. No one can quarrel with that; it has been the theme of most of the preaching in the Church since Christ founded it.

There is really no cause to quarrel about anything, but there are a few considerations which your letter makes necessary if it is to be answered adequately. For instance, it calls for the literal fulfillment of an isolated text of scripture. Since you referred to Luke 10, 3-12, let me say that John 12, 8, is just as relevant to your question.

This is where Mary, the sister of Martha and Lazarus, pours precious oil on the feet of Jesus. Judas objects that the oil should have been sold and the money given to the poor, but the Lord says to leave her alone. "For the poor you have always with you, but me you have not always."

There are sidelights to this conversation, such as the insincerity of Judas, but spiritual writers have usually seen here the point that wealth can be used for the direct worship of God (as it was in all the sacrifices of the Old Law) as well as for the indirect worship of God as it is when given to the poor. You can worship God either way, according to your choice, but it would seen unreasonable to require everyone to worship God according to the way you yourself prefer.

There even seems a danger in giving too much importance to money when you want to "cash in" all the treasures of the Church. Take, for example, a fine solid gold reliquary as a typically useless treasure. (Relics are pretty much out of fashion.) When the Church sells a reliquary, there is always a hidden loss even when a great price is received. The reliquary's full value is not in the dollar price of the gold it is made of — its value comes also from the hours of workmanship expended by its maker. In the vast majority of cases these were hours employed in the direct worship of God. All memory of these hours vanishes when the vessel is melted and sold. When it is sold "as is", the admiration people have for it in a museum collection is for the workmanship or artistry of the maker perhaps, but certainly all thought of the worship of God is lost.

I'm sure you know there was a great wave of this selling of the treasures of the Church in Europe in the late 60's, and on a lesser scale, of "obsolete" Church fittings and furnishings (like statues and altar rails) in this country.

Whenever a cathedral or great church is built, you will hear the action called a waste of money. The money collected for the building could be given to the poor. But this is seldom, if ever, done and there are reasons why it is not.

If you are a Catholic and believe that Christ founded his Church as a visible organization of human persons, there is a distinct value in such things as visible cathedrals. They make for continuance of ritual by providing a permanent site for the enactment of the various traditions of the faith: celebrations of feasts, ordination of bishops and clergy.

The effect is preservative. If you do away with cathedrals and even churches, and go in for such things as "home" Masses in somebody's recreation room you do save money and the money could be given to the poor but you do so at the risk of endangering necessary traditional practices. When ordinations are held in home parishes or small missions instead of in cathedrals the importance of the sacrament is diminished in the thoughts of the general public accustomed to a degree of pomp and circumstance in a ritual so necessary to the continuing life of the Church.

Besides calling for a distinction between the direct and indirect worship of God, Clara, your question brings up the need to define the "wealth of the Church" and the needs of "the poor."

If by "vast wealth" you mean everything that every Catholic owns added to everything owned collectively in the Church, I would have to agree that this wealth is vast. But *vast* in your expression is a loaded word. It seems to carry the connotations "idle," "unnecessary," "expendible," and "shameful."

The wealth of the Church is none of these. It consists mostly of churches to worship God in, hospitals for people to get well in, schools for children to learn about God in, and retirement homes for people to prepare to meet God in.

Total up all the money needed for their construction and you would arrive at an enormous sum. Total up what you could sell them for and you would get a lesser, though perhaps respectable sum.

But the real difference would not be expressible in money terms; it would be the same as in the reliquary before and after it was melted and sold. The purpose, the visible, external worship of God, would be lost, even though the money were given to the poor.

The satisfaction of the needs for food and shelter is not the only purpose in life. As a matter of fact, if you took some wild, bloodthirsty, murderous tribe of savages and supplied it with food and shelter your result would be a well-fed, well-housed, wild, bloodthirsty, murderous tribe of savages. Man has needs beyond physical necessities. You shouldn't have sold those schools and churches because that is what this tribe, along with the rest of mankind, will need as much as it ever needed food and shelter.

Part of the Christian understanding of charity is that it does more good to the giver than to the receiver. The good to the giver can come whether he gives food to his neighbor, schools to the ignorant, or churches to those who haven't heard what the purpose of life is or of the God who was the first giver. I really can't see, Clara, why gifts like these, "given to God," should ever seem empty to you, even compared with gifts of food and drink given into the physical hands of the needy.

Just to add a final reflection, we could consider the Church in relation to the modern welfare state. Most of the charitable functions undertaken by the Church in former ages have been taken over by the state in modern times. I think the Church can take some credit for having taught our Western civilization this aspect of social justice.

In a sense, even communism in its purely economic aspects got its inspiration from the early Christians of the time of Ananias and Sapphira, when the community supported every-one in it on commonly owned funds — voluntarily. The communists make community giving compulsory, not vol-untary, and this, from the Christian point of view, takes all the merit out of it for the vast majority of the people.

Human nature being what it is, Clara, your suggestion if carried out would only add the Church to the agencies of the welfare states in eliminating any suggestion of charity and the love of God. The cathedral, the golden reliquary, the gift given to God or man in perfect free will and with the warmth of charity all stand as answers to the implications of your question.

As always after reading over what I have written I find that I have overanswered. You, personally, Clara, could answer back on most of these points because they do not apply to you. You said in your letter only that the Church should "take care of all we can" and you are most certainly right in that. But I am going to let it all stand anyway, because there are so many people who do need these additional considerations pointed out to them.

Reverence for the Blessed Sacrament

With the new Mass ritual there came such innovations as lay ministers of Holy Communion, a change very hard for persons reared in the old traditions to accept. There were also many relaxations in the meticulous regulations on the physical treatment of the Blessed Sacrament. All such change inevitably gave rise to suspicion as to whether those priests and lay persons abandoning the old ways of utter reverence still believed that Christ was present, Body and Blood, Soul and Divinity under those appearances of bread and wine. As it has turned out, there were some who did not so believe, decided to quit pretending and quite properly, given all the circumstances, left the Church. But those who did believe were still faced with what seemed an outrageous relaxation of reverence and they certainly had the right to ask about it. There is an answer, one going back to the early Church and source in ancient tradition.

THE QUESTION:

I am 66 years old, was raised a Catholic, attended a Catholic grade school for eight years and have gone along with many of the changes in the Church in the last ten years but one I am unable to accept is the extraordinary ministers. When I receive Communion, I find myself getting in the line receiving from the priest rather than the lines with the extraordinary ministers, especially the women with short skirts.

We were taught in the Catholic school that the first three fingers of the priest's right hand were consecrated and only he could touch the Blessed Sacrament. If the Host accidently dropped to the floor, a cloth was dropped over it until all had received Communion and then the priest would carefully pick up the Host.

I was at the Mass the day the priest in our parish prepared the extraordinary ministers to administer the Blessed Sacrament to the parishioners. He just read a few words to them and that was it. Nothing was done about blessing their fingers and it is hard for me to accept such a cold way of preparing someone to give Communion to a congregation of devout Catholics. I am very puzzled about the touching of the Host. I would appreciate a good explanation of how this change took place and what happened to the old teaching that the Host was too sacred to be touched by hands other than a priest's.

Mary J. Anderson

THE ANSWER:

Mary, along with a good many other persons, you are suffering from religious-cultural shock. You have my sympathy because of my memory of the time my Sunday-Mass assignment was changed from a parish where we did everything the old way to a parish that tried to keep just a little ahead of everyone else in promoting change. Anyway, I was taken by surprise. I was ready to distribute Communion and was feeling a little put out because no priest had come to help when a bevy of nice old ladies came up to the altar and filled the cereal bowls they carried with Hosts from the large ciborium. One of them said kindly, "You take the middle-aisle station, Father." They helped to distribute Communion, and the time required for it was much shortened, but it took me a much longer time to get over the religious-cultural shock. Maybe the reflections I made at the time will help you too, Mary.

Let me say first that this is neither an argument for, nor an argument against, the employment of lay persons in the distribution of Holy Communion. The permission is now ecclesiastically legal and everywhere accepted, though the official restriction to occasions of necessity is usually met with knowing smiles.

I realized at the time of the little ladies' intervention that whatever my personal reaction might be I would have to get used to the new state of affairs. I took thought of what Father William Busch had told us in the seminary. He taught history, but of course is more famous for being one of the founders of the liturgical movement in this country. It occurred to me that he, most likely without meaning to promote change, had touched upon the germinal doctrines which eventually brought about the use of extraordinary ministers of Communion. At any rate he taught us that in the Eucharist doctrine as professed by the Catholic Church, there was a *"Res"* (thing) aspect as well as a *"Persona"* (person) aspect. Most of us seminarians at the time were unacquainted with this thought and had from childhood devotionally considered the Blessed Sacrament only as a Person. However, we felt no surprise as it was evident that the Eucharistic species had to be handled, cared for and in many ways treated like an inanimate thing. What did surprise us was his telling us that in earlier ages (he specified the time of Charlemagne — circa 800 A.D.) treaties between rulers were sometimes signed not with ordinary ink, nor even with the blood of the treaty makers but with the Blood of Christ — wine consecrated at Mass. Giving this kind of importance to the

"*Res*" or "thing" aspect would, I suppose, give pause even to the most avant-garde theologians of our own time, but it is a plain fact of history, as was the carrying of the Eucharist by lay people not only to the sick but to stay-at-homes.

Such practices were given up after the rise of scholastic philosophy and theology which placed more emphasis on the "*Person*" aspect of the Eucharist. We know that devotion to the Real Presence of Christ in the Eucharist was flourishing at the time of St. Thomas Aquinas (1225-1274 A.D.). As later defined by the Council of Trent (1545-1563) Christ was present in the Sacrament in his body and blood, soul and divinity. Such emphases on the "*Res*" aspect as Luther's "consubstantiation" (Christ is present with, in, or under the bread) or his disciple's "impanation" (a hypostatic union between Christ and the bread) were rejected in favor of "transubstantiation" (the total conversion of the substance of bread into the Body of Christ and the total conversion of the substance of the wine into the Blood of Christ. Of the "*Res*" aspect the Council admitted only that the Eucharist had the appearances, color, taste, etc. of bread and wine. In opposition, many sects have now gone over to the belief that there is only the "*Res*" aspect to the Eucharist; it is only bread and wine with a special meaning.

Within the Church there has recently been some writing by theologians using words like *transignificance* instead of *transubstantiation*. They do not seem to be denying the Real Presence but want to express it in terms other than those of scholastic philosophy. They have not been condemned but they must face the fact that the scholastic concept of perceptible things being composed of "substance" and "accidents" is well-suited to the mystery of the Real Presence. Color, taste, etc. are "accidents" of the substance, something like adjectives to a noun. Every perceptible thing has its substance, but our senses tell us only of the "accidents." We can't perceive "substance." We can't perceive "accidents" in isolation from substance. We never see "white" or taste "sweet"; it has to be, e.g., a white cloud or a sweet food. In the Eucharist the substance is the Body and Blood of Christ, the "accidents" are those of bread and wine. The philosophical doctrine cannot be scientifically demonstrated but the more important point is that it cannot be scientifically disproven either, and thus the religious doctrine is kept in the realm of the supernatural where it belongs. "Transignification" seems to put it into the realm of human psychology and to put the change in our senses rather than the substances. All this terminology emphasizes the "Res" aspect.

But be all that as it may, Mary, since the passing of the dark ages the emphasis in the Catholic Church toward the Eucharist has been on the "Person" aspect. As the doctrine became appreciated by more and more of the faithful, devotional practices sprang up which were the opposite of such things as using the Precious Blood to sign documents. Until just a few years ago the priest, between the Consecration and Communion of the Mass, was required to keep his thumb and right forefinger joined at the tips, lest any infinitisemal particle of the Host should fall to the floor or be wafted away. Incidentally, the instance of reverence you mention was not correct in all details. The priest was to pick up the fallen Host immediately. The spot where it had fallen was to be covered and later washed with a "purificator", a cloth that was itself to be still later washed three times in water which would be run into clean ground, not the sewer. The fallen Host, whether or not soiled in the fall, was usually placed in a little gilded purification cup of water to dissolve, lose the appearances of bread, and thus cease to be the Body of Christ.

There was a recommendation, if not a prescription, in the front of the Missal to the effect that should an insect fall into the chalice after the consecration the priest was, if he could do so without nausea, to swallow it whole, lest some tiny fleck of the Precious Blood should be lost.

In reference to your question, Mary, the ordination ceremony of the priest does include an anointing of the hands, which popular devotion always interpreted as consecration for the touching of the Host. I am unacquainted with the idea you mention of the three fingers of the priest's right hand being consecrated to the touching of the Host, but it is an example of how people devised devotional ideas out of a deep sense of the Real Presence, the "Person" aspect of the Eucharist.

Liturgically, emphasis on the "Person" aspect led to the placing of the tabernacle for the reserved Sacrament on the main altar of every church and to an elaborate etiquette of lights, veils and curtains to indicate the reservation of the Host. I first noticed the rise in emphasis on the *"Res"* aspect of the Eucharist when the younger priests of the parishes where I helped discontinued the use of the ciborium veil, and began filling the ciboria with unconsecrated altar breads without "purifying" the vessels before re-use. One of them, I remember, began carrying the ciborium in one hand with his arm hanging down at full length, as he would a football, a practice, I am glad to report, which does not seem to have caught on. With the publication of the new rite of the Mass, the need for the chalice veil, and the burse for the corporal disappeared and priests who continued their use did so out of a desire to emphasize, a while longer, the "Person" aspect. I tell you all this, Mary, because you, I am sure, know what all these things, burses, veils, etc., are. They are only archaic terms requiring explanation for most of our population of teen or younger age.

The point I am trying to make, Mary, really has to do with your question. If someone wants to emphasize the *"Res"* aspect of the Eucharist he gets rid of things like veils, scrupulosity about invisible particles and the use of *ordained* ministers of Communion, such as the priest, in favor of extraordinary ministers, such as lay people. Mine is only a private appraisal and I certainly speak with no final authority but it seems to me that a change in emphasis from the "Person" to the *"Res"* aspect is being engineered by those now in the Church who have the power to do such things. I am guessing, but it also seems to me that this change is being effected in the interest of ecumenism, closer union of Catholics with other men. Whether that is good or bad is for everyone to decide for himself. It may be that in the emphasis on the "Person" aspect the Church did render the Eucharistic doctrine less intelligible to those who came to it with absolutely blank minds as do so many modern persons. It is possible that such persons may be more readily attracted if they are told of the Eucharist as a "thing" before they are given its explanation as a "Person."

At any rate, and as always, danger to Catholic doctrine comes from overenthusiasm for change and reform. Emphasis on the *"Res"* should not exclude the "Person" or the fall will be into heresy with those who think of the Eucharist only as bread and wine with symbolic meaning. This might be the point at which to add that a lesser intensity of faith is required, if indeed any faith at all, if the Eucharist is to be treated exclusively as a thing *(Res)*.

Another conceivable reason for the present change of emphasis from "Person" to *"Res"* might be found in the parallel desire to teach "community." This term is used loosely to mean that we should pay more attention to our fellow man than we do to our private devotions. I don't think anyone means we should pay less attention to God, but that is the impression that some of the zealous proponents of "community" give. In reference to the Eucharist the community-preacher would put more emphasis on the function of the Sacrament in uniting mankind that he would on its uniting us with Christ in a supernatural way. For the purposes of the community preacher the *"Res"* aspect of the Eucharist is all that is necessary; for someone seeking to emphasize union with Christ, there must be emphasis on the "Person" aspect.

I'm sure you will join me here, Mary, in wondering why on earth there has to be excessive emphasis on either of the aspects. What is annoying to both you and me is an excess of emphasis rather than a departure from the true doctrine of the Church. The trouble is further that the persons promoting the changes claim them to be only attempts to restore a balance of emphasis. As in all human arguments, you have to make a choice. But let no one distort the true doctrine. We must not accuse anyone of sin, but it does seem obvious that the people who have stopped genuflecting to the Blessed Sacrament, stopped bowing or tipping their hats when passing a church, who now "talk out loud in Church" (that dear old stand-by of the devotional confession) or who distribute Communion wearing skirts short enough to scandalize people are tuning out Christ's revelation to us: He is present, Body and Blood, Soul and Divinity in the Holy Eucharist.

Chewing the Host

In the course of devotional changes in the Church some things which used to be reprehensible have become desirable. This change has become possible through the increased use of symbolism, which can be sometimes good and sometimes bad. Old attitudes of reverence can be disrupted by new emphasis on a symbol which in itself does not promote reverence so much as a doctrine. Christ is truly present in the Eucharist, which should therefore be swallowed with reverence; but the Eucharist is food and therefore should be treated like food and chewed. Both the people who are offended by the chewing and those promoting it, should learn that the chewing can be reverent, and will be, once the symbolism is properly evaluated.

THE QUESTION:

When I was a youngster, I was taught not to chew the Host when receiving Communion. It was to dissolve in your mouth and not touch your teeth. Now one sees the priest chewing after he takes the Host during Mass and people of different ages, mostly the younger ones, leaving the communion rail chewing as hard as they would if they had gum in their mouths. Has the rule about the Host dissolving in the mouth been discontinued?

Mrs. A.M.

THE ANSWER:

Strictly speaking, Mrs. A.M., there never was a "rule," that is, any universal law about not letting the Host touch your teeth. As your letter shows, it was widely taught as a pious practice and act of special reverence. But only, I should think, since we started (about the 11th century) using unleavened or "flat" bread for the altar. In the very old days when regular bread in large pieces was used it would have taken too long for the Host to soften for people to follow that form of devotion.

Your question is not exactly one that the whole world is debating, Mrs. A.M., but it does show how people react to unexplained changes in the Church. The teachers who are doing the changing don't bother to tell the children the way things used to be done and have no contact with the older people who react to a change when they see one.

Many of the newly introduced customs, such as chewing the Host, seem outrageously irreverent to persons brought up in the old tradition. For us old timers, one of the most edifying sights in all the Catholic ceremonies was that of the little children at First Communion: eyes downcast, hands folded, walking slowly with measured steps, hardly breathing in the overwhelming thought of what they were about to do. Now it is not a rare occurrence to have them come to the altar with their hands in their pockets, carrying on a conversation with a chum. They have been taught, I suppose, "not to be afraid."

But this matter of chewing the Host, as you say, can be puzzling. For some as yet unresearched reason there has grown up among many teachers of catechism an unreasonably bitter opposition to the custom of swallowing the Host without allowing it to touch the teeth. Now I do remember being warned at about college age that there was a real danger of not receiving the Sacrament if the Host was totally dissolved in the mouth before it was swallowed. This warning was theologically sound; the Real Presence ceases with the appearances of bread and wine.

But the insistence on chewing seems not to come from this consideration so much as from the idea of treating the Eucharist as food. The logic runs that since you ordinarily chew food, you should chew the Host. It's a matter of symbolism. But somehow this minor point has received attention all out of proportion to its importance. What is primarily important is only that the Host be not totally dissolved.

I remember reading, during the first fine flush of independent thinking after Vatican II, at least three manuscripts submitted for publication in *Catholic Digest* of the "This-was-the-way-before-we-knew-better" type. They each had reminiscences of how "Sister" used to stage whisper at the childen returning from Communion, "Stop chewing the Host!"

Now I never witnessed anything like that and am inclined to credit the imaginations of the would-be authors. They were using this type of ridicule in their zeal to change the old Eucharistic manners. What the zealots overlooked, of course, is that obvious jaw-rotating chewing is not necessary to carry out the symbolism of eating nor for insuring that the Host will be "received," that is, swallowed before being dissolved.

I suspect that the whole procedure was originally just a teaching trick, something physical for the children to do to help them remember the abstract symbolism. When the children make caricatures out of the act, the true teaching has missed fire. After all, good table manners, as they were taught in the long ago, tended to discourage any vigorous activity in the act of eating. You were supposed to be slow, quiet, and unobtrusive. I can't see why the same rules should not apply at the Eucharistic meal.

The idea of noticeable chewing even reached a commercial phase. I was once consulted by the Mother Superior of a group of nuns who were supplementing their income by providing altar breads for neighboring parishes. She had been visited by a salesman who wanted her to change to a new type of altar bread which required a special machine for its manufacture. The machine produced a peanut-shaped, crispy-crunchy piece of bread which could be easily picked up by the fingers for self-administration of the sacrament and which rivaled the TV-advertised chip and cereal foods in chewability.

The salesman threatened her: unless she signed a contract for the purchase of the machine immediately he would put her on a blacklist and when the official order to use this type of altar bread was issued she would be then unable to purchase the machine and would be driven out of the altar-bread business. I gave her what comfort I could by assuring her that even the most zealous chew-the-Eucharist reformers were unlikely to require the use of a patented process in the production of altar breads. She stayed with the old method and product; so far she had no trouble.

I didn't bother to explain it at the time to the good Mother Superior but the whole imbroglio is an outgrowth of the inept use of symbolism. So let me explain now.

In simple terms, a symbol is a visible thing or action standing for or signifying something else, usually something invisible or abstract. Symbols are much in use in all religions. Curiously, the word *symbol* and the word *devil* come from the same Greek word (*ballein* — you could look it up). Symbols can be effective or ineffective, that is, good or bad. They can be simple or complicated — and so on.

Symbols are the basis of most poetry. All the intricate and subtly distinct figures of speech, metonymy, metaphor, and so on, are only subheadings of the topic *symbolism*. Symbols served their purpose well in the Catholic Middle Ages in instructing the illiterate in the abstract truths of the Faith.

There is a kind of continuance of this type of teaching in "lodges." I remember as a boy gaining entrance somehow to a building used by several secret fraternal insurance societies and being mystified by the paraphernalia stored in the meeting rooms: golden balls and stars on poles, banners with inscrutable designs and impenetrable inscriptions, books of great size bound in purple velvet, maces, halberds, and so on. They were all symbols and used in symbolic action to teach something or other.

The universal use of symbolism in human life would seem to be a reason for extremely careful use in the realm of religion, especially in the Catholic faith. There must be careful use and careful understanding. In the Christian religion symbols have caused considerable trouble by their profusion, for instance, in the Book of Revelation, where almost anyone can see his own enemy described as God's enemy. Seeing too much symbolism in things can be bad.

All the sacraments are symbols but the Eucharist is not only that. Were it only a symbol its meaning would be only that God nourishes us. Bread and wine do not by themselves symbolize the presence of Christ for us; we know about the Presence from the direct unsymbolic words of Christ at the institution of the Eucharist.

The little children who used to come up to Communion reverent to the point of seeming frightened were conscious of the Presence and probably had no thought at all of acting out the food symbolism, but they had their minds on the more important truth. If the teachers insist on a minor point of symbolism to the point where the children lose a sense of the Real Presence of Christ, the direction is toward the old 16th-century heresies.

One of the perennial dangers to true religion is the habit skeptics have of reducing all religious belief to a set of symbols. The Resurrection of Christ, they would say, does not have to be

a literal fact of history. It is a symbol of the recurrent flowering
of life in nature and as such its story is beautiful enough to
warrant telling a story of a dying God who comes to life again.
Or, they say such things as that the Apostles saw in the teaching
of Christ truths that shouldn't be allowed to die with Him, and
were so impelled to tell a symbolic story about his return from
the dead to show that his doctrine lived on.

Within the Christian religion something like that has been
said of the Eucharist — Christ, they say, was only using the
symbol of life-giving food to signify our dependence on God
the Father. He said the bread and wine were his flesh and blood
only to make vivid through the use of symbol the truth that our
life comes from Him. (Note well: skeptics say such things, I am
not saying them.)

Mrs. A.M., what all this has to do with exaggerated chewing
is this: symbols should only be signs of the truth; an historical
truth itself, like the Resurrection, should not be made a symbol
of something natural. If the children are truly receiving Christ,
it is putting things in reverse order of importance to make them
conscious primarily of the fact that they are eating.

Symbolism can be sublime or ordinary. Offhand I would say
that the more widely understood the symbol is, the more
sublime it is likely to be. The symbol of the physical union of
the Body and Blood of Christ with the body and blood of those
who believe in Him is sublime, and so widely accepted that we
can say it explains the entire growth of the Church.

The more ordinary a symbol is the less widely appreciated it
probably is. As a symbol, chewing the Host is a rather recent
development, hardly thought of or mentioned in Christian
commentary until now. So when people like yourself do not
immediately grasp the significance of the children chewing the
Host, I would say that the symbol is an inferior one, better
discontinued unless everyone, the children included, can be
made to understand the subordinate importance of the chewing symbol.

All in all, Mrs. A.M., we mustn't conclude that anyone is
trying to teach the children to be irreverent, but I think we can

say there has been a mix-up in the evaluation of symbols when children going to Communion seem to be casual and thoughtless rather than reverent and God-fearing.

The Permanent Deacons

What seem to be reforms in the modern Church are sometimes restorations. In the Sacrament of Order, the office of deacon had degenerated to merely a preliminary step on the way to the priesthood. Now the Church proposes to restore the former glory of the diaconate by ordaining men to it who do not intend to go on to the priesthood but to do their part in its restoration by remaining deacons and doing the tasks anciently associated with that office. The diaconate has so long been thought of as a "part" of the priesthood that the first question many people ask about it is "What functions of the priest will the deacon take over?" The question should be changed to "What should the new deacons do?"

THE QUESTION:

As an ordained permanent deacon and the editor of a small newsletter for the diaconate I have a question for you. What is the present status of deacons with regard to sacramentals? The last we heard was that the Bishop's Committee on the Permanent Diaconate had petitioned Rome for several "permissions," especially blessings. To many of us it does not seem logical that we can celebrate the sacraments of Matrimony and Baptism but cannot perform the less important sacramental functions like blessing rosaries.

Raymond L. Sanders, Jr.

THE ANSWER:

Your question, Reverend Mr. Sanders, touches on so many points of current interest that I hope you will forgive my branching out from it. I can't answer it directly or definitely because by the time my answer would be printed one with considerably more authority may have reached you from Rome.

But I can venture to explain why you were not automatically invested with the power of blessing things at the time of your ordination.

In the old pre-Vatican II ritual, the official list of all the blessings given by the Church, even priests were restricted in their power to bless things. Exorcisms, for instance, could be used only with prescribed permissions. Other lesser restrictions were to bishops and members of certain religious orders. Sometimes these restrictions were relaxed by a particular bishop and the ordinary parish priest was permitted, for instance, to bless rosaries even though the reservation in the ritual was to members of the Dominican Order.

I remember that on one occasion when we parish priests wanted to install Stations of the Cross in a new church, we had no "faculties" and had to arrange for a Franciscan friar to do it, for in those days (and for all I know maybe even now) only a member of the Franciscan order could bless and install Stations. In the sense that only a priest could bless things all blessings were of the "reserved" variety.

It was all part of that marvelous network of authority that permeated the Church, until the reformers broke the windows to let in the winds of change. It is the stubborn persistence of the authority-network that would tend to delay or possibly prohibit the new permanent deacons from doing any "blessing" in the formal sense of the word. The Bishops Committee you mention is asking for the relaxation of a long-standing rule.

As you indicate, blessing things is a small item compared to witnessing marriages and solemnly baptizing. To be concerned about it seems to me to be missing the point. The Church doesn't really need permanent deacons to bless rosaries. The fields the Church had in mind for the new deacons besides participation in the various liturgies are religious education, ministry to the sick, aged, widowed, divorced, the young, — pastoral counseling in general. Should the opportunity for such activity be lacking there is work in hospitals, nursing homes, rural life programs, and among the handicapped, the chemically dependent and the racial minorities.

It would be too bad if the general public got the idea that the deacons are a kind of second-grade priests. The concept of the Church is considerably more glorious than that. First of all, the deacons do receive the Sacrament of Order. They are, as were the first priests, ordained representatives of the bishop in the fields designated for them by him.

The bishop's ministry in the early Church, as now, included the offering of the Eucharistic sacrifice and the works of mercy we now label as social service. He delegated to the earliest deacons the social services; to the priests the primarily spiritual offices.

Read the passage at the beginning of the sixth chapter of the Acts of the Apostles. It does not in its own text establish that the seven chosen to assist in the "care of the tables" were also ordained deacons (St. John Chrysostom in 400 A.D. said they were not). But the overwhelming majority of interpretations by both Catholic and Protestant theologians as well as a number of liturgical references favor the belief that Stephen and the other six were indeed the first deacons.

The deacons began as waiters. The verb form of the name *deacon,* I suppose we could say "to deacon," is used in the Gospels to describe Peter's mother-in-law serving Christ at the table and also of Martha, who worked while Mary, her sister, listened to the Lord. The verb form was generally used also in a figurative sense for any good works, including the spiritual, but it meant chiefly the corporal works of mercy. We learn that from complaints in the book *The Shepherd of Hermas* (150 A.D.) to the effect that some deacons kept goods for themselves that were intended for the poor. But, of course, from the same age we have the contrasting example of St. Lawrence, the deacon who could tell the persecutor that as custodian of the Church's funds he had none, since all had been distributed to the poor.

The deacons first came to give Communion because it was their basic function as waiters to take the offerings of the people, select the bread and wine to be used for Mass and distribute what was left to the poor. It was a natural step for them to help in distributing the Eucharist itself. The highest liturgical point reached by the deacons is found in the Offertory prayer of the Pre-Vatican II High Mass, "We offer ..." The *We* was spoken by both the priest and deacon.

Tertullian (250 A.D.) makes the first reference we have to the deacon as the extraordinary minister of Baptism. Deacons were also charged with keeping proper order in the liturgical ceremonies and leading the "Prayer of the Faithful." The deacon was expected to be the expert and model Christian in those days when the world was turning to the Church.

The function of the deacon in these early centuries as the public reader of the Gospel developed from a commission to teach and evangelize. Of the original seven deacons we know that Philip and Stephen openly sought converts and it was this activity on the part of Stephen that led to his arrest and martyrdom.

We might add that the Fathers of the Church compare the deacons to the prophets of the Old Law and poetically to the scven angels with trumpets and the seven thunders in the Book of Revelations.

On a lower level of dignity than this but still in indication of importance, the deacons were an early version of present-day chancery officials. They accompanied the bishop on his official visits and were sometimes used as intermediaries when the bishop was investigating the conduct of priests. Some of them came to regard themselves as above the simple priests, as we know from a letter of St. Jerome. I don't know too much about present-day organization of churches other than the Catholic, but there seems to be a precedent here for the importance of deacons in some Protestant sects, where the deacons "call" a pastor of their choice when there is a vacancy in the parish.

There was no such practice, as far as I know, in the early Church but it is true that when a bishop's seat fell vacant his successor was often chosen from among his deacons, and just as often his archdeacon ruled the diocese until the coming of the successor.

Famous names are associated with the diaconate. Athanasius was a deacon when he attended the Council of Nicaea. Hilary, later Pope, was a deacon when he was sent by St. Leo the Great to the Council of Ephesus. Gregory the Great when he was the ambassador of Pope Pelagius to Constantinople was still a deacon.

We have no census figures on it, but from the extent of the activity of the early deacons, they would seem to have been almost as numerous as the priests. At the time of the Council of Arles (314 A.D.) Mass could not be celebrated without a deacon. Deacons were often sent to places in which there were no priests, to distribute the Eucharist, preach, baptize, lead prayer and in general take charge.

This is the point at which to ask "If the deacons were doing so fine a work, why was their office discontinued?" It wasn't exactly done on purpose. About the year 400 canon law began to insist that the clergy "live by the altar," that they have no secular occupation. It would seem that over many years thereafter whenever hard times or civil commotion decreased the number of "livings" or salaried positions for the clergy, it was the deacon rather than the priest who was let go or left voluntarily. A married man with a family would not work for nothing.

A century earlier, the prohibition of marriage, or at least the use of it, was beginning to be extended to deacons, and it became harder for the Church to recruit them.

A third reason for the discontinuation of the permanent deacons is connected with your question about blessings. Despite the high regard of the Church for its deacons and the bishop's dependence on them for so many things, there was always a clear distinction made between their work and office and those of the priests.

Hippolytus, author of what is now the second Eucharistic Prayer in the revised Missal, lived in the second century and in his jurisdiction deacons distributed the Eucharist only when there were not sufficient priests. In his writings is found the put-down that the deacon was "not ordained to the priest-hood."

With this as a starting point, theologians changed the original idea that the conferring of the Sacrament of Order brought varying charisms, or fields of work (social for deacons, sacrifical for priests). It brought only an increase of sanctifying grace. No new power was being granted deacons at ordination. Even the priest was only a witness at Marriage, and the deacon could not confect the Eucharist, only distribute it. He could baptize, but Baptism was a sacrament that anyone, in case of necessity, could confer licitly and validly.

With this kind of thinking, it seemed to the theologians that a good deacon should be interested in going higher, getting more sacramental grace through the reception of the priest-hood. One who was reluctant to do this came to be looked on as unworthy, unzealous.

This is how the high office of deacons became only a step on the way to the priesthood. It was not abolished but was made less important and only transitory, no longer a permanent state.

Priests took over some of the work of the deacons, lay persons took over some. This was a bad thing because the original deacons were not just priests of a lower rank who helped the priest in the liturgy by distributing Communion or substituting for unavailable priests at weddings and baptisms (or blessing rosaries) but men of specific rank and stature in the Church. And their dedication was far above that of even good lay people who took over for them.

The reason for the restoration of the permanent diaconate is the same as the reason for the original institution of the diaconate. The story is the same today as it was on the day told of in the first verses of the sixth chapter of the *Acts of the Apostles:* there is more work to be done than can be accomplished by the priest-clergy alone. Some priests have heard this need crying so loudly that they have given up the specific work of the parish priest to go into government social services and politics. Except in cases where they also gave up the Faith, they can be faulted only for mistaking the work of the deacon for the work of the priest. There were no "working" deacons.

A strong, fervent, permanent diaconate could become a powerful force for good within the Church, carrying out as the bishop's representative the corporal works of mercy. The bishop has, as has the Church itself, the duty of providing for both the spiritual and corporal needs of his subjects. Like the Twelve Apostles, he cannot personally fulfill all the duties he is burdened with. For the spiritual work he has his priests; in the mercy of God, he will in the future have adequate help in his other set of duties from his deacons.

The permanent deacons, even in the unlikely event that Rome would not relax its "reservations" and allow them the privileges of blessing, should certainly feel no disappointment.

Their call is to the different and more exacting fields of social service, which is only the modern term for the corporal works of mercy, which in turn means only the outward physical expression of love for fellow-men. I can't resist a final anecdote because it illustrates a sense of values. I was "on call for emergencies" my first day as resident chaplain for a hospital. Things were quiet. I needed a haircut but I carefully left the barber's phone number at the desk before leaving for his establishment. Sure enough the phone rang. It was for me. Wondering with the Cure d'Ars, "What poor soul needs me now?" and listening for sirens that might tell me there was still time, I left in mid-haircut and jogged back to the hospital. It was little Mrs. O'Something on floor 3-C. She wanted a medal blessed.

Cardinals

Once reformers have an initial success their problem become one of deciding where to stop. Sound reforms and soundly thinking reformers are self-limiting. Advocates of change for the sake of change who are merely tired of the ways things have been are in danger of pushing their ideas to the point where the carrying out of their reforms would mean the abolition of the institution they started out only to change. So it is in present times that even such basic items in the constitution of the Church as the election of the Pope by the cardinals has been suggested for reconsideration by those with a reforming cast of mind. I don't know of any who used the specific question, "What good are cardinals?" but in the context of other suggestions that is what is being asked.

THE QUESTION:

My question is about the cardinals. What purpose do they
serve besides electing the Pope? And why are they called, for
example, "Terence, Cardinal Cooke?" Why isn't it "Cardinal
Terence Cooke"? Also I have one of those Papal blessings with
the picture and signature, Paul VI, PP. I suppose the PP means
"Pope" but am I right?

Laurianne Reinhart

THE ANSWER:

One way of understanding the form of a cardinal's name,
Laurianne, is to notice how it emphasizes the Christian name
by putting that first. It minimizes the title of cardinal by putting
that second. The general idea is that all persons with Christian
names stand equal in the sight of God, though from a
secondary practical viewpoint there have to be distinctions in
rank.

This form is used in signatures and echoes the usage of the
Pope, who never signs himself officially as *Pope John Paul*
but always with the simple Christian name taken at his
election. He follows the Christian name with the capital letters
PP, which, as you thought, mean Pope. The letters stand for
Pater Patrum, Father of Fathers, to indicate supremacy, just
as emperors call themselves *King of Kings.* The double capitals
are a form of shorthand dating from the time when all writing
was done by hand. They are still used in *SS. Sacramentum,*
meaning *Most Holy Sacrament* and *PP. Sanguis,* meaning
Most Precious Blood when these terms occur in the names of
religious orders. The use of *PP* in manuscripts to mean *Papa*
(Pope) dates from the eleventh century.

But humility is more probably the reason why the form for
cardinals is kept rather than why it was originally adopted. The
latter reason goes back to medieval times and the usages of the

courts of the kings which were imitated by Papal court. In
those times members of the nobility held their positions by
reason of inheritance from the previous generation. The social
strata were well defined and any passage upward was rare
indeed. This circumstance led to great pride in family and the
association of titles with the family name rather than with the
Christian name, even in the case of cardinals.

In more recent times the emphasis on family would have
little meaning so we usually put the title in front of the full
name, President Jimmy Carter, for instance. Since the Church
doesn't always follow such secular trends, the old form of the
name for cardinals has persisted.

All that was in answer to your second and third questions.
Your first question, Laurianne, could be put less formally:
"What good are cardinals?" In this form it sounds like it comes
from someone conscious of the revolutionary and anarchistic
movements of our time so we better try to answer it.

Besides electing the pope, cardinals head various govern-
mental units in the Church, some in dioceses as pastors, others
in Rome as heads of what we could call departments. As
cardinals, though, all this is spare time activity — their primary
function is to elect the Pope. If cardinals never did anything
else, this function alone would justify their existence.

In the wake of Vatican II voices have been heard crying for a
widening of the electoral basis. Bishops and theologians and
laity should all, according to these voices, be represented by
persons from these various groups with the power to cast votes
along with the cardinals. This electing body would be more
democratic certainly, but anyone seriously proposing it has to
ignore a lot of practical matters and a lot of possibly repeatable
history. The present system is the reaction to sad experience
with mobs, rapacious noblemen, kings and emperors having
their preferences respected in the choice of the Pope.

It is true that the present method of the election of popes is
utterly undemocratic in the eyes of today's world. A group of
about a hundred men, chosen for the purpose years ahead of
time, determine who the leader of the millions of Catholics will

be. But whether full democratic election is in the interest of the Church's unity is the pertinent question. In Catholic theology the Church is a visible organization of men with free will. The same free will which casts their souls in the image and likeness of God also gives them an ineluctable propensity toward politics and power struggles. Politics and power struggles do not of their nature lead to unity, and unity the Church must have if it is to continue as a visible organization here in this world of men.

In the medieval kingdoms, political unity was preserved by making the eldest son king on the death of his royal father. Even in the wildest days of English history no tyrant upstart could claim kingship in the face of a legitimate hereditary claimant to the throne. Cromwell, ruler of England in the 17th century, who lost his popularity for other reasons and finally had his skull used as a football, never dared to call himself King, only Lord Protector. The laws of succession were so strong that a man with the right heredity could be king of several nations at once, even though he were feeble minded.

The gravest threat to the Communist establishment in Russia and China is the lack of provision for the orderly transition of power on the death of the dictator. Each time one dies, a power struggle must settle the issue, usually with the deaths of the losers.

Though most Protestant theology holds that the Christian Church is *not* a visible organization and that its unity is in some inward agreement not outwardly expressed, non-Catholic Christians continue to group, regroup, divide and subdivide, sometimes with considerable acrimony.

The Catholic Church can't go along with this kind of unity. It believes that its outward religious and political unity is one of the marks by which it can be identified as the true Church. In a visible organization that mark of unity becomes more visible with any increase in the numbers of members. That is why just a touch of triumphalism is not too bad a thing.

That is also why the Church clings to the undemocratic method of electing the Pope. A relatively small group of preselected cardinals secretly, efficiently and in most cases quickly, present the Church with a new leader. There is no drawing up of the tank battalions as at the death of Stalin, no wall-newspaper campaign of calumniation as at the death of Mao, there is no passage of power to incompetents as so often happened in the ages of hereditary kingship, there is no fragmentation of the Church into smaller units as has happened to the Protestant denominations over the years.

Election of the Pope by cardinals is, of course, only a practical means to unity. The Church ultimately has to rely on the guidance of the Holy Spirit for its unity, not on any humanly devised method of preserving it.

As a matter of fact, the election-by-cardinals system broke down during the Great Schism when there were at one time three claimants to the Papal throne. Each one had his own set of faithful cardinals and the scandal finally had to be removed by the Council of Constance where not only the 29 cardinals but the five nations: Germany, France, Spain, England and Italy, with six votes each, elected Martin V in 1417. The claimant living in Rome voluntarily resigned, the two others were deposed by the Council. The one living at Avignon was recalcitrant and when he died years later had only one cardinal left. This cardinal thereupon elected himself Pope, but no one paid any attention.

In these days of the H and neutron bombs the Pope and all the cardinals could conceivably be killed at once so one cannot claim election by cardinals as the only way to elect a Pope. This kind of election has been a matter of law since 1059. Before that time possession of the Papacy came from the support of one faction or another of the Roman nobility, who thought of the office in secular rather than religious terms, and were thus responsible for scandals.

Before this type of noble politicians took over control of the Papacy the office had been filled through election by the clergy of Rome. Of course, Peter, the first Pope, was given the office by the Lord himself.

The history of the cardinalate goes back into the mists of

early Church history. The Apostles, soon after the Ascension of the Lord, had chosen seven deacons to assist them and the first Popes in Rome did something much the same. The tradition is that Pope Evaristus (97-105) appointed 25 priests to assist him in the growing city of Rome, each with a specified territory to care for.

When these parishes eventually required more than one priest for each, the pastors, or at least the head ones, became known as the *cardinal* priests. The word is still used in this sense, it means "indispensable" or "necessary." It came from the Latin word for *hinge*, something necessary in the operation of a door. Also the *cardo* in the Roman army was the company street of the camp, essential to good order. So eventually the head deacons, priests or bishops even in cities other than Rome would sometimes receive this informal appellation, *cardinai.*

In the ninth century *cardinal* became an official title. Seven of the bishops with sees near Rome were allowed to officiate in the Lateran bisilica otherwise reserved for the Pope alone. They participated in the Papal elections though they were not the only ones voting. It was only in the days of St. Peter Damian and Hildebrand (later Pope Gregory VII) that the efforts of a noble family to install its own candidate in the Papacy first aroused vigorous clerical opposition. By the decree of Pope Nicholas in 1059 only the cardinal bishops, though in consultation with the other cardinals, could validly elect a pope. In 1179, at the end of the great investiture conflict between the pope and the emperor about who should appoint bishops, Pope Alexander IV at the Third Lateran Council extended the right of voting to all the cardinals.

The system didn't work very well at first. As we saw, it led to the Great Schism. The cardinals' dignity grew during the last part of the 13th century when there were 12 Popes in 40 years with some intervals as long as two years between Popes, so that much of the time the cardinals ruled the Church. They grew rich and powerful and their politicizing led to the sad spectacle of two and three men at a time claiming to be the Holy Father.

But eventually they learned their lesson and since the time when the election ending the schism had to be held by a general council, rather than the cardinals alone, the system has been all to the advantage of the Church.

Procedures have been polished. When Cardinal O'Connell in 1922 didn't get to the conclave on time, not through his own fault but because of the quick election of Pius XI, the rules were changed so that all cardinals would have time to get to Rome. When Cardinal Rampolla in 1903 seemed to be the favorite of the conclave before the election of Pius X, the Austrian emperor sent in his veto. The emperor could no longer positively influence the conclave but even this lesser power of veto, respected at the time, was thereafter taken away.

In modern times there has been no questioning of the propriety of procedures in the elections. Once at the Catholic Digest we reprinted an account of the election of Pius XI which said that at one time he was behind Cardinal Laurenti in the voting and implied that Laurenti had been elected but refused. We got a gentle but firmly reproving letter from then Papal Secretary of State Montini, later to reign gloriously as Paul VI, quoting the exact statistics from the official record. So even the appearance of irregularity is checked out.

After Renaissance times, during which the morals of ambitious cardinals were no better than those of the corrupt society in which they lived, the system of election of the Pope by cardinals alone worked out very well. No really bad popes were elected and the list since then contains not only good reformers and excellent administrators but many genuinely pious men some of whom have been beatified and canonized. There can be no worthy argument raised against the present system on the grounds of poor product.

The chief argument for retaining the system is that it avoids throwing the church into the kind of political turmoil in which the world in general usually revolves. It would be fatuous to deny that there is political activity within the sacred college of cardinals — if you're not liberal you must be conservative and vice versa. But confining political activity to an expert and dedicated small group eliminates mass hysteria, physical power ploys, ecclesiastical Fuehrers, opportunities for journalistic deceptions and so on, in short, most of the ills to which one-man-one-vote democracy is heir. For instance and hypothetically, the defeat of a French candidate would not lead to the defection of any cardinals from the Church, much less the defection of the French nation as might very well happen if everyone in a unanimous French populace were voting for a Frenchman.

So, Laurianne, while the present system of electing the Pope is not a matter of dogma nor a part of divine Revelation, it is the end result of a great deal of trial and error on the part of the Church. It is the best system yet achieved and should certainly not be done away with in any fit of change-for-change's sake fervor.

To get back to your question, in their daily life cardinals have the same occupations as bishops in general, they are pastors or administrators. But as the only papal electors they are the Church's insurance against international politics, military might, mob violence and the growing power of the communications media, notably TV, to control world opinion. It seems to me that to change the system would be to tear down the gates of the City of God in the face of these besieging evils.

Indulgences

The Church's dispute with Luther over the doctrine of indulgences was the starting point of the Protestant Reformation. While the overall debate spread to many other topics, the one over indulgences sputtered on for centuries until it became practically academic when Catholic devotion no longer gave a central place to the doctrine. Extremists hoped that Vatican Council II would treat the subject with benign neglect or perhaps even discontinue the granting of indulgences. However, the Church authorities, who can be credited with a better grasp of theology than have the extremists, reaffirmed the integral doctrine. So to speak, they had to, because of its foundation in the greater concept of the Communion of Saints. There was a not-quite-sweeping revision of indulgences, a change in some of the terms used in their promulgation and an explanation of their meaning in the Enchiridion, *the official publication which answers all questions people can now ask about indulgences.*

THE QUESTION:

As a convert to Catholicism since 1973, I have taken every opportunity to learn more about the Church. I teach the First Communion class with a "born-Catholic" lady in our parish Confraternity of Christian Doctrine program. So you can see that I would like to be well informed on everything to do with the Church.

However, there is one puzzler that no one has explained to my satisfaction: the indulgence. I have a prayer book printed in the mid-60's that offers a "plenary indulgence" for prayers recited over a period of time, and I also have some old medals that give an indulgence in terms of days.

My understanding of an indulgence is that it sort of "buys time off" for a soul in Purgatory. But the next world is certainly not restricted to days and nights like Earth is; "days" of indulgence seem meaningless in a place where there is no time.

Also, with my Protestant upbringing, I always thought that indulgences died a natural death after Martin Luther so vehemently opposed their sale in the 16th century. I am confused as to their function now that we don't hear so much about Purgatory any more.

I remember that when I was a child my Catholic friends told me that after we all died we would have to go to Purgatory and pay for our sins before entry into heaven, but that I would have to spend a lot more time there because I was not a Catholic. Now I am one, but I am still very confused on this subject. Please clarify it all for me.

Mrs. Brownie Gritzmacher

THE ANSWER:

It won't be easy, Brownie, but here goes. You cover the whole subject pretty well. If I restate your questions correctly you are asking: 1. What is an indulgence, anyway? 2. What does "plenary" mean in connection with indulgences? 3. What does "40 days" actually mean? 4. Didn't Martin Luther do away with the whole idea of indulgences and especially with their sale in the Catholic Church? 5. What's the connection between indulgences and that state called Purgatory which we don't hear much about anymore?

To start with your number one question — an indulgence is the taking away of the need to suffer punishment in the next life for sins we have committed in this one. Only God can do that, but Catholic faith is that He delegated the power to men. There are of course Christians who do not believe that Jesus did that. To such people the whole concept of indulgences is outrageous and they look upon indulgences as impious frauds. There is no point in discussing indulgences with them until you come to some agreement with them on the nature of Christ's Church — was it founded as a visible, working organization or as a kind of meeting of minds? Did Christ hand over his own power to Peter and the men who were to succeed him as heads of the Church?

Catholics say Yes and consequently believe that the Pope is in charge not only of the artistic and monetary treasures of the Vatican but has the far higher charge of dispensing spiritual treasures, the merits gained on behalf of mankind by Christ, the Blessed mother Mary and all holy people.

The thought is that many saints suffered here on earth far more than enough to satisfy God's justice in punishing their sins. Christ and the Virgin didn't have *any* sin and yet suffered. The Pope in the name of God's mercy gives credit for this suffering to persons who have repented their sins. Thus he *indulges* these persons, not in their sin, but in taking away punishment for the sins. That act is what is called an *indulgence*.

Of course, all such considerations are lost on people who have been taught that indulgences are *only* devices to raise money, attract tourists to shrines, or support an indolent clergy. I would be straining any historian's credibility were I to say that indulgences have never been used for these purposes.

But we don't do away with all social welfare programs because
frauds have been perpetrated; neither does the Church do away
with this beautiful concept of indulgences because of its
occasional criminal misuse.

So your number-one question, Brownie, can be answered by
saying that an indulgence is a declaration by the Pope (or
delegated bishop) that if good works specified by him are done
with the proper dispositions, punishment that would justly
come even to the repentant sinner in the next world (Purgatory, that is,) will not be inflicted.

To go on to your next two points, "plenary" simply means
that all the punishment a sinner had coming to him will be
remitted. "Partial" indulgences take away only a part of the
punishment a sinner has coming. Maybe this is the point to say
that no punishment can be taken away until the sin has been
forgiven in the Sacrament of Penance (confession, that is). A
misconception on this point is widespread among those who
are outraged by the very idea of indulgences. Indulgences are
not permits to commit sin, as they think.

Anyway, most pre-Council Catholics have a nostalgia for
the old books of devotion presenting prayers foot-noted with
"Forty Days", or "Seven Days" together with the name of the
Pope and the date of proclamation. Those that have been
taught the Baltimore Catechism learned what these periods of
time meant. It was intended, since there could only be an
approximation in any case, that the indulgence take away as
much punishment as would have been remitted by God for that
many days of public penance as performed in the early church
before the days of private penance. Public penances could be
very severe, involving such things as standing in front of the
church in the place reserved for penitents in admission of your
sin and in testimony of your sorrow. Just like the penances of
old, some of the indulgences ran to seven years or seven
quarantines (period of forty days each).

There were, you can be sure, devotees in modern times who
added up and kept count of the indulgences they gained. I
remember that just half a century ago when I was in the

seminary there was a group of students (nick-named "the intelligentsia") who openly decried this practice and as a result got the reputation of being very broadminded indeed.

But of course they didn't oppose the validity of indulgences, only the mixing of arithmetic and spirituality. The arithmetical side of indulgences became prominent over the centuries because each Pope would grand his own list of indulgences and none would ever be withdrawn. They piled up. I can't remember my source but I know I have read somewhere that one of the Popes forbade anyone to total up the indulgences attached to the Rosary. By his time there were many separate indulgences attached to every prayer recited in the course of the devotion, and the total would be so great as to cause ridicule if it were computed. When Pope Pius XII used to bless and indulgence rosary beads all inquiries as to exactly what indulgences were being granted were answered, "All possible." No arithmetic was allowed to intrude.

But the Popes never stopped granting indulgences. The doctrine was sound, despite the quarrel with Luther and the defection of his followers. There was even a reaction toward more indulgences and in 1669 a new Papal Congregation of Indulgences was set up to regulate and promote them. This subject leads us into your fourth point, Brownie, about Martin Luther putting an end to indulgences. He did not, but it would not be wrong to see in him an instrument of God for putting an end to the *abuses* connected with indulgences.

Abuses were widespread before his time and we learn of them chiefly through the condemnations by the official Church of such practices as the granting of erroneous indulgences by local bishops. (For instance, the pretense that their indulgences remitted both the punishment for sin and the *guilt* of sin so that the sinner didn't even have to go to confession. No Pope or Council ever granted such an indulgence.)

There was also traffic in the income from indulgences. Some of the indulgences required a giving of money to pious institutions; some of the money would end up in impious hands. Pius V in 1567 cancelled all indulgences which required donations of money to anything at all.

Then there was the matter of completely false indulgences. Religious houses, without any authority to do so, might deceive the faithful by proclaiming indulgences to be obtained by money gifts to their house. This kind of caper seems to have been one occasion for the setting up of the Congregation of Indulgences and was undoubtedly the reason for the publication of the *Raccolta* in 1807 which listed officially approved and valid indulgences. The prayer books of the first part of this century usually gave this publication as the source of any world-wide indulgenced prayers they printed. In 1904, by which time all flagrant abuses had been eliminated, the Congregation of Indulgences was merged with the Congregation of Rites.

But there was still room for improvement, not in the doctrine of indulgences but in their administration. One of the documents of Vatican Council II, issued January 1, 1967, was the Apostolic Constitution, *The Doctrine of Indulgences*. It directed that a new list of official indulgences be drawn up which would be attached only to "the most important works of piety, charity and penance." This work was finished a year and a half later and appeared as *Enchiridion of Indulgences*. (*Enchiridion* just means "list.") The decree, issued by the Sacred Apostolic Penitentiary, revokes all indulgences it does not specifically name. There are only 70 items on the list, compared with the uncomputable number of indulgences that were previously in force.

We have already talked about two kinds of indulgences, plenary and partial, but indulgences can still be classified as universal or local, meaning that some can be gained anywhere, others only at Rome or other specified place. There are perpetual and temporary indulgences, meaning that some can be gained any time of the year, others only in certain seasons or on certain days. Dropped were what used to be called "real" indulgences, those attached to certain things like a crucifix, rosary or medal. "Personal" indulgences formerly could be gained only by members of specified groups, usually confraternities or religious orders. Some could be gained for the souls in Purgatory, others only for the person performing the good works.

The new Enchiridion makes many of these distinctions unimportant by beginning with three general grants. The first gives a partial indulgence just for raising one's mind to God in the performance of duty or in bearing the ills of life; the second for giving (in faith and mercy) any services or goods to persons in need. These two grants are more or less for "good works" as were all indulgences ever granted up to now. The third, however, is brand new. It gives a partial indulgence to anyone who voluntarily deprives himself of anything licit and pleasing. This grant has as its purpose the keeping alive of the spirit of penance among the faithful who have been freed of the obligation under pain of sin to abstain from meat on Fridays and to fast on certain other days.

The Enchiridion then goes on to the 70 indulgences too much beloved or too important to be lost in any reform whatsoever. The items include such things as old favorite prayers, litanies, hymns, psalms for recitation; actions such as kissing the Cross on Good Friday, visiting a cemetery, *devoutly* using a blessed crucifix, rosary, scapular or medal; listening to sermons, making retreats and missions, visiting churches and renewing baptismal vows. This list is not complete; you have to read the *Enchiridion* to learn them all.

There isn't much new in all this, except that specific lengths of time like those you referred to, Brownie, have been omitted. Indulgences which are not "plenary" are now simply "partial". I guess the scholars in charge of writing the Enchiridion saw the same difficulty as you did in speaking of time in Purgatory. The old expressions had a meaning, as we saw, but it was easily missed and not readily grasped by everyone. So now you can gain only a "partial" indulgence, meaning one which takes away part of the sin's punishment, not one of so many days or years. The old effort to indicate the relative amount of punishment each indulgence would remit has been abandoned.

That amount is now thought of as depending on the sincerity and fervor of the one trying to gain the indulgence, rather than on the prayer said or the action done.

To come to your fifth point and mention of Purgatory, Brownie, the distinction among indulgences whereby only some of them could be gained for the souls there has been abolished. Now any indulgence can be so applied. Purgatory, like indulgences, is still part of sound Catholic doctrine. You correctly point out that we don't "hear so much about it" any more, but that doesn't take away its reality. Neither indulgences nor Purgatory as we now understand them are specifically set forth as doctrine in the Bible. As many Catholics know all too well, many door-to-door proselytizers of various sects are ready and willing to point this circumstance out.

But it works like this, according to Catholic thought: the Bible is not organized like a modern text-book or reference work. Yet it does present all truth by proclaiming basic teachings and ideas which can be logically developed and more deeply comprehended by human reason. Purgatory and indulgences can be so arrived at. The Bible, in Catholic interpretation, teaches: 1. that Christ (who was God) appointed Peter to take his place in administrating the Church He founded. 2. that God is both just and merciful. By his nature He must both punish and forgive, to our human minds a contradiction. The Church reasons that the doctrines of Purgatory and indulgences bring us about as far as we can go in reconciling the infinite mercy with the infinite justice of God.

Both doctrines begin with the need of satisfying God's *justice* by punishment. In the case of indulgences, this punishment is suffered voluntarily by persons who don't deserve it but God's *mercy* is shown when the credit for the suffering is given by responsible human authority (the Pope) to guilty but repentant persons like you and me.

In the popular mind this same kind of thought is expressed by saying that God is merciful till you die, then He is just. The statement won't hold up against deep theological scrutiny, but since no amount of theologizing can reconcile infinite justice with infinite mercy on the level of finite human minds, it is perhaps not a bad way to think. Indulgences and Purgatory answer, within the limits of our understanding, questions we ask about the next life.

Both indulgences and Purgatory are inescapable conclusions in the Catholic way of thinking. We reason to them from the more fundamental truths of faith found in the Bible.

The doctrine of indulgences is closely connected with the doctrine of the Communion of Saints. There is a lot of talk today in amateur theological circles about *"community"* in religion and worship but this transfer of merit through indulgences is a greater act of community than any envisioned by the present-day reformers who regard indulgences and Purgatory as hopelessly old-fashioned.

From the viewpoint of Christian practice, indulgences as we know them grew out of the custom in ancient times of bishops remitting some of the public penance imposed on sinners, particularly apostates during the persecutions. The penances were often so severe that the sinner would or could not accept his penance. In a process in some ways comparable to our modern plea-bargaining ("plead guilty to manslaughter and I won't indict you for murder") bishops begain to remit part or all of the punishment required by the penance originally imposed for the apostasy. This reduction often kept a person in the Church and could be thought of as saving his very soul. Later, when the whole system of public penances had pretty well died out and there was no punishment here on earth to be allieviated, the punishment to come in Purgatory was removed from repentant sinners.

This was sound thinking, but as we saw, abuses crept in. In the time of Luther a great division of Christendom occurred largely over the matter of indulgences. In his mind, you had to get rid of the doctrine to get rid of the abuses.

We shouldn't leave the subject without pointing out that such things as raising one's mind to God, patiently bearing the ills of life and doing good to one's neighbor always benefited the person doing such things in the eyes of God. Indulgences, in a way of speaking, only make the benefits official. The Catholic doctrine of indulgences is a middle ground between the teaching of those sects which think all spiritual authority is fraudulent and the practices of Medieval and Rennaissance times when some Catholics apparently could be fooled into believing than an indulgence by spiritual authority was automatic and got you out of Hell and Purgatory whether you deserved that or not.

This latest decree on indulgences (1968) has as its main thrust the idea that the pious dispositions of the indulgence gainer are of paramount importance. It even abolished "real" indulgences, those attaching to things or objects. Too many people gave the wrong emphasis to the special rosary or medal by not understanding that the important thing was the mental action that accompanied its use. A good many of them let their practice degenerate to superstition.So in the new decree you can still gain indulgences by the *pious* use of medals and so on but a bit of metal must not be thought of as having any value apart from the mental action associated with it. The indulgence is gained by prayer.

I don't know, Brownie, whether your reaction to what I have been able to say about indulgences will strike you as being a clarification or just the stirring up of the stale fumes of old theological controversies. Indulgences shouldn't be thought of as something to argue about. More happiness will result if we try to see them as one manifestation of the Communion of Saints, that great disposition of God whereby the Church consists of the blessed in Heaven, the sufferers in Purgatory and the strugglers here on Earth, each part relating to the other two with help or requests for help as appropriate. The motive in every case is love, because God himself is Love. Nobody can argue with that.

Traditionalists, Tridentinites and Ultraconservatives

Unity within itself is the first need of every organization. In human affairs, politics for instance, organized parties make fragile and transitory alliances to get a temporary unity sufficient to gain their immediate purposes. Often they must compromise with the original purposes of their own organization. This the Church cannot do, though many think it can and should. The Church's purposes are supernatural and oriented toward eternity and its principles simply cannot be compromised. Internally the problem boils down to deciding what things within the Church are immutable and which changeable in view of the Church's sempiternal character. This is the issue around which conflict arises with ultraconservatives every time an up-dating of rite or custom is entered upon.

THE QUESTION:

I was recently alarmed when I heard about a faction within the Church that is totally against the changes in the Mass. They say that the changes are sacreligious and they do not represent Church Tradition. As evidence they cite the Council of Trent, Canon Law and Pope St. Pius V (*Quo Primum*). They even go to the extreme of saying that the people who go to the Mass, as we have it today, are in sin by their attendance, because the bread and wine are not changed, the words of consecration are invalid according to tradition.

I certainly hope that these accusations are false, but how does the Church refute these very grave charges?

James W. Connell

THE ANSWER:

You really shouldn't be alarmed, James, because the protests of which you speak are only examples of history repeating itself. The Church has lived through so many similar difficulties that our reaction should be only a prayer for resignation, not an outcry of fear.

Before getting around to the specifics of your letter let us fortify ourselves with a little background. The problem with the super-conservative groups came up after the calling of Vatican Council II. Councils have usually been called to straighten out differences in doctrine and to proclaim the official teaching of the Church.

Vatican II, oddly enough, seems not to have been called "against" dissenters to any Church doctrine but, if I can express this properly, "against" the whole Church itself.

The idea was to bring the Church up-to-date, to get away from procedures and mannerisms that were intellectually embarrassing to Catholics who had daily dealings with the outside world.

Take, for instance, the *Index of Prohibited books.* Modern intellectualism had made the idea of any man controlling the very thoughts of another man repulsive. Even though the old *Index* did a pretty good job of indicating what writings were against the Catholic Church and a very poor job of preventing the reading of such works, it was being called a form of brainwashing and censorship and was, in the course of Conciliar events, done away with.

I suppose there are still good arguments for having an Index but monarchical control of books has given way to democratic tolerance under which everyone is entitled to have his say, no matter what the people in charge think of it.

To take a less important example, consider the dress of priests, monks, and sisters. Even Pius XII, long before the Council was thought of, had suggested the "simplification" of what nuns wore. In most cases the sisters were wearing the "dress-up" clothing of noble medieval ladies, differing from sisterhood to sisterhood as the European towns of the Middle Ages differed in clothing styles. The ceremonial robes of the pre-Vatican II Monsignor were simply what was in style for the gentlemen of Louis XIV's court for state occasions. In no case was this clothing ecclesiastical in its origin, it was only what the stylish man or woman wore long long ago. The simpler garb of the monks (Franciscans, Benedictines, Dominicans) was originally just what the well dressed peasant was wearing. There are present-day parallels to this practice of wearing the styles of previous generations in the Amish sects and Hasidic Jews. Even the vestments worn by the priest at Mass are preservations of 4th-century styles. Wearing such clothing is a testimony to conservatism, wearing what has "always" been worn.

Just like the Index, specifically religious clothing had real advantages in preserving the Faith but the arguments in its favor were not winning ones in modern religious circles, where being old-fashioned was something to be ashamed of in your fellow religious and ruthlessly corrected in yourself.

Now, religious garb and even the *Index* are minor matters. They are not the reason for Pope John's *Aggiornamento,* only aspects of a far more necessary up-dating. Since the time, let us say, of the Council of Trent (16th century) or even of Vatican I (19th century) there has been a vast expansion of human knowledge, much of it directly affecting religious thought. Religious thought, as we saw from the Index and religious clothing, tends to be conservative in nature, and properly so, since God's public revelation, though it began with Adam and continued to the death of Christ's longest living Apostle, was a definite body of knowledge. We can make inferences from it and draw conclusions from it but we cannot change its content. We must conserve it, be conservative.

We need not and should not be super-conservative. We must remember that not all our inferences and conclusions are necessarily correct just because we started from the authentic deposit of faith. Often they are arrived at by the use of scientific data. Of all things on earth scientific "facts" are the most likely to go out of date. When that occurs, some of our religious stances may need revision if they are not to be subjected to modern ridicule.

For instance, the edition of the Rheims-Douay version of the Bible which my seminary class was using in 1930 contained a list of dates for the patriarchs going back to Adam, the date of whose creation was given as 4004 B.C. Of course our professor explained that the editors had cribbed the date from the work of Anglican Bishop Ussher, who had scientifically but erroneously computed it from cross references in the Old Testament.

So even 50 years ago, the date was widely regarded as laughable, but there it was in our Bible, a fantastically telling example of too much conservatism. I'm sure that Bishop Ussher, back in 1650, was highly regarded for the scientific exactitude of his research, but right now it is only the very, very conservatives like the Fundamentalists who hold his work in any high regard.

Frankly, but without any desire to be offensive, the Church does not want to remain on the scientific level of the Fundamentalists. They are good people and will get to heaven in their own way, but as human knowledge of this world increases, they will have a harder and harder time in gaining converts and holding their membership.

The Church believes that scientific Biblical work like that of Bishop Ussher must be up-dated. Since his time, archaeological discoveries have been made, previously inscrutable inscriptions and even whole languages have been deciphered, historical records have been re-evaluated, new records have been found, texts have been corrected even in the manuscripts the Bishop worked with, so that even without dragging in that specter, Evolution, the Church cannot now go along with 4004 B.C. as the date of Adam's creation.

Until Vatican II, every Council has occasioned some flaking off of membership from the Church. It was a matter of considerable self-congratulation on the part of those promoting Vatican II that no heresy nor even schism resulted from it. Whether the defections of the present ultra-conservatives will ever amount to an offically pronounced heresy can't be determined for sure just yet.

I don't know who totaled up the figures but it is quite generally said that after the Council of Nicaea (4th century) two-thirds of the Church fell away. No trace of the Arian church remains, except perhaps in those cases where a modern theologian's thoughts accidentally coincide with the ancient errors. And after the Council of Chalcedon, the Monophysite heresy flourished for centuries, but is hardly heard of anymore. These ancient heresies have faded away. Some newer ones have not.

The Council of Trent was called to "counter-reform" the Catholic Church, and the doctrines denounced as heresies there persist today in the dogmatic teachings of the Protestant churches. The great fear of the Catholic ultra-conservatives in Vatican Council II was that Protestant teachings, which were the "liberal" opinions of the 16th century, would finally find entrance into Catholic dogma. Their fears were not entirely groundless, since the "liberal" positions of today only too often echo at second or third bounce things the Council of Trent condemned. Happily, changes in the Catholic Church in the direction of Protestantism are so far confined to such things as more hymn singing, starker churches, relaxation of ritual and other outward aspects. Inwardly things have been conserved: the new canons of the Mass still speak of the Mass as a sacrifice and the Vatican II documents speak of the "deposit of faith" and use the term in its traditional sense.

It was the change in secondary things by Vatican II that unduly alarmed the ultra-conservative Catholics and brought some of them to the brink of schism. After Vatican Council I, (1870) some of the ultra-conservatives had gone over the brink. An example can be found in the "Old Catholics" would could not accept the Pope's infallibility as defined by that Council and set up their own church with parishes and state financial assistance. A curious chink in their conservatism was the use of their mother tongue, German, instead of the traditional Latin in their liturgical services. Their reactions to change in the Church were otherwise like those of the present Traditionalists. There are very few left today.

So, James, the present ultra-conservatives' disobedience should be a cause for concern but not for alarm. What is going on is a pattern of events the Church has witnessed and endured many times before this. During and after every Council conservatism has prevailed, but not ultra-conservatism. Always some kind of middle ground has been measured off, given boundaries defensible against all further attacks. The central Church always survives, though she never shakes off all opposition. Her old enemies fade away to be replaced by new ones who must be arraigned in new Councils.

That is one reason why the present ultra-conservatives may be faulted for appealing, as you point out, to the Council of Trent. Laws and ordinances of Popes and Councils do not remain in effect forever but only until changed by succeeding Councils or Popes. What they decree is always related to their own time in the history of the Church: Vatican II did not take up the Arian problems of Nicaea nor did the legislators of that 4th-century council have us in mind when writing their decisions. When the Council of Trent cleared up its contemporary liturgical problems by decreeing exact procedures for Mass (the Tridentine Mass) it was addressing the difficulties of its own day not those of our 20th century. It was solving problems by that decree just as Vatican II solved problems by prescribing the present procedures at Mass and allowing it to be said in the vernacular. To be consistent the ultra-conservatives would have to insist not only that the 400-year-old Tridentine Mass should not have been changed by Vatican II but that it should not be changed for another 400 or for that matter 400,000 years. I don't think any of them really propose that, it's just that they prefer the old Mass to the new one.

There is a term in English common law, *mortmain,* meaning "dead hand", i.e., what a king proclaimed in life cannot be changed by those who survive him nor by his successor. Leaving things the way they were has been beneficial to survivors and successors in so many cases that present authority is thought sometimes to depend on deceased authority. Of course, it cannot be so based, power to rule comes from power to subdue or from the consent of the governed. The appeal of the Traditionalists to the *Quo Primum* of Pius V calls for a rather heavy-handed but apt comparison. George Washington and Thomas Jefferson had slaves but Abraham Lincoln freed all slaves. Can anyone validly appeal to the authority of the earlier Presidents in an effort to restore slavery?

Your remaining point, James, is about the validity of the words of consecration. The answer is the same as for the question about the power to make changes in general. I'm not sure you saw the same literature that I did, but on this subject I think the point the Traditionalists make is that in the English version of the new Liturgy, *pro multis* in the Pius V formula for the Consecration has been translated "for all men" instead of literally: "for many." It is typical of the ultra-conservative attitude to think that a secondary phrase, if mistaken, could invalidate a whole formula and that translations to be valid

must be absolutely literal. It's the question of *mortmain* all
over again. The power of a living Pope to formulate the words
for the Consecration is not limited by the decrees of dead
Popes.

The literature I read said that the change was made from
"many" to "all" to effect a change in doctrine. When one says
that Christ died for many you imply that there were some for
whom his death did not bring salvation — they refused it and
went to hell. When one, according to the literature, says that
Christ died for all men one is saying that all are saved and that
there is no hell. Speaking for myself now, I think this logic is
pretty good but it ignores the possibility that the new Liturgy is
referring to Christ's intention in dying. He certainly wished his
salvation for all men, whether or not all in fact accept it. I'm
pretty sure that this shading or change of meaning *was*
deliberately intended by the commissioners in charge of the
translation — it was an emphasis of the mercy rather than the
justice of God — but they had the authority, in my thinking, to
make the change. I don't see how it could invalidate the whole
formula for changing the bread and wine into the Body and
Blood of Christ.

But however mistaken we may think the Traditionalists to be
in particular matters I think we up-daters should extend the
same consideration to them as we do to the positively
Protestant element that insists on remaining in the Catholic
Church. Respect for the freedom of consciences should extend
to both ends of the doctrinal spectrum.

It is difficult, and to some impossible, to march to someone
else's drum. When you have loved the beauty and pageantry of
an ancient Church for decades of your own life, off-hand and
even insolent proposals to snap out of it are not well received.
One should of course give in to proper authority, but in judging
people who have difficulty doing that, one should remember
that even Adam thought (in conscience?) that he was excused
because Eve had put him up to eating the apple. Sincere
Traditionalists find excuse in maintaining rites and customs
that the whole Church once found right and true. They just
can't see anything wrong with that.

The Six Precepts
of the Church

In any time of change, whether within a society or within a church, the first institutions to be attacked are the rules of that society or church, the things "everybody had to do." In pre-reform times the penalty for not doing what was expected by a church or society was exclusion from its membership. In times of change the reformers always try to eliminate the rules but to keep their membership, do what they want but accept no penalty. In the case of the six precepts of the Church, the reformers' effort has been not so much to attack openly what even they must recognize as essential laws as to explain them away or just change the subject when such matters as the obligation under sin to attend Sunday Mass comes up. Among the complaints of plain Catholics called upon to teach the faith to children are that the newer text-books seem to give more space to the reasons excusing Mass attendance than they do to the need and reasons for Mass attendance and that the newer texts seem often to be simply incomplete in their exposition of the Catholic faith. Most frequently eliminated from consideration in these "reforming" texts are the traditional six precepts of the Church. Confraternity of Christian Doctrine teachers should ask and should be told why.

THE QUESTION:

My chief occupation is teaching emotionally handicapped children in the public schools but I have been teaching religion for 24 years in parochial schools. I am sure that many Confraternity of Christian Doctrine teachers like myself would like a definite answer to my question: "Are the precepts of the Church still in vogue?" Priests have told me they are not. I do not see the precepts listed in the newer catechisms. I do not remember seeing them mentioned in the *Catechetical Directory* of 1971.

If they are not in vogue, problems arise, such as; "What is our obligation to hear Mass on Sunday and to go to confession and Communion once a year?" What are we to teach if we have no authority to quote?

Elsie Dembowsky

P.S. Just today a priest did find *one* publication for me, *A New Cathechism of Catholic Faith* by Father John P. Schrol that lists the precepts but gives no explanations. There must be some reason why the other catechisms are omitting the precepts.

THE ANSWER:

You have asked a good question, Miss Dembowsky. To take the last sentence of your letter first, let me say that the nonappearance of the precepts in the newer catechisms as a neat set of six laws may be caused by caution. All authors of catechisms hope that their books will remain current and useful for a long time, but they must be in accord with the Code of Canon Law, which is now under revision. If a new Code appears soon, and if the canons on which the six precepts are based are noticeably changed, catechisms reprinting the precepts from the Baltimore Catechism will become obsolete. Cautious authors do not want that to happen to their work, so they omit the precepts.

I think we ought to list the precepts of the Church right now so that all readers will know exactly what the subject is. The 1886 Baltimore Catechism reads:

"Question: What are the chief commandments of the Church?

"Answer: The chief commandments of the Church are six. 1. To hear Mass on Sundays and holydays of obligation. 2. To fast and abstain on the days appointed. 3. To confess at least once a year. 4. To receive the Holy Eucharist during the Easter time. 5. To contribute to the support of our pastors. 6. Not to marry persons who are not Catholics, or who are related to us within the third degree of kindred, nor privately without witnesses, nor to solemnize marriage at forbidden times."

If these precepts are not in the catechism you are using and you believe in teaching the children that they must go to Sunday Mass and obey the other precepts you can quote Canon Law as your authority. You can tell your students the six precepts were taught as a unit for centuries before the Canon Law went into effect in 1918 and that they may still be found in the Code as follows: Mass on Sunday, canon 1247: fasting and abstinence, canons 1251 and 1252; yearly confession, canon 906; Easter Communion, canon 859; church support, canon 1496; marriage with non-Catholics, canon 1060.

Their absence from current catechisms does not mean that they have been repealed. Their absence from the General Catechetical Directory (issued by the Sacred Congregation for the Clergy) is explained by the fact that that document was not itself a catechism. It was a "directory," as its title says, a set of guide lines for persons instructing converts or writing catechisms.

You called these six laws precepts. The Baltimore Catechism used the word *commandments*. Either term is usable. Instructors like to use *precepts* because it is easier to teach the children that there are Six Precepts of the Church and Ten Commandments of God than to stop every time a *command-*

ment is mentioned and explain which list of commandments is under discussion.

Precept has the same technical meaning in Catholic legal terminology as *commandment;* it is a law binding under the pain of sin, mortal or venial, according to circumstances. But since the Ten Commandments were specially revealed by God to Israel and the Precepts of the Church are only formulations by Church authorities, the latter are on a lower plane of dignity.

This difference is evident in the dispensations from the precepts which the Church rather readily grants, especially from the sixth precept about marriage with persons who are not Catholic. It might be said here that Catholics married "in the Church" to persons not Catholic have not broken the precept because they have been dispensed from keeping it. It should be unnecessary to say here that no dispensation can be granted from the Ten Commandments and that this circumstance sets them far above the Precepts of the Church.

However, just as the Ten Commandments (except keeping the Sabbath) can be arrived at by man's reason without the special revelation of God, so can the precepts be arrived at without special proclamation by the Church. They are not just particular laws (like keeping to the right in traffic) but rules necessary for the very survival of the Church.

That statement remains true even though the precepts vary, as the Commandments do not, in number, according to the country where they are published. For instance, in countries where the clergy are paid out of tax money the fifth precept is not put into catechisms because the clergy are already being supported.

For the U.S., six precepts were published by the Third Plenary Council of Baltimore in its catechism to take care of the special needs of the American Church. Take again the sixth and fifth precepts. In 1886 Catholics were in a small minority and interfaith marriages would usually work against the propagation of the Catholic faith. Monetary support of the Church had to be insisted on because, far from supporting the

Church, the state was constitutionally against any aid to religion. The idea of supporting the Church was actually new to many immigrants from Catholic countries. Accordingly the bishops at Baltimore included the provisions of the fifth and sixth precepts in the U.S. list of chief commandments. A German catechism (Herder), as late as 1957, omits both from its list of chief commandments.

And so we got six precepts from the Council of Baltimore. The bishops used a set of the precepts already published in the then current catechism for the Catholics of England (where Catholics were also in a small minority). That set in turn went back to Cardinal Bellarmine of counter-Reformation times (1598). Centuries before him the precepts are found (900 A.D.) in German books of instruction. Way back in the time of Constantine (300 A.D.) we know from still extant sermons and writings that Catholics were expected to go to Mass on Sunday, pay tithes, and obey laws about the liturgical seasons in contracting marriage.

You see, though, that in listing the chief commandments all these historical bishops, legislators, writers, and preachers were attempting to draw up a kind of rule of life for practical Catholics. They were trying to set forth the basic observances for any person who claimed the name *Catholic*, especially in times of religious chaos. If you were not among those who kept these commandments in addition to the Ten Commandments of God you could not reasonably call yourself a Catholic. The Catholic Church would survive only through people who kept the precepts.

A further point is that the six precepts are supportive laws, that is, they specify a time or manner of obeying greater laws such as the one to adore the true God. Going to Mass on Sunday is only one way of adoring God, but when it is required of Catholics, it assures that both a minimal and perfect fulfillment of the greater obligation will be made.

Fasting and abstinence are expressions of sorrow for sin, in turn a form of the adoration of God. The second precept is not so much an addition to the Ten Commandments as a means the

Church takes to assure that God will be adored in one more way. Of course, human legislators wrote the precept, so human legislators can change it, but so far they have changed only the specifics of fasting and abstaining.

It is a sobering thought that the Vatican II relaxations in fasting and abstaining were just relaxations and not repeals. The Church ceased to specify exactly what fasting and abstaining should be done but did not do away with the whole idea of mortification. The idea was that each Catholic should choose for himself what self-denial he should undertake. It makes the imitation of Christ harder really, but that was part of the idea; do something harder and gain more merit; adore God in one more way, gain yourself one more right to call yourself Catholic.

It could be that the present oblivion of the second precept prompted your thought that the precepts may possibly have been all repealed. So next, Miss Dembowsky, I would like to call further attention to your thoughtful use of the phrase "in vogue." Taken in its strict meaning that phrase in your letter would make me answer your question with "No, the precepts of the Church are no longer in vogue." By that I would mean that teaching them by rote is no longer fashionable, or that not much religious writing is being done in any effort to have the precepts observed.

Your phrase is equivocal in that it implies the meaning. "Are the precepts in force?" that is, "Do the precepts still exist as laws binding Catholics under pain of sin?" My answer would then be Yes. They are in the present Code of Canon Law, each in its own place, though not as a set to be memorized. They do not have to be in the catechism to be laws. Yet your question "Why are they not in the catechisms?" calls for a longer answer than the one I gave about cautious authors.

To begin with, not all catechisms are, like the Baltimore, the product of a council of bishops, teaching with authority. Anyone can now sit down, write, and publish a catechism and call it Catholic. Catholics careful of their faith have to be careful about the source of what they read, even in self-proclaimed "Catholic" catechisms. Significantly, the first thing the recent reformers within the Church succeeded in was the suppression of the Index of Forbidden Books. I suppose there were abuses and politics involved in compiling the old prohibitions, but at least when an author was on that black list, you knew there was some question about his perfect ortho- doxy. With the Index suppressed, you have to judge for yourself in matters requiring expert knowledge you may not have.

The suppression offered the reformers the opportunity of putting the label "Catholic" on books questioning even the basics of Christianity. No official, ultimate, public denuncia- tion could follow routinely, since there was no longer an Index.

Something like this has happened in the catechism field. We have catechisms now with, as you say, no mention of having to go to Mass on Sunday, Communion once a year, and so on. The *Dutch Catechism* was among the first to become (in)- famous in this way, being notable for what it skipped over rather than for teaching outright heresy. What was in it was all right; the falsity was only in the implication that it presented the entire Catholic faith. Some of the new catechisms are wrong in the same fashion and the General Directory that you mentioned was an effort to correct them. Section 38 of the Directory insists that the whole of Catholic doctrine be taught by speaking and writing catechists.

It is risky to impute wrong motives to the authors of the truncated catechisms but at least the possible reasons for their leaving things out can be listed. One motive recognized by the authors of the Directory could be called false or pseudo ecumenism, a desire to make friends and achieve unity with other Christians by concealing, or leaving out of public professions of the Catholic faith, those items which might turn the outsiders off. Now, one can no more oppose sound ecumenism than one can oppose motherhood or free beer; it is the pseudo variety which would deceive non-Catholics about the full content of our belief that is reprehended in Section 27. Among the precepts of the Church, the sixth, about marrying non-Catholics, could be considered offensive to pseudo-ecumenical ears and thus be left out of a catechism written by a so-inclined author. The fifth precept, requiring monetary support of the Catholic Church organization, when there is so much "world hunger," might also be considered offensive to non-Catholics.

Another motive for omitting the precepts might very well be found in the idealism of the catechism authors. They want every Catholic to go to Mass on Sunday, for instance, but believe that one should do so out of pure desire to adore God. To emphasize a law requiring attendance under pain of sin by putting the precept in the catechism would, in the opinion of such authors, spoil the motivation of the children. There must be only promise of reward, no threat of punishment, in this psychology of teaching. The old catechism made an opposite point when it distinguished perfect from imperfect contrition for sin and insisted on the validity of the lower motive, fear of punishment. The catechisms in question would seem to skip over the whole matter of punishment for missing Mass on Sunday.

As with sound ecumenism, it might be better not to take issue with such high motivation; certainly it is better to act out of love than out of fear. The twin troubles with this approach are that 1. many people need enforced law and threat of punishment as well as persuasion to bring them to salvation, and 2. too strong an insistence on high motive leads to a desire to abolish the law.

Msgr. Ronald Knox's famous book, *Enthusiasm,* presents a series of historical characters who have made just this regress in the pursuit of sanctity. They begin by believing in their own worthiness so much that for them there is no need of law. Then they proceed to act as though there were no law (especially for themselves) and typically end up obviously insane, often to the point of believing themselves divine.

Heaven forfend that any catechism writers should come to any such sad fate, but as I said, we are counting out only their possible motives.

I would not bring up the next possibility myself, but as you say, Miss Dembowsky, there must be some reason why the precepts are being left out of the new catechism. If it is not pseudo ecumenism nor an excessively high standard of moral motivation, it could just be that the author's commitment to the traditional faith is weak.

Anyone who kept the old six precepts was an easily recognized Catholic, and anyone who would leave them out of the instruction of Catholic children must be, to put it delicately, a less fervent Catholic. Keeping the precepts on public occasions was a showing of the colors, a profession of faith, even a training for martyrdom.

Just a few decades ago, keeping the precepts publicly in many parts of the U.S. could mean social ostracism, the loss of job opportunities, promotion, or the job itself. Worse, in the more rarefied intellectual circles, was the implication of your mental inferiority. I remember my rage (as a newly ordained priest) at one doctor of psychology who patronizingly, though in his mind charitably, explained he didn't want to go further into our discussion of confession because he didn't want to destroy my faith.

I am just theorizing now, but I think the overall effect of all this petty persecution was to cause some of us to become in outward habit like unto the unbelieving.

In view of the petty persecutions many Catholics rather easily dispensed themselves from obligations which tagged them as Catholics. Dispensations are now so easily obtained from valid authority that the continued existence of the precepts has come into question, at least in the minds of some of the catechism writers.

If all this seems like too much answer for just one question, Miss Dembowsky, let me make a kind of summary of what I have been trying to say. The teaching of the precepts has been de-emphasized and that is a bad thing because the precepts were more than a list of chief commandments. It was by our following them publicly that men could learn that we were Catholic followers of Christ.

It has been the constant dogma of the Church that she is a visible organization, not just a gentle philosophy or an attitude toward life. Observance of the precepts makes the individual members of the visible organization themselves visible, and unless Catholic children are taught a practical rule of life, such as the six precepts, by which they are marked as members of the Church, the future visibility of the Church, not to say her survival, will be at stake.

Racism

Crusades, whether we are talking about the old ones that tried to recover the Holy Land for the Christians or new ones that try to establish racial equality in our society, are difficult to keep going at full steam. Even when the general thrust of the latter kind has won wide acceptance, crusades are subject to "benign neglect" from administrators, mental fatigue on the part of listeners to sermons and quiet despair on the part of enthusiasts. That it should be so is part, I suppose, of the general human condition of having fallen from original grace. Yet, full steam, half steam or only a little steam, the good Catholic must struggle on because the principles which call for racial equality are found in the very constitution of the Church. The level of effort may at times simmer down to what is being done for morality in general, little enough in view of the present scene, but the struggle can never be abandoned unless our purpose is to abandon our Catholic faith. The most highly and best motivated persons in the struggle against racial inequality are those who suffer from it patiently as this letter from a black man indicates.

THE QUESTION:

I am a third generation black American, 62-years-old, widower, a father of eight grown-up children. I live alone. The good Lord has been very good to me. I have seen many things during the years, enough that nothing can shock or surprise me anymore.

I was raised a Catholic. How good a Catholic am I? I cannot answer that question but, still, I am a Catholic. During my lifetime I have never missed a Sunday Mass when I was able to *get into* a church. Of course, there were days and times when I was not permitted *into* a church because of my color and race. Even in church, where people supposedly go to wash their spiritual dirty linens, clean up their hearts, and purify their souls, some expressed hatred of my being there. That used to bother me when I was young. Then I told myself that I should not blame the Lord for that.

Later, things changed a little. I did not have so much difficulty in getting *into* a church, but did have difficulties in finding a seat. Then, that also changed, although occasionally, someone changed their seat when I sat down next to them. Finally came this idea of shaking hands and offering the "Peace of the Lord" toward the end of the Mass. That created a new problem for me. I notice some people jerking away after offering their hand. That made me uncomfortable since I never go to church to make anyone feel uneasy.

I solved the problem by always finding an isolated place in the church. Every now and then an usher might walk up to me and offer the "Peace" or someone from a far-away pew would look at me, smile, and bow. That was all right.

A few days back I was on vacation and I went to church in a strange place. I was unable to find an isolated seat, but settled myself in one of the back pews.

When the time came to offer the "Peace of the Lord," a little girl of five or six years of age in the pew ahead, suddenly turned around, not knowing who was sitting behind, put out that hand, then, suddenly pulled it back as if she was frightened.

She looked at the young man next to her and asked innocently, "Daddy, is it all right if I offer him the Peace of Our Lord?" I was able to keep the smile on my face while all the folks around us turned pale.

My question is: Two thousand years after Christ preached, two hundred years after Thomas Jefferson declared that all men are created equal, more than a century after Abe Lincoln signed the Emancipation Proclamation, at a time when we claim to be standing at the peak of civilization, what can the Church do for that nice little girl?

K.D. Mathew

THE ANSWER:

The simplest answer to your question, Mr. Mathew, is that the Church can teach her the words of St. Paul: "There is neither Jew nor Greek, there is neither slave nor free, there is neither male nor female, for all are one in Christ Jesus." It is what the Church has always taught; it is not what all hearers of the Word have taken to heart and put into their lives.

As a matter of fact, your letter does not say what the little girl's father said to her in return. If he said something like "Why not?" her education was in good hands and the Church's teaching had gotten to him. If he hold her to be quiet, to turn around or not to bother people, the question becomes not what the Church can do for the little girl but what the Church can do for the father.

Your question is really a rhetorical one, by which I mean that you and I and nearly everyone concerned know the answer without its being spoken or written down. Whether in politics, sports, or religion, people take sides with complete commitment outwardly but nearly always with inward and secret reservations. What the Church can do for them is a question without a specific answer. The Church does all she can; it is seldom enough.

It has been said so many times that it is a cliche, but the truth is not that in our civilization Christianity has been tried and found wanting; the truth is that Christianity has been tried, found difficult, and dropped — or professed with secret reservations.

I think that is the difference between your Christianity, Mr. Mathew, and that of those who wouldn't sit next to you at Mass. You, judging from the overall tone of your letter, seem to have learned and accepted the fearsome admonition of Christ to love those who hate you. I think you did it by realizing that God, for his inscrutable purposes in this world, allows what we call evil. You sort of echo King Charles I of England when he said of Cromwell, who had him beheaded, "God made him, therefore I love him."

In point of fact, the benefits of learning the doctrine of the Church have accrued to you and not those who discriminate against you.

One of the less noted paradoxes of Christianity is that according to its doctrine an attempt must continually be made to improve the spiritual, mental, and physical well-being of all men, while acknowledging that all human effort will be forever ineffectual. Our "progress" seems only to be from bow-and-arrow to atomic war. The Christian explanation of the paradox, Mr. Mathew, I think is exemplified in your reaction: an infinite God knows, understands, and in his own good time will take care of all things evil. But, don't let go of the other half of the paradox — we can't in God's plan leave it all up to Him.

Besides St. Paul's statement that we are all one in Christ, there is the well-known Scriptural teaching on the equality of men in the second chapter of the first Epistle of St. James. That's where he talks about showing respect to the poor as well as to the rich men wearing golden rings. There was not enough mixing of races in the days of James for him to explain his lesson in terms of racism, but he certainly meant to say that true Christians must not discriminate against their fellow men, whatever the circumstances of their lives must be.

For a final consideration of Christianity in our present

civilization we might remember the days of the Gnostics. These original Gnostics were rather queer Christians and wildly heretical but they were well-named. They claimed to be the "knowers," the people with "inside" information about the doctrine of Christ.

With due allowance for the errors of the old Gnostics, I would say that what the present Christian church needs is some *good* gnostics. These would be people who would be "knowers" of the pure doctrine of Christ. In the face of the millions who only outwardly accept the Christian creed, these would be those who accept the doctrine of Christian charity without secret reservations, without cynical discounting and allowance for special circumstances.

These people would by that acceptance become saints, but they would not form a new kind of saints, they would only join the vast company of those already bearing the title "officially." Analyze the life of any famous saint of God and you will find its chief ingredient to be exactly the simple acceptance of the meaning of charity as Christ taught it.

The Old and New Mass

There are, at this writing, enormous numbers of persons old enough to vote who have no memory at all of the "old" Mass. There are even larger numbers who remember it fondly and two groups, much in the minority, one of which remembers the old Mass with scholarly distaste and the other which remembers it with fanatical love and loyalty.

The ritual legislated at the Council of Trent more than 400 years ago became so firmly established that, before the Council of Vatican II, to change it in any respect seemed to border on sacrilege. Yet the Council of Trent, too, was only updating thousands of local variations for its own time. It was successful because it was part and parcel of the Counter-Reformation struggle against heresy, in which all participants realized the absolute need for unity.

The urgency of the times was at least partly responsible for the inclusion in the Tridentine Mass of procedures and customs not perfectly understood nor, as we would say now, entirely thought out. The elimination of such imperfections in the new Liturgy, for people of deep sentiment but unscholarly disposition, made the Mass almost unrecognizable in its new form. But presumably if the new Liturgy retains its facade for 400 years it will be as venerated as the old Mass was and may even need updating and studious correction by that time. The whole point is that, while the ceremonial trimmings are devised by men, the central Act is divine and in it there can be no change.

THE QUESTION:

My mother and I go to church but the changes in the Church hold my father and my sister back. They do not attend Holy Mass.

My question is: Do you think that if Mass returned to the old way, more people (or the rest of the people who stopped going to Mass) would begin to go again? Thank you.

Tony Harvey

THE ANSWER:

First, Tony, I will just say to you that it might take a little prayer to get your father and sister back to Mass even if it were all "changed back" again. And a little prayer also might bring them back even if the Mass is not changed back.

The answer to whether the Mass *should* return to the old way is, all in all, No. Just to start with the crass commercial side of the question, the cost of re-editing and reprinting all the liturgical books would be beyond estimate. Also on the practical side is the consideration that every organization loses some membership every time it changes. The splintering of the Protestant sects into ever smaller units after and since the Reformation proves pretty well that each change of doctrine drives out part of the membership.

The trouble with the sects was that once they accept the principle that change was necessary, they couldn't stop changing and therefore couldn't stop diminishing into smaller and smaller units. Every tourist knows that changing his money into that of another country means the loss of some of it through exchange charges. If he changes all of it every time he crosses a border, he eventually becomes penniless.

Your question, Tony, doesn't involve doctrine so much as ritual, but the same truths hold. Changing the Mass back now would only alienate many present members of the Church, and

while some former members might return, the number would
be highly debatable.

But this whole question should be answered on a level much
higher than that of considerations like the above. For, despite
what we said about the inadvisability of change, we can't deny
that a lot of change has taken place over the centuries in many
things concerning the Mass. (An example right there. A lot of
good Catholics like to say "Liturgy" now instead of "Mass"
which is all right with me as long as we are talking about the
same thing.)

In the case of the Mass, changes were effectively stopped for
some 400 years by the Council of Trent and the Missal of Pius
V (1570). The then current prayers and rubrics (directions
printed in red for the priest) were, so to speak, frozen, with the
result that it has taken years of research to discover why the
ritual existed at the time in the form it did.

There are still a few things which we cannot completely
explain, like the word *consecration* in the old prayer at the
breaking of the Host. The priest used to put a fragment of the
Host into the chalice and say "May this commingling and
consecration of the Body and Blood of Christ be eternal life for
us receiving." The word *consecration* was removed from the
prayer in 1969. The consecration had already taken place, so
this prayer could certainly not be regarded as effecting the
consecration.

What did it mean? We still don't know. So, in the course of
the Mass reform in 1969, the prayer was changed. And to
reverse the change, Tony, would be to use a prayer one word of
which would be without any meaning for us.

Another example of what should certainly be an irreversible
change is the procedure at Communion. Older people will
remember how, in the Pius V Mass (1570-1969), the altar boys
used to say the *Confiteor* prayer, ("I confess.") They do not say
it anymore because of another change. They were reciting a
medieval addition to the Mass, the formula for Communion of
the sick.

Back in the 13th century, Communion by the laity had

become very infrequent; our law obliging Catholics to receive
Communion at least at Easter time dates from this period
(1215). The reasons why people stayed away were good or bad
according to your viewpoint: the obligation of Confession
before Communion had just come in; continence was a
requirement for married persons before Communion; and the
growing practice of using unleavened bread meant that the
people no longer could bring ordinary bread from their homes
to be used for Communion.

So few persons came to Communion that an odd theological
theory appeared, to the effect that the priest could receive
Communion on behalf of the people. That way it didn't really
matter that they did not come. A reaction to this sad condition
of affairs occurred later in the same century, but by then all
official memory of the ceremony in which the people had
received Communion had vanished. So the rite for Communion of the Sick, which had been preserved and used
regularly, was taken up as a ready-to-hand formula for use at
Mass.

Now, Tony, again you would have to agree that it would be
pointless to return to this ceremony at Communion time, since
it was established in ignorance, if not carelessness, in the first
place. Communion of the people was never an addition to the
Mass (which this ceremony made of it); it had always been an
integral part of the Mass.

This kind of comment could go on past the point of
boredom, Tony, but just one more obvious example of justified
change in the Mass can be found in the practical elimination of
the offertory prayers. For centuries the offertory ceremony was
taught as one of the three essential parts of the Mass, the other
two being the Consecration and the Communion. To hear
Mass one had to get there at least in time for the Offertory. In
popular devotion, the people at this point offered "themselves"
while the priest offered the bread and wine.

The prayers the priest said were beautiful and, among those
who followed the Mass with a missal of their own, the loss of
these prayers in the 1969 reform were sharply felt. Only vestiges

of them remain.

But of course it was not just to shorten the Liturgy that these changes were made. The reasons are many and complex, perhaps summed up in the fact that the name of this part of the Mass has been changed from *Offertory* to *Preparation of the Bread and Wine.*

Before we decide to go back to the older prayers, we should consider how some of them got into the Mass in the first place. We had the 399 years of untroubled tradition in the Tridentine Mass. But it, too, had a beginning and drew on other sources for the prayers and ceremonies prescribed for it in 1570.

It is easy in the 1570 Ordinary of the Mass to pick out prayers in the first person: *I* instead of *we, me* instead of *us.* There was, for instance the "I confess." The "I" shows that originally this could have been a private prayer of the priest, most likely said before he began Mass and only in later times said at the foot of the altar. Incidentally, it was never said *at* the altar. The shorter form of this now optional prayer is still in the first person although the *Credo* "I Believe" has been changed to "We Believe."

Soon after the "I confess" in the 1570-1969 missal came a private prayer speaking of "my" sins as the celebrant kissed the altar. The prayer before the Gospel was in the first person, as was the first offertory prayer and the three prayers just before Communion.

Obviously all these first-person prayers had their origins in the private devotions of the priest and were frozen into the community Liturgy because of their popularity, not to say excellence. The 1969 reform was largely motivated by the sense of community but it compromised in the case of the "I confess" and the one remaining "quiet" prayer before Communion in allowing the prayers to stay in the first person.

The point of reviewing all this, Tony, is to check whether we want to bring back this element of private devotion to the community Liturgy by "changing back."

The old Offertory prayers had a background of offertory precessions, bringing and offering of gifts, sharing of the offerings, and blessings of the offerings, so diverse in different times and places that it must have been a magnificent achievement by the Council of Trent to establish a ritual that was ultimately enforced and followed for four centuries.

For instance, in Rome in the late 8th century the celebrant Pope personally received some of the gifts of bread and wine from the people. But by the Middle Ages the rite had disappeared — while the reciting of the processional psalm the people used to sing persisted. In the time of Justin (150 A.D.) there was no procession of the people bringing gifts but gifts could be left for the poor near the altar. In the time of Hippolytus (200 A.D.) offerings of oil, cheese, and wine (for the clergy and the poor) were brought to the altar, but after the celebration of the Eucharist.

In the time of Theodore of Mopsuestia (350-428 A.D.) the offertory procession was a grand affair and finally came to symbolize the placing of the body of Christ in the tomb! This seems to us an extraordinary symbol but in the Eastern Churches then the common belief was that the Resurrection was signified by the Consecration of the Mass. Accordingly what we would call the offertory procession was thought of as the burial ceremony of Christ, the unconsecrated bread and wine representing his dead body.

In Africa in the 4th century the faithful brought bread and wine into the sanctuary (or up to the altar) not *before* the Eucharistic prayer but at the moment of the Eucharistic action.

In the face of such divergent precedents the Council of Trent probably followed the offertory procedure most familiar to the bishops in their own dioceses. At that time in the Western Church there were no offertory processions. The only action of the people which signified their participation was their presence.

Accordingly the Council of Trent approved an Order of the Mass which made public the private devotional prayers of the priest and included prayers which confused (because of the prayers' origins in various other ceremonies) the bread and wine and the gifts for the clergy and the poor with the Body and

Blood of Christ.

Examples of this confusion were found in the first offertory prayer of the 1570 Missal ("this immaculate Host" before the Consecration) and in the ending of the Roman Canon where the priest blessed with signs of the cross the already consecrated species and seemingly calls them only "these good things." The explanation is that at one time this blessing was for the gifts for the poor.

So we ask again, Tony, whether or not we should "change back" and readopt mistakes, however honest. As you see, it would not be as simple as it sounds. What most people have in mind when they yearn for a return to the old ways is the sense of wonder, awe, and adoration that the long tradition of the Tridentine ritual built up in the Mass. Who can quarrel with that? I would go so far as to say there were sound arguments for making no changes in the old Mass. But, of course, once they were made, I would not reverse them.

As a priest who said the old prayers for many years I must admit that the objections to them by the modern reformers never bothered me, though largely because of my ignorance of the research in which the reformers were engaged. When you didn't scrutinize the prayers word by word they certainly seemed to fulfill their purpose and the inconsistencies were not obvious enough to cause distraction.

What we can hope and pray for is that, despite the occasional hustle and bustle in the 1969 Liturgy as opposed to the 1570 Mass, its ritual will gradually endear itself to the whole people and they will again come to offer the Sacrifice in the numbers they boasted in the days of Pius XII.

Mass Stipends

Although St. Paul could have been self-supporting at the trade of tentmaking, he recommended that those who served at the altar should derive their living from that service. Yet the sad fate of Ananias, who tried to hold out money from the Christian community while pretending that he was giving his all, was a counter-counsel to the early Christians.

There is no question, in view of recurrent scandals among religious fund raisers, that mixing the spiritual with the financial can be very rewarding, both for sincere and insincere promoters. Consequently even so pious a custom as giving money to a priest so that he will offer Mass for some departed loved one of the donor rouses suspicion that money and religion are being improperly associated. We must suppose that any pious custom which can be abused has been abused somewhere or other, but that should not prevent our defending the basic custom.

THE QUESTION:

My question is about Masses for the deceased. First of all, I am glad to be a Catholic and believe in Purgatory because as one priest said, "I ain't so bad, but I do goof up once in a while."

1. But what about the Protestants who do not believe in Purgatory or praying for the dead? After my mother died we had Masses offered for her but not for my deceased mother-in-law who wasn't a Catholic. Do the Protestants escape Purgatory because they don't believe in it? Of course I know many people pray for the deceased in general and God in his mercy uses prayers and Mass intentions where and as needed.

The big complaint I hear in this vicinity is "Father does not get to say the Masses for so long after the funeral when someone in the parish dies." 2. Does the deceased get the benefit of the Mass when the money is given or when the pastor gets around to offering the Mass?

After my mother's funeral the priest was very kind. He had the Month's Mind Mass offered with money brought into the rectory before I asked. 3. Is that and Week's Mind a tradition that is fading away? 4. How much Mass money is really necessary? Our envelopes at the funeral home say "For Masses to be used according to the wishes of the family." I heard one priest say that in the place where he was stationed the envelopes all said the money could be used for whatever the family wanted and he liked that because when his Dad died they got hundreds of dollars of Mass money which he thought was too much and some of the money could have been donated for such things as vestments or other church items.

Irene Kraske

THE ANSWER:

I put the numbers into your letter, Irene, just to keep the answers lined up with the questions. There really is not much new to say in answer, but plenty on which to reflect.

1. Granted that this is a Purgatory, what happens to deceased Protestants or even total unbelievers will be the same whether they believe in Purgatory or not. Nonbelief will not excuse them from spiritual penalties they might have incurred in life. The doctrine of Purgatory, in a sense, is an effort to reconcile for human understanding the infinite mercy and infinite justice which are God's. It is a doctrine developed by theologians because of a dilemma. The dilemma is that if God is infinitely merciful, it would seem to us that He will forgive everybody everything, but if He is infinitely just He will hold everybody absolutely accountable for everything.

The doctrine of Purgatory, theologically tied in with the Catholic teaching on the sacramental forgiveness of sins, is a kind of double gesture in the two opposite directions of mercy and justice — it satisfies both demands of logic without destroying either. According to the doctrine you are both spared and punished. The other common-sense prop of the doctrine is that, since the Church attributes sinlessness only to the Lord and his mother, everyone else has sin to expiate but not everyone is so guilty as to be banished from God forever. Being in Purgatory assures your final going to Heaven as it *purges* you of sin and all its effects.

One of the difficulties in getting this doctrine accepted, apart from the fact that the word *Purgatory* does not occur in Scripture, is brought up by your question No. 2. The unreflecting answer to it, I suppose, is that the deceased gets the benefit when the Mass is offered for him. But this answer bypasses the rather stupefying consideration that the deceased is no longer in time but in eternity, which St. Thomas called *totum simul,* "everything at once." In eternity there is no time.

Our difficulty is that we can't think practically in those terms, though we can use them in expressing thoughts about theoretical matters. So just *when* the departed soul gets the help from a Mass offered for him wouldn't matter to him, though we believe it would be better for him to have the Mass than not to have it.

Your third question gets us into the subject of devotional offerings of Masses for the dead. The Masses said on the third, seventh, and thirtieth day after death along with the anniversary Mass are not part of any liturgical prescription, although special Mass readings for the anniversary were supplied in the Pius V (1570) Missal. Some editions of the "Black" Missal (containing only Masses for the Dead) had rubrics about the third, seventh, and thirtieth day. I would have to say, Yes, the practice of Week and Month's Mind is fading away since there is no mention of them in the new (1969) Missal.

Your fourth question about the money offerings for Masses brings up the heart of the matter as far as controversy and misunderstanding are involved. Your particular question here presumes that at funerals people leave money or money and Mass cards (stating for the information of survivors that a Mass or Masses will be said for the deceased). In many places, by direction of the bishop, such money, called Mass stipends, now goes to the local church bank account, not to individual priests, as also do offerings for weddings, Baptisms, and other "stole fees." The income loss to priests is ordinarily made up for by a salary increase.

Just a few years back it was universal custom that Mass offerings went directly to the priest who "said" them, that is, satisfied the obligation of saying the Masses imposed by the person who offered the money. This money was regarded as being a part of the income of the priest to be used for his personal needs and support. In places where this old practice still holds this money amounts to perhaps 5% to 15% of the priest's total income, but I remember the Great Depression days when it ordinarily amounted to more than 50%. In some places it was the only income. Right now in some mission countries the offerings for Masses from home still are the chief income of the priests working among the very poor.

I learned in the seminary that it would be a mortal sin to accept a stipend and not to satisfy the obligation of offering the Mass, even though the money amount was only a dollar. Every so often in those days there would be a scandal in which some poor "suspended" renegade priest would try to collect stipend money when he had no right to accept it nor any authority to fulfill the obligations he assumed. Canon law imposed severe penalties for any trafficking in Mass stipends, such things as getting the Masses "said" in places where the stipend was lower and keeping the difference.

The whole system smelled of simony to those who hated the Catholic Church, and I suppose that is why the present tendency is to depersonalize the offering, but the offering of Mass stipends to individual priests is not now forbidden. It had a legitimate origin in the history of the Mass.

It's a long complicated story, beginning with the theologians of the 11th century. They wanted unleavened bread (the kind we still use) at Mass because they reasoned that our Lord had used that kind at the Last Supper, where the Jewish Passover ceremonial called for it. (The Jews used it to remind themselves of their sudden Exodus from Egypt. They couldn't wait that day for their daily bread to "rise" and get bubbles in it from the effect of the yeast or leaven. They had to bake it in a hurry and got flat bread).

In centuries previous to the 11th either kind of bread could be used for Mass, and the people could bring up to the altar in the Offertory procession the leavened bread they baked at home. When they were not allowed to do this anymore, they seem to have lost interest in receiving Communion and the procession eventually died out. In the 1570 Missal all that was left of the processional ceremony was a single verse from the psalm formerly sung during it. Even that was recited at Low Mass by the priest alone.

In some places of course, the procession was maintained for more years than in other places. Variations developed. The one variation pertinent for us was that at funeral Masses in many places money offerings were brought in procession to the altar. Researchers tell us that is why in the old (1570-1969) Requiem Mass both offertory verse and refrain were kept and sung instead of just the single verse as was the case in other Masses

— there was time to sing during the offertory procession at funerals, but not at other Masses.

Of course, everybody realized that this was only a "collection" with ritual. The old link of the people with the Mass action — in their offering the materials of the sacrifice — was broken by the substitution of money. Finally the collection was taken up at all Masses without any ritual notice at all being taken of it by the priest or his ministers.

The Mass stipend (to get back to it) originated at this point. People began bringing their money offering to the priest at times other than that of Mass. Quite probably, they wanted their offerings noticed and acknowledged. Also, this was in the Middle Ages when the practice of prayer for particular intentions became popular. Money payment obliging an "intention" from the celebrant became associated with the Mass.

The idea was that the lay person would provide the money for the purchase of bread and wine for Mass and also contribute to the support of a priest to say the Mass. The priest in return would have a particular intention (that of the stipend payer) when he said Mass.

This understanding and explanation of the Mass stipend is still valid but in the 1969 Missal a diminished version of the pre-11th century bread and wine procession is provided for, obviously to restore the idea that the people should furnish the immediate materials for the sacrifice, not just money. The "offertory verse" which was the only relic left of the post-11th century money procession has been taken out.

In addition to the answers to your questions, Irene, it seems to me that a few general observations are called for. Mixing the practical and the spiritual as happens in the case of the Mass stipend can make for awkward situations but it is human nature and not Church rule which bring them on.

When money is left at the funeral parlor there can be misunderstanding because of the widespread custom, especially among the very poor, of friends and neighbors helping with funeral expenses. If money donated at funerals is intended to be used as Mass stipends, it should be properly labeled or accompanied with a printed "Mass card" stating that purpose. In relatively prosperous communities, where there is not likely to be a family need for monetary help, it would seem doubly wrong to use money intended by the donors for "Masses for the deceased" (spiritual charity) for anything else, such as church furniture, morticians' fees, even donations to the poor (material charity).

Until, which is not an immediate prospect, the whole system of Mass stipends is eliminated officially, a priest who personally accepts money to offer a Mass or Masses is gravely obliged to follow the intention of the donor. In places where the bishop has directed that incoming Mass stipends be used for church expenditures, the money amount of the stipend is specified and the corresponding number of Masses must be said.

When so many intentions are requested that the local parish priests cannot take care of all of them, the intention and the stipends can be sent to the missions, to deprived priests in countries where the Church is being persecuted, or to impoverished parishes in our own country. When this is done the justifying purpose of the Mass stipend is fulfilled. Catholics and their priests have no reason to be ashamed of it, although, as idealistic reformers rightly point out, the stipend certainly is not, and should never be, the reason why Mass is offered.

Mysticism

The average Catholic says his prayer but rarely gets into its higher forms. Those that do reach prayer's higher level do so out of a desire to become closer to God and to be numbered among his saints. The mental processes by which a person attains sanctity and sometimes ecstasy are not entirely distinct from those used by Hindu sadhus, Buddhist monks and psychological experimenters. But we can't for that reason dismiss the writings of the great Catholic mystics as mental delusions, since they had purposes beyond those of the psychologists and even the non-Trinitarian mystics. In their case things like charity toward fellow men, adoration of the eternal Father, purgation of all vice, acquisition of specific virtues were all pre-requisites for serious prayer and their attempt to come closer to God. Things like mental peace, mental strength, and mental pleasure were not among their objectives as they are among the objectives of the presently well advertised transcendental meditators.

THE QUESTION:

What is mental prayer? I wish someone would write a pamphlet explaining the difference between simple, traditional meditation and transcendental meditation. It should explain that in simple meditation, the mind, the imagination and the will are employed but that in transcendental meditation there is a sort of negation of intellect and concepts. It should define these terms so that one can better understand what he reads about prayer. It should be for the unlearned, like myself, and even for children.

J.M.

THE ANSWER:

Until I came to your last sentence, J.M., it didn't occur to me that your question could be the source of an article here, since mysticism and the higher forms of prayer are not of universal interest. Though there is presently a rash of mystical sects preaching various kinds of meditation I thought at first any attempt to confute them was beyond my abilities and inclinations. It was your point about defining the terms that changed my mind. I won't write the pamphlet you suggested but I can run over the terms which come into any discussion like this. Once Catholics can be precise in their own minds on the meaning of the terms they will have much less difficulty in avoiding pseudo-spiritual fads. There might even be less brainwashing, deprogramming, kidnaping and rescuing of the young people fascinated by ideas apparently new to them.

"Transcendental meditation" is a term that has taken on a new meaning rather recently. It used to be just two good English words meaning, I suppose, a thought process above the ordinary, a mental dwelling on things religious which brought the thinker into the realm of the divine. Now it is practically a copyrighted name, usually abbreviated to TM, used for commercially marketed lessons in therapeutic psychology. It may be, J.M., that you did not have this modern usage of the term in mind at all, but since so many people have heard of TM and wondered at what relation it might have to Catholic mental prayer we had better describe it.

The one who hopes to "meditate transcendentally" puts in two sessions of 20 minutes each day, with his eyes closed, repeating his own secret *mantra*, some Hindu word for love. He concentrates on inhaling and exhaling, dismisses other thoughts that come and go in his mind but does not force himself to "concentrate." Simple, but it is harder than it sounds and may require a course of lessons to get results. One result can be "cosmic consciousness," which could be described as a state of being physically relaxed as in sleep, while being mentally alert. This consciousness leads to a feeling of mental energy so that it is easy to do things like giving up smoking. Among observable physical results can be lowered blood pressure, more alpha brain waves (the best kind), and improved metabolism.

All this is obviously a far cry from anything religious even though it is called transcendental meditation. But it does come from Hindu mysticism, being a distilled form of spiritual exercises that take Hindu holy men a lifetime to learn well and practice expertly. The cosmic consciousness arrived at in TM is often thought to be identical with the high contemplative states of Trinitarian mystics but it is, as we shall see, not the same.

There isn't much emphasis on the contemplative approach to God in modern social spirituality. The lack is being countered on the popular level by such substitutes as TM and the "mystical" sects which fall far short of satisfying man's real need to know God more directly.

It might then be enough to outline standard Catholic spiritual procedures and contrast them with the ersatz mysticism outlined above, defining, as you suggest, J.M., the terms as we go along.

You have to begin with having the Catholic faith so that you realize that *prayer* is lifting your mind and heart to God to offer him the honor due him from you and to advance his glory on earth.

Prayer can be vocal or mental. When it is mental it is possible to make some distinction between it and meditation. In *mental prayer* the mind is chiefly reasoning, in *meditation* the mind is chiefly devoted to pious feelings and to the use of the will in making good resolutions. Unless one follows a developed method of prayer there is likely to be confusion. Without a map the person addressing himself to God may not really know whether he is growing closer to God or sinking deeper into self-delusions. The craziest people in the world have been mystics gone wrong.

Practically every canonized saint who ever wrote anything put down his or her favorite method of prayer. For practical purposes in the training of religious personnel, the methods of St. Ignatius Loyola and of the Seminary of St. Sulpice in Paris cover most of the possibilities.

They have in common the requirement of triple preparation for prayer and meditation. The remote preparation is found in a daily life conducive to prayer. The proximate preparation is in reading or reflecting ahead of the time of prayer with the desire to glorify God and become better. The immediate preparation is to place oneself in the presence of God.

The fundamental mental acts common to both methods are 1. rendering to God the submission owed to him, 2. consideration of the need to acquire virtue, 3. self-examination, 4. requests for the help of God's grace and 5. good resolutions.

The conclusion of the meditation is pretty much the same in both methods. There should be thanksgiving, a check-up on how well the meditation has been performed, a final prayer for God's blessing, the choice of some dominant thought to carry through the day.

The differences between the Ignatian and Sulpician methods might be called only technical. The Spiritual Exercises (Ignatius) have the meditator separately apply each of three "powers" (memory, understanding, and will) to each of the points made in the meditation. In the Sulpician method the three essential acts are adoration, communion and cooperation, with each of these terms having its own specialized meaning. The adoration is, so to speak, of one of the virtues of God; the communion is in drawing this virtue to ourselves through prayer; the cooperation consists in resolving to practice the particular virtue the same day.

The Ignatian method calls for the person praying to take an *active* role; the Sulpician method encourages *passivity* in the reception of grace requested of God. But of course the two methods tend to overlap each other. Either method can get pretty involved compared to the two 20-minute sessions of the TM-er, but as far as Catholic mysticism goes, we are still only on the threshold of the house of God. The practitioner is only beginning when he has mastered such techniques of prayer. It is in fulfilling his resolutions for a better life that he begins what is called the Purgative way. He has not only to do penance for his sins but acquire habitual penitence, achieve a hatred and fear of sin. This is done through mortification, the suppressing of even lawful desires. Mortification is directed against the seven capital sins which must be conquered one by one: pride, covetousness, lust, anger, gluttony, envy and sloth. These are the sources of sin giving rise to temptations which must be resisted until all affection for things not of God is done away with. It gets harder and harder.

But once this shedding of vices is accomplished the practitioner of Catholic mysticism is ready to start on the second stage of his journey, the Illuminative way, on which he must acquire virtues. His prayer is no longer based chiefly on the tedious use of reason and the reaching of conclusions but has a spontaneous quality. The practitioner no longer feels the need of any reasoning to convince himself of the need and desirability of his search for God. He feels free of sin and moves toward God without any self-persuasion. In fact, he finds it difficult or even impossible to go back to reasoned prayer. He is habitually in agreement with the will of God, whatever it may be for him. At this stage, which is much more pleasant that the previous purgative one, he may receive spiritual consolations from God, feelings of love and joy so intense that spiritual writers and hymn composers feel obligated to use the word *sweet* to describe them. There is a rough parallel here to what the TM-er is shooting at, but the true Christian mystic finds this a place of danger from which he must press on. The dangers are in taking pride in what he has so far accomplished, and neglecting duty to remain in, or return to, a spiritual consolation. He avoids these dangers by striving for the moral virtues of prudence, justice, fortitude and temperance as well as the theological virtues of faith, hope and charity. All this, I'm sure you will join me in remarking, J.M., is easier said than done.

For the Catholic mystic there remains the Unitive way in which he may add *contemplation* to the meditation and the sweetly consoling prayer he has learned.

It is only here, J.M., that we can go on to your reference to "negation of intellect and concept." I find no trace of this in the popular practices such as TM but it is essential to transcendental meditation, in the old standard use of the term. At this point we can start calling it *contemplation* instead of transcendental meditation, to underline the difference between psychological mind tinkerings and the action of Almighty God in the minds of true mystics.

Text books on mysticism or the spiritual life work mostly from the writings of Teresa and John of the Cross, both canonized saints and proclaimed "Doctors of the Church." The text books have a more orderly arrangement of facts in presenting the highest stages of the spiritual life than do mystic authors. This for the reason you mention in your letter — negation. The mystics know they can't say in ordinary human speech what this Unitive way is like, they have recourse to saying what it is not like. No matter what sublime ideas of God come to them in their prayer, they have to deny to themselves that they have reached Him.

The text books, in connection with the Unitive way, speak of the gifts of the Holy Spirit coming to the soul of the mystic. These are Wisdom, Understanding, Counsel, Fortitude, Knowledge, Piety and Fear of the Lord. All, of course, are

forms of God's grace first enumerated by Isaiah but granted to
the mystic as he or she approaches the closest psychological
union with God possible to man here on earth. There is nothing
the mystic can do (notice the idea of negation) to gain these
gifts, God gives them. The mystic uses a sail on his boat, instead
of rowing it. He will come next to a stage called variously the
prayer of simple regard, the prayer of simplicity, the prayer of
recollection or, more technically, acquired contemplation. In
any event it is not yet the prayer of infused contemplation,
which is the highest stage and called by various mystics the
prayer of full union, the transforming union, the ecstatic union
or spiritual marriage.

It is this state which is impossible to describe partly because
it includes darkness (negation) as well as light, and desolation
(negation) as well as joy. On the positive side, the most explicit
thing that can be said of it is that the mystic has *certainty* of the
presence of God in his soul. While this at first thought should
bring only joy, the mystic has intervals of agonizing sorrow —
presumably because he still feels the infinite distance between
himself and God.

So your "negation" element is found all through the life of
the mystic. He has nothing of sin or pleasure in his life. As he
progresses he finds that even spiritual joys must not be sought
for as ends in themselves and when he has at long last arrived at
infused contemplation, it too, has its elements of dark
negation.

All through his life, the *nada* (nothing) of St. John of the
Cross enshrouds him. One of the greatest Christian mystics
significantly entitles his masterwork "The Cloud of Unknowing." Both these authors are in the tradition of Dionysius the
Areopagite, a Syrian monk of the 6th century. He pointed out
that since the human senses and the human intellect are
incapable of attaining God, they must be emptied of creatures,
i.e., of all feelings and thoughts, if they are to be made ready for
the reception of the Creator. The only "knowing of God" that
the mystic can have is knowing what God is not.

The difference between true mysticism, the effort to unite

oneself with God, and psychological routines designed to make oneself feel better thus was explained as far back as the 6th century. In Catholic teaching the highest mystical state is not attained by human effort by is granted by God.

A not inconsiderable number of the new meditation methods are plainly agnostic. There is talk of altered states of consciousness, of higher states of consciousness and enhanced awareness, all of which are purportedly brought about by the practitioner (or by drugs) and so differ absolutely from the religious concept of God working on the individual soul. In Catholic mysticism the practitioner must be active up to a point, cooperative beyond that point and passive in the ultimate stage.

We must not overlook the possibility that in all the stages previous to the transforming union, the psychological processes may be the same in the TM-er, the Buddhist monk, the Hindu holy man and the Catholic mystic. Very probably the alpha wave output of the brain fluctuates in the same way and degree in all four, blood pressure and heart rates may be the same in the ecstatic states of all four, the joys and agonies may correspond exactly in degree, but the TM-er is looking for more mental energy or whatnot, the Buddhist for union with the ground of being, the Hindu with the cosmos, the Catholic mystic with the Blessed Trinity.

Thomas Merton was investigating the similarities of pagan and Christian mystics by interviewing the holy men of Asia at the time of his death. But even in cases of pagans who attain high mystical states we must, if we have the Catholic faith to begin with, distinguish between the way God acts in them and the way He acts in those who have accepted his revelation through Christ. The author of the *Cloud of Unknowing* sees the high mystical state as the logical outcome of Catholic theology worked out to its ultimate conclusions. The devout Catholic and the contemplative mystic are both on the same road, the difference is only in how far each has traveled. For the good Catholic, TM and Asiatic transcendalities can only be detours.

You called yourself unlearned, J.M., but you are not if you begin your mystical investigations as a practicing Catholic. In God's dispensation, ignorance is the lot only of those who lack the faith to see the working of the Blessed Trinity in the minds of men and seeing only the working of the "laws of nature" or "cosmic consciousness," in the mystical states men can attain.

Appendix —
The Perennial Questions

Problems arising from Church law on birth control, divorce, cremation, Bible interpretation, and lately, intercommunion come to so many people that questions on these subjects are sent in oftener than any others. Even though they have been answered more than once in the Catholic Digest *they continue to come in and deserve to be answered as often as necessary. The next five Q and A's in this volume are reprints, after updating and second editing, from the first volume in this series, "What Would You Like to Know About the Church?" Their inclusion here will make the present volume of greater use to persons of all faiths seeking to know why the Church stands where it does on matters of concern to our whole society.*

Birth Control

THE LETTER:

I take the *Catholic Digest.* However, I am not a Catholic. I
have an aunt by marriage and several friends who are Catholic.
I certainly agree with the Catholic Church's stand on abortion,
but I do not understand the Catholic Church's stand on birth
control, with overpopulation such a problem today; and the
people with the most children seem to be those on welfare or in
those countries where there is starvation. Would it not be
better if these children were not born? Can you explain this to
me? This is what I would like to know about the Church.

Mrs. R. Austin, Jr.

THE ANSWER:

Anyone who takes the *Catholic Digest*, Mrs. Austin, cannot
be all bad. You agree with us on abortion, too, so I welcome the
opportunity of trying to explain why Catholics who follow the
reasoning of traditional morality still oppose artificial birth
control.

They are not really as pigheaded as they seem to many of
their contemporaries, but to show that I must begin with
background considerations. Just what is the issue? Let me say
first that it is not a case of the Catholic Church working for an
overpopulated world, devoutly hoping that everyone will have
as many children as physically possible. Birth control by moral
methods is not only permitted by the Church but can be an
obligation of the sincere Catholic. The point, of course, is that
there is a difference between natural and artificial birth
control, the first being allowable and the second sinful.

Despite the implications of those opposed to her stand, the
Church is not really relying on starvation, war, and natural
calamities to keep population down and the world habitable.
Certainly such factors have operated locally in the past and in

view of atomic proliferation may well operate on a world scale in the future, but the Church does not rely on them to solve the population problem. The traditional Church regards irresponsible parenthood on a family or national scale as immoral because she believes that God has provided man with a nonsinful, natural birth-control method. I must add that it requires at least intermittent sexual self-denial for successful operation.

It is at this point that I lose all those people who consider they win the argument by exclaiming, "This is the 20th century!" They say it as though the numerals were oversize and underlined. The society we live in lacks any built-in lessons in self-control. Deliberate self-denial of any attainable pleasure is looked on as idiocy. This effect shows through even within the Catholic Church in the agitation to move away from celibacy of the priesthood and the old monastic vows of poverty and obedience. The basic gripe against the Church is that she requires the foregoing of pleasure as a means of controlling population.

I'm sure that you were not even thinking of things like that, Mrs. Austin, so let's go on quickly to a second consideration directly brought up by the question in your letter, "Would it not be better if these children were not born?"

To be or not to be? If life is only a period of agony followed by a return to nothingness, the unbelieving world has the better of the argument — it would seem better "not to be." If, as the Church believes, God creates each person with the ultimate purpose of that person's eternal happiness, the period of suffering between creation and physical death is literally unimportant. This was the thought in Pope Paul's mind when he reproved those who would limit the number of those admitted to the "Banquet of Life."

A second background consideration is in the realm of fantasy. Suppose that all the world were Catholic and that by a greater miracle, all the people followed the Church's traditional teaching about birth control. The population problem would disappear! People would have only as many children as the planet could support.

The rhythm method, known with such great good humor as
Vatican roulette, is fallible in a percentage of single family
situations. But if the whole human race practiced natural birth
control, population could be certainly controlled; in the total
world situation the method would be (dare I use the word?)
infallible.

In fact in that world of fantasy there would be easier
attainment of control. The current complaint of the birth
control societies is that people, despite the effectiveness of
modern artificial methods of contraception, are continuing to
have as many children *as they want,* not as many or few *as they
should have* for the best balance of population with world
resources. A world of obedient Catholics would not present
this problem. So the Church does not see herself as interfering
with the march of human progress.

The fantasy approach to the practical problem only annoys
and does not dissuade the nontraditional moralists. But from
the viewpoint of the Church, the artifical birth control societies
want to abolish the natural law. The Church holds that the
natural law cannot be abolished, any more than God can be
abolished. Both Hitler and Stalin avoided what were to them
population problems by genocide, which was basically wrong
because it was against natural law, not just because their
respective countries had statutes against murder or even
because of the "Thou shalt not kill" commandment published
in the Bible. They could ignore statutes, but could not repeal
the natural law. If natural law and a statute coincide in scope,
abolishing the statute makes no essential difference in the
morality of the action.

So political power cannot do away with natural law. Neither
can majority opinion. If Vatican Council III were to convene
tomorrow and by a 99.4% majority declare that there was to be
no canon law against artificial birth control, the action would
not change the natural law. No matter how many confessors,
canon lawyers, or episcopal false prophets announce themselves in favor of artificial birth control, nothing changes in the

realm of right and wrong.

Majority opinion is not the source of natural law. This natural law we are talking about is nevertheless written in the heart of man. It means that there are some things, at least, that a man with his wits about him can discover to be wrong. I would regard my own murder by another as wrong. If I am mentally healthy, I go on to the consideration that it is also wrong for me to kill other men. This mental attitude is natural in man; it is not natural to other carnivorous animals. Natural law is not self-enforcing. It is often broken by the free will of man, its application is subject to further reason as in the case of self-defense. But this sense of a natural law is one of the things, along with self-reflection and free will, that raises man above the animals.

Patience, Mrs. Austin, I realize that since you said you were against abortion, you go along with me on natural law, murder, and self-evident wrongs. All this has to be said first.

Artificial birth control is not so self-evidently wrong, since you said you didn't understand the traditional Catholic position. Again, no one will understand the foreground without knowing the background. It might help to say that the Catholic vision of life is greater than the social security type of outlook.

In the rise of the welfare states, the social philosophers began speaking of government care from cradle to grave or from womb to tomb, their definition of the total life span. A more religious definition would be that new life begins with the twinkle in the father's eye and continues eternally in the Beatific Vision.

Such things are beyond government control and of little interest to its agencies, but the traditional Catholic faith is that interference at any point by man in the continuum of human life is against the natural law. Just as abortion is a breaking of the continuum, so is interference with the life forces used by God to create new eternal life. And just as it makes no difference morally whether the Supreme Court provides for the killing of the person at three rather than six months of age, it makes no difference morally whether interference with life comes at the time of its production, in its later stages through euthanasia, or in the premarriage intention to control it artificially.

Imagine, just for the moment and for the purpose, that you are God, planning the production of a particular human life. Where do you begin? Is it at emergence from the mother's womb, at six or three months of fetal life, at the moment of conception, at the physical union of the parents, with the intention of the parents to have children, with the previous production of the parents themselves? It would seem that man's interference with your plan at any of these points would be in opposition to your will.

In Catholic tradition the intention to have and rear children is inherent in the marriage contract, for the contract's alternative, promiscuity, while satisfying the sex and companionship drives, would take little thought of the children needed to continue, not the life of the parents, but the life of the human race, part of God's continuum. So, in a very real sense you could say the marriage contract and the intention of the parties are, in God's view, the beginning of new life. If you accept all this reasoning, you must agree that artificial birth control is wrong. It interferes with the continuum of life.

Opponents of the Church's position are often infuriated with her seeming inability to appreciate the urgency of the immediate problem. Old-line Catholic moralists are equally infuriated with the pooh poohing of her philosophical and logical arguments. One of them is that no faculty of man should be abused.

In the traditional Catholic moral context, saying that the sex faculty should not be abused implies that its primary purpose is procreation. When those contrary point out that it has also the purpose of mutual comfort and give this purpose more importance than procreation, they are only proclaiming "This is the 20th century!" A single look at God's total creation shows that procreation is the primary purpose of the sex faculties. The second purpose does not even exist in the lower, unfree-willed, unself-reflecting animals who actions are ultimately controlled by body chemistry rather than willingness or unwillingness to observe law.

Yet the Church insists that the secondary purpose of marriage be fulfilled as strongly as do the new moralists. For instance, it is not fulfilled by artificial insemination, any more than the first purpose (procreation) is fulfilled by a contraceptive act. The Church is against artificial insemination even when the parties are man and wife because there is no human comfort and no expression of conjugal love in it.

The force and fundamental importance of this abuse-of-a-faculty argument are seen more clearly in its disregard by the new morality than in its presentation by traditional Catholic morality. In the new morality, masturbation (called self-abuse in the older, more genteel, manuals) though obviously the abuse of a faculty, is not reproved. It cannot be reproved, and the new moralists must join the liberated women's magazines in encouraging what used to be called solitary vice, because artificial birth control is, physically, mutual abuse.

Vasectomy and sterilization, both mutilations or the destructions of a faculty, are necessarily O.K.'d in the new morality. The chief trouble is that there is nowhere for the new moralists to stop. If these methods of population control fail and their purpose must be achieved, they go on logically to abortion and euthanasia as acceptable methods of population control. The only sins left are things like dumping tailings into Lake Superior or not using electronic smoke controls in your smokestack.

It is not a reassuring simile, but it is a fact that Catholic moral principles, like Catholic dogmas, are related to each other as are the cards built into a house by a child. Pull out one of the bottom ones and the whole edifice tumbles, as it has for the new moralists.

That is why the Pope is his encylical *Humanae Vitae* didn't care that he so bitterly antagonized the fatuous enthusiasts who expected him to give in to the pressure of majority opinion. He couldn't give in without wiping out the whole structure of Catholic morality, adherence to the natural law, and belief in the God of Judaeo-Christian tradition.

Mrs. Austin, your letter shows you to be a fair-minded, sincere person, so after that outburst you, and thousands like you are entitled to ask: "If you're so smart, why haven't you persuaded the errant Catholics and, for that matter, the whole world to give up artificial birth control?" The answer is that the official arguments are abstract and while logical, are not as persuasive as the artificial birth control societies' arguments.

I said our arguments were not as persuasive; I did not say they were not as good. They are in fact better. But the societies can point to the millions of starving babies, we only to a principle to which logic has brought us. They can point to women in real fear of death if they follow the traditional morality; we can only call for heroism in the pursuit of sanctity.

We suffer from the lack of a coercive argument, one that forces peoples' assent. Of course, even the arguments for the existence of God do not coerce everybody. It comes to a question of value; which is more important in our lives, heaven or earth? The new moralists can't see why we cannot have the best of both worlds, but they have to blind themselves to the whole picture of command and obedience, of sacrifice of the temporal for the sake of the eternal, found in traditional Catholic morality.

The new moralists seem now to be the molders of what has become majority opinion. But ever since Adam joined the majority formed by Eve and the serpent, majority opinion can be looked on as a test of right or wrong only with the closed eyes of the new moralists. If you don't understand how they can see anything with their eyes closed, neither can I.

Majority opinion is all in favor of improving the "quality of life" in living populations at the expense of life itself for future generations. Sort of reminds you of Jack Benny, God rest him. His most famous joke held up the radio program for ten minutes with studio audience laughter. All he did was hesitate overlong in reply to the bandit demanding his money or his life. The audience, obviously with the right set of values, thought it hilarious that anyone could ever consider preferring money to life, but that is not the way the world is now. Present majority opinion chooses for itself a more comfortable future (money, really) while denying any future (life, really) to what would ordinarily be a large percentage of the human race.

Divorce and Remarriage

THE LETTER:

From time to time lately I read of the relaxation of the Church with regard to divorce and annulment — just slight reference and no detail. My question: What are the church's current rulings on annulment and divorce? Are they really any different from what we have always been taught?

I am a happily married wife and mother and I do not ask for myself. But a first cousin of mine insisted upon marrying a boy who was still in the service. My aunt and uncle gave their permission because they were afraid they would run off and possibly go to a justice of the peace. When he was discharged, they came to live with my aunt and uncle, but he was unfaithful.

My cousin learned of his affairs but because of the condition of my uncle's health (he had had a second serious heart attack and the family was advised absolutely no shocks) she never spoke of what was going on. Almost a year went by. Then my aunt answered the phone one day and a female voice said, thinking she was talking to his wife, "Keep your rotten husband away from my daughter." Of course, the whole thing came out and he was almost thrown from the house. My cousin was urged to start annulment proceedings and went through the entire procedure. But an annulment could not be gotten because of the impossibility of proving that he never had the intention of remaining faithful before the marriage. She got a civil divorce.

My cousin eventually "married" the man she was working for during all of this time. Before this "marriage" her husband met her outside the office building one night and gave her a severe beating and this was the only time she has ever seen or heard from him to this day.

Eighteen years have passed. My cousin attends Mass every Sunday. Her present husband is a wonderful husband and father and their two girls are active Catholics who (one is 17, and the other 14) still ask why Mother doesn't receive Communion. She is tearing herself apart. I am certainly not going to judge her. Since we started to subscribe the *Catholic Digest* and I discovered your "What Would You Like to Know About the Church," I've wondered if this might be the source of further information.

I'm not looking for an easy way out for this girl, but I'm convinced that she had a rotten deal. She was headstrong and very young; but she is paying a terrible price, and I wonder if the good Lord in his mercy would help us find a way for her to return to the sacraments.

M.C.

THE ANSWER:

Letters like yours and situations such as the one you describe, Mrs. C., are very moving and disturbing. They make nearly everyone wonder why the rules can't be changed. Just before your letter arrived, it was reported in the secular press that three priests' senates in the eastern United States had petitioned for the readmission to the sacraments of divorced and remarried Catholics whose original spouses were still living, with permission to continue in their second marriage. They were undoubtedly thinking of persons who really wanted the sacraments again.

We can begin by taking up your question about the relaxation of the marriage laws. The answer is that there have been administrative changes which in some cases can speed up annulment procedures by eliminating automatic appeals and by delegation of authority to lower levels. But in the Church's doctrine of sacramental marriage there has been no change.

What you, judging from your letter, have been taught still has the force of law. Civil divorce, agreed to by both parties, of itself does not prevent the guilty or nonguilty from seeking absolution and Communion. It is remarriage, which is *prima facie* evidence of a determination to remain in what the Church declares to be a state of disobedience, that makes canonical reconciliation with the Church impossible. Strict law makes the official Church seem cold and inhuman to those who really suffer from its enforcement. Relatively few people can by themselves understand the need for it or have the ability to "take it."

My one-time best friend and worst golfing partner was deserted by his bride within hours of the wedding ceremony, yet waited 14 years for a Church annulment. It came through, but by that time he had lost all desire for another marriage, and considered that life had passed him by. Church legal procedures then seemed slow to the point of injustice, but he never questioned the basic law. He got the point that the Church really doesn't have a choice between being "strict" and "permissive."

A presentation of lawmakers' difficulties will not be as moving as the recital of the difficulties of your cousin, Mrs. C., but before any final attitudes can be reached, the Church's dilemmas must be considered. As an example, take her stand on the validity of Protestant marriages, or, to be more exact, marriges between validly baptized non-Catholics. Because of the Baptisms, the Church holds these marriages valid and a Catholic may not marry the divorced party to such a marriage. To change the rule would be a grave insult to millions of sincere Christians because it would amount to calling their happy marriages less than Christian, and their children illegimate. Yet the same rule must seem outrageous to a divorced non-Catholic who wants to marry a Catholic. It must seem to him that the Church is trying to exercise authority over a non-member. It's easy to say "Brush away all the technicalities" but brushing away technicalities would harm as many people as it would help. The Church has only the choice of saying "This is the law" or "Anything goes!"

In civil law, failure to live up to a contract can be established by the usual rules of evidence and the case settled. The trouble with Church law cases, so to speak, is that they so often involve the mental intentions of the litigants. The Church holds that conscience (a judgment here and now about the morality of an action about to be performed) is supreme. The Apostles choosing a successor to Judas said only that he had gone "to his own place," not that the betrayer of the Lord had gone to hell. The Church has no ceremony of condemnation that is the opposite of canonization. She excommunicates (or rather, used to) by bell book, and candle, but does not imply anything more than a judgment on the morality of the excommunicated person's action. She does not declare him lost forever. Even if he does not outwardly repent, he may have been acting according to his conscience.

In practice, of course, if every man were allowed to follow his own inward conscience without being required to accept outward legal consequences, the abolition of law and complete anarchy would result. So the Church, while for matters of eternal import, such as heaven and hell, insists that conscience is supreme, for matters of temporal import such as Christian marriage, must enforce laws. She could not exist in anarchy.

That is all in the face of compassion for those to whom the enforcement of her laws is painful. The priests' senates which petitioned for readmission to the sacraments of remarried divorcees were asking the Church to abandon law. It may have seemed to individual members that they were only asking for a change in law but *de facto* they were asking that the Church give up all sanctions, allow individual conscience to rule temporal as well as eternal affairs, and surrender herself to anarchy.

At this point I image myself presiding over a joint meeting of three priests' senates and hearing the cries that this wasn't what was meant at all. Some hold that the Church can dissolve marriages as well as witness them; that marriages can die of themselves and that the Church can be witness to their dissolution. If the new moralists are talking about the dissolution of marital love, common purposes, and so on, marriages certainly do die of themselves. But there can be no dissolution

of the original contract in which the parties agreed to a
Catholic marriage.

If the parties can prove in law that that was not their
intention, there never was a Catholic marriage and the
supposed marriage can be annulled. If it was the intention of
the parties to contract a lifetime union, the new moralists, to
declare their marriage dead, would have to deny the plain
meaning of the contract. That way lies chaos.

As an aside, I suppose the new moralists are proposing a
conditional marriage contract for future use in the Church. But
that would take us into the metaphysical realms of the natural
law on the question of whether a conditional contract could be
the basis of a true marriage. The standard Catholic teaching is
that marriage *as a sacrament* comes under the regulating power
of the Church. But because marriage *as an institution* is based
on the natural law, the Divine revealed law, and the Apostolic
law, mere ecclesiastical law cannot change the elemental
requirements of monogamy and indissolubility: one man —
one woman — till death.

By this time, Mrs. C., I can hear you saying something like "I
know all that, but what can be done for my cousin?" I don't
know. I have to admit there is no comfort in telling anybody
"That's the law" whether you are talking about an overtime
parking ticket or a life lived out in agony of conscience.
Sympathy for a man on trial for his life, sympathy for the man
imprisoned, sympathy for the good cause a criminal represents
can all make the administration of justice and the enforcement
of law painful to enforcer and enforcee alike. But abolishing
law to do away with lawbreaking makes no more sense than
abolishing hospitals to do away with disease.

In such painful cases as that of your cousin, Mrs. C., the only
"out" would seem to be reliance on the Catholic doctrine of
conscience. Whatever disobedience caused her present status,
her conscience may tell her that it is morally impossible to leave
her partner. God's judgment will be the same as any sincere
judgment she makes of herself. But the doctrine of conscience
must be properly understood. Most people take it to mean that

you can follow your own will (they think that is their "conscience"). The doctrine does not mean that. It does mean being so certain of your position that you take your chances in not going to Confession or Communion and being willing at death to face God without having made use of the sacraments that He has provided for you.

Technically, that is the sanction of the law: obey — or no sacraments. Honestly following your conscience means weighing your judgment against that of the teaching Church, which is based on the studies of learned theologians, and deciding that you are right and that they are wrong. It can be done but it is not simple. It would seem to require the same degree of heroism as fully obeying the law. Conscience is an "out" but not an easy one.

To abolish the law and its power to bring ordinary people into obedience to God and Church, to allow the disobedient to go to Communion, which is the symbol of unity of discipline as well as belief, would be to destroy the whole concept of the Church as a governing institution. It would be unreasonable.

To raise all this to a more philosophical plane we have to admit that the opponents of reason are in the ascendant now. They do what they please, shout "Why not?" and refuse to listen to the answer. This attitude accounts for the popularity of birth control, abortion, euthanasia, disbelief in dogma, irreverence in worship, and a lot of lesser things I could think of. I do not accuse, Mrs. C., your cousin, nor anyone caught in the toils of the law of being against reason. I can only offer my unworthy prayer that the trend toward unreason in our present society may be reversed and obedience to the Author of all good law be resumed on a world scale.

Cremation

THE QUESTION:

I am a senior sociology major at South Carolina State College, a native Southerner, Afro-American, and convert to Catholicism. I converted at the age of 13 and have never regretted my decision. I am presently 21 years old.

I often contemplate death and the hereafter and often feel a desire to be cremated after death. My question is "What is the Church's official position regarding the cremation of Catholics?" If the Church does not allow cremation, then why not?

Ronny A. Baston

THE ANSWER:

The Church doesn't forbid cremation anymore, Ronny, unless it is done to symbolize denial of the Catholic belief in the resurrection of the body.

Cremation was common in ancient Rome, but the Christians didn't practice it. The great Christian Emperor Charlemagne forbade it under pain of death (and burial) and there was little or no cremation in Europe for a thousand years. The convenient modern process was invented in 1869, and cremation was thereupon taken up by the anti-Catholic Masonic societies as a symbol and forbidden by the Holy office in 1886. The new Code of Canon Law continued the prohibition in 1918, but the anti-Christian symbolic use had pretty well died out (excuse the unintended pun) by 1963, and an Instruction was issued, permitting cremation except when it was symbolic. Since then the Church attitude has progressed or regressed, according to your viewpoint, so that the new Rite of Christian Burial makes provision for the funeral ceremonies being performed in the crematorium itself.

But while your question, Ronny, makes these snatches of history necessary, it turns my mind to the newspaper obituary column. That feature is one of the prime reasons why so many people still buy the paper, filled as it is with news even more disturbing than that of the tolling bell. I was taught in my college journalism classes that as people grow older, they get more and more addicted to reading the "obits," and that a good many people turn to them first of all. I took up obituary reading rather early in life and have always indulged in the usual speculations about relationships and in gossipy checking out of who was buried in, and who out of, the Church.

I think I give the column a more thorough reading than necessary, and perhaps that is why I have lately noticed the growing number of nonfunerals. I find not only the time-honored requests to omit flowers, but statements that there will be no reviewal, and no visitation. This means no wake, no prayers, no farewells, and most likely cremation, or donation of the remains to medical science. If Catholics are not involved, I don't suppose it makes any difference. But sometimes I think they must be, since there is a notice of a commemorative Mass to be offered later. But Catholic or not, cremations and donations for transplants are increasing in number. There is no right and wrong to be argued out here. It is a good thing to receive the full rites of Christian burial, and a good thing to give them up so that someone else can live a longer life. In point of fact, though, not all cremations are necessary, and not everyone's body is needed for transplants. So there is room to evaluate the traditional Catholic final rites and their place in the total framework of the Faith.

Catholics believe not only in an afterlife but in the resurrection of the body. About all we know about that resurrection we have learned from the resurrection of our Lord. His risen Body was palpable; it could be touched and felt, as the doubting Thomas learned. But is was unaffected by space and time. The Lord did not have to walk to Galilee to meet his Apostles there after He rose from the dead; but He ate food with them after He rose; his face was recognizable. This aspect of the Lord's risen Body gave rise to the Church's traditional respect for the bodies of the faithful departed. The human body was not a piece of clothing to be discarded by the immortal soul. It was part of the Risen Christ. It will be part of the faithful follower of Christ in the final resurrection.

Just how this is to be accomplished remains one of God's mysteries. The story is somewhere in the old Roman Breviary about the martyr who proclaimed his faith by pinching the skin of his hand and declaring that he expected to rise again with that very flesh. That would seem unlikely. To use a mechanical term, the turnover in material in the human body is such that, at the end of an average life, the organism will have used many times the amount of material needed for the fabrication of one body.

And then there is the question of the constitution of matter. The solidest stone is ultimately fashioned of elusive energy particles. So when we pass beyond this realm of space and time and our bodies have reached their ultimate dissolution, it would seem that God would have at his disposal pure energy from which to reconstitute our bodies.

The average human being, however, does not think of such possibilities; he thinks of the body he now has. Christian devotion has tended to take this unsophisticated approach. In its extreme form I suppose it is best seen in the famous Capuchin Catacombs of Rome where the mummified, un-buried, religiously robed bodies or skeletons of long-departed monks wait patiently for the last day.

The elaborate embalming procedures of modern Western society are based at least partly on respect for the remains, although health laws certainly play their part. The very existence of cemeteries, tombs, and grave markers attests to a natural human reverence for the dead. I can remember Sister telling us in grade school that China was poverty-stricken because it had so many well-tended cemeteries that good, straight railroads could not be built. Maybe, maybe not. But even around New York City the enormous burial grounds that you pass on the way to the airport show the prevalence of this human instinct.

I think it would be safe to say that people who have this respect for the dead are people who believe in God. Some of those who do not believe nevertheless use death and burial symbolically. I am not too sure of its truth, but I have heard the story that the French statesman of the 1st World War, Clemenceau, insisted on being buried in a standing position. Apparently he meant that this resumption of the standing position was the only one he expected for his body, a kind of joke or play on the word *resurrection*.

In the last century, in the days of the "freethinkers," cremation was a symbol of the same kind for them. Somehow the immediate fiery return of the body to its elements symbolized for them man's identity with the material earth better than the Christian "dust to dust" and the slower process of burial. This pagan or materialistic symbolism is generally acknowledged to be the source of the Church's previous prohibition of cremation (Canon 1203), although certainly the expectation of resurrection entered into it.

But the modern popularity of cremation arises not so much from denial of God or immortality as from the ordinary pressures of life. Those who spend time convincing others of the universal feasibility of cremation say we are running out of space for cemeteries. In many modern cities there is truth in the statement, although I have read that all living and dead members of the human race so far could be contained in one cubic mile of space, a minute percentage of the earth's volume. Other considerations are those of expense, though again the saving is minor.

Funerals, despite the cliche, "This is the only time we relatives see each other any more," are no longer social occasions. Obviously no one any longer has time for the leisurely all-night wake afforded our fathers and grandfathers.

There is no question but that cremation and "donation to science" is the coming fashion in disposal of the dead. In England a few years ago more than 55% of all deceased were cremated, and the percentage has surely increased since then.

Besides the inclinations to save space, money, and time by cremation, many famous people, romantically or pantheistically inclined, have requested that their ashes be spread over the place they loved most in life, or the sea or the mountains or the desert. Now all these factors have considerable, not to say determining force in the decision for cremation on the part of pagans. But, Ronny, I don't think they completely outmode the traditional Catholic practice.

When I was chaplain at the county hospital, I dutifully went along with the resident doctors on the matter of autopsies. That is, when the survivors of a medically unsolved death would refuse the routine request for an autopsy, the doctors would ask me to ask them again. I would, but my heart wasn't in it and I can't remember ever changing a decision. Of course, an autopsy is not the same as cremation, but the same sense of reverence for the human remains is involved. Nowadays if the request was for organs for transplant I suppose in special cases I could work up more enthusiasm. But I'm still glad I don't have such problems anymore.

In the face of cold scientific reason, it still seems to me that I will keep bodily integrity and identity if I eventually attain that glorious risen body St. Thomas Aquinas writes about (everybody a perfect 30 years old, constant physical ecstasy, freedom from the limitations of space and time: all in participation in the Beatific Vision).

I suppose the beautiful words of the *In Paradisum* ("May the angels lead thee into paradise, may the martyrs receive thee at the coming") can be just as appropriate in the crematory as in the church. They will not, though, ever be as consoling to me as when they accompany the slow procession with the casket down the center aisle, even though they are followed by the devoted local soprano quavering "Nearer My God to Thee." The difference is in the reverence of an act designed to preserve instead of destroy the human remains.

Your letter, Ronny, didn't say why you felt a desire to be cremated. Any consideration of a private nature can now justify a decision for cremation. But the Instruction of May 8,

1963, encourages Catholics to follow the "old and better" custom of burial. That is the "official" and, may I add, my personal, attitude.

The Bible

THE QUESTION:

I am a 16-year-old junior, attending a Catholic high school.
In grammar school, I was taught to believe that the Bible and
all its stories were recorded fact and were to be believed.
However, in the past three years I have been told by my
theology teachers (two of them Sisters) that the Bible is not
fact, merely stories that deliver a moral. Although these
teachers did explain that Christ's life on earth was recorded
history, they said the way events are presented in the New
Testament are exaggerations of the truth. Are they?
Kathy S.

THE ANSWER:

No. But I think, Kathy, that I will have to restate your
question, and I hope I get it right. You are asking not only
"Why did some teachers tell me one thing and others another?"
but also "Which teachers are right?"

On the basis of exact quotes from your letter I would have to
say that both sets of teachers are wrong and thus mess up the
whole discussion a little more. Taking you at your written
word, one set of teachers taught you "the Bible and all its
stories were recorded fact" and the other set of teachers taught
you "the Bible was not fact." Now unless all of these teachers
were very high up in the tree, they did not come out as flatly as
that. At least I don't think so. The first set must have known
that there are poems and parables in the Bible, and the second
set must have known that there are historical books in the Bible
well-supported by secular documents and archeological
studies. But, Kathy, you did very intelligently catch the gist of
two sides of a great continuing discussion and you made simple

— at least in the asking — the question "Is the Bible true or false?"

Some people insist the Bible is false because it says a fish swallowed Jonah when no fish in the Mediterranean Sea has a gullet larger than six inches. Literal interpreters of the Bible will say there was at least one fish that big because it says so in the Bible. From this type of argument we have to back away immediately. It is the kind of ignorant clashing by night that the Church has always tried to avoid. We at *Catholic Digest* once had a letter from a lady Jehovah Witness denouncing us for something we said in favor of Christmas trees. She pointed out the passage in Jeremiah (10:3,4) "decked it (a tree) with silver and gold"; applied to the passage to the modern Christmas tree (it referred to making wooden idols); and accused us of false religion.

You see, Kathy, when you sit there with that large Bible in your lap it is not an easy thing to get the truth of it. Its parts were written in ancient times, in cultures differing from ours as Brooklyn differs from Babylonia. It was written in various languages, none of them the modern English you and I most easily understand. Even if you trust the translator and he is not trying to shade the meanings to support his own convictions, no translator can do more than paraphrase a poem. Shades of irony and sarcasm may escape him. He cannot possibly catch and transmit the meaning of references to persons, events, political and religious circumstances, mentioned nowhere else in all the world's literature. Sometimes the part of the Bible you are reading has been translated through several languages before coming to you in English and each translator has made his guesses and perhaps had his eye wiped by the next interpreter.

Within a single language the text has often been copied and copies made from copies. Sometimes what the scribe meant for an explanation gets copied into the texts. Sometimes by mistake, he leaves something out. Now, none of this destroys the validity of the Bible, but you will have to admit that trying to read it with *full* comprehension would be as difficult as getting the full force of Shakespearian tragedy in a German dialect translation. Everyone concerned in the translation has done his best, but you just do not have the original. The point of my saying all this is to show the perils of literal interpretations — and offhand decisions that the Bible is false.

It is very easy to come across a text or phrase in the Bible which reassuringly confirms some belief you already have and to take the phrase as proof of the belief. From the time I was a small child, I lisped the Hail Mary with its praise, "full of grace." As a priest for many years on the Feast of the Assumption I started from "full of grace," and explained in my sermons to the people that if she were *full* of grace, there was, so to speak, no room for sin in the Blessed Mother; that no sin meant no corruption of the body (one of the penalties of original sin), and hence the assumption of her body into heaven upon her death.

All that I said was true, and faithful Catholics, among whom I want to be numbered, believed it then and still believe it. But now we believe it even though there is a new translation of the Bible in which Mary is declared by the angel not to be "full of grace" but only "singularly favored." The new translation does not destroy the doctrine of the Assumption, but it does eliminate what I thought was a good argument from Scripture for it. Of course, I had the customary dark suspicions of translators inserting their prejudices into the Scriptures. But as a matter of fact my personal knowledge of the language in which the angel spoke is limited, and I cannot confute the new translation. So my reminiscence should be a warning to you, Kathy, against reading your own convictions into the text of Scripture.

So, if you are still sitting there with a big Bible in your lap, Kathy, you can be sure that almost any meaning you discover there for yourself may be subject to correction by people who know more about the text than you do, and that you should be cautious in jumping to conclusions. But a bigger problem, and I think here we are getting closer to what you had in mind in your question, is that even if by some miracle of scholarship we

could be sure we had the exact text as it was first penned by the
original human author, we would still have the task of
determining what the author *meant*. Sounds silly, but it's true.

You see, the way you express things depends upon what you
are expressing. When you are chatting with your friends, you
are likely to use the latest slang. Giving the valedictory address
at your high school, you skip the slang and keep your speech
solemn. In written matters there would be similar differences
between a letter to a chum and an application for a job. The
authors of the various books and parts of the Bible didn't have
so free a choice of styles and forms in which to write. In Old
Testament days, the languages were not as full of abstract
words as our modern tongues. Generally, even when the
authors were trying to communicate abstract truths, they used
the story form for which the words came easily. Also,
generally, they were very good story tellers.

Noah and the Flood, Jonah and the Whale, Judith and
Holofernes are such good stories that the question as to
whether they were written to record things that in fact
happened or written to preserve entertaining folk tales
becomes secondary. They fit very neatly into the times and
places of their origins and in so doing show they have *meanings*
beyond the bare story. Thus the Noah story means that God
punishes sin and rewards obedience; the full Jonah story means
that the Jews should share their religious truth with the
Gentiles; the Judith story means that the weak Jewish people
should not give up hope of final victory over their powerful
oppressors.

Considering that the day of the paperback had not yet
arrived and that there was no financial or other advantage in
publishing either fiction or fact it becomes most probable the
stories were written to teach lessons. Taken as plain history,
they have obviously mistaken details. Noah's ark could not
have been big enough to hold a pair each of all the animal
species on earth. Nineveh could not have been all that big,
either. (In the story it took Jonah three days to walk across it.)
Nabuchodonosor, Holofernes's monarch, was never king of

Assyria as the story says he was. But, of course, if the stories
were told only to teach religious lessons, the problem of their
scientific or historical accuracy vanishes. This kind of explanation is not too hard to follow and should be rather easy to
accept as long as we are talking about certain Old Testament
books. It is when we come to the life and works of Christ that
we have to dig just a little deeper into what authors *meant*.

One of the most disturbing terms the average casual Bible
student runs into is the word *myth*. Only 50 years ago its
meaning was confined to pagan and ancient tales which
wondrously accounted for the world as the ancients knew it.
Thunder was the voice of Jove and so on. Then, in the wave of
new archeological and linguistic knowledge, the word *myth*
was increasingly applied to the Jewish and Christian stories in
the Bible. Scholars became able to translate ancient inscriptions that had been indecipherable. This ability gave them
better understanding of equivalent passages in the Bible. It
became apparent, for instance, that the story of the Flood was
not unique to Hebrew Scriptures but was found in several
other and earlier cultures. *Myth* was the reasonable term to use
when you had to write about this whole class of stories. It was
not intended in the use of the *myth* to imply that the Jewish and
Christian stories were untrue. But that certainly is what it
sounds like to the average casual Bible student.

Kathy, if this second set of teachers you had really said what
you said they said, it was words like *myth* that made them say
it. They must have kept on thinking of a myth as a false tale,
rather than as a class of literature as the competent Bible
scholars did. Such a mistake can be destructive of Christian
faith if you are going to call the Bible passages about the
miracles of Christ *myths* without having the scholars' classification in mind. Pagan literature is full of stories about dying
gods and their return to life. The stories are poetic per-
sonalizations of the dying, dormant, renewing, and flourishing
seasons of the year. The question is whether that is all the story
of Christ's death and resurrection means.

At this point we should remember, Kathy, that the chief

difficulty in understanding the Bible is finding out what the author meant. To stay only on the subject of death and resurrection: Did the author of the Gospel mean to personalize the passing seasons with the story of Jesus Christ? Did the authors of the pagan tales mean that such characters as Tammuz historically lived, died, and lived again? I would say No to both questions.

It is all right to identify some of the stories of the Bible as being forms of literature contrived to teach abstract religious truths, but there is no need to say that all stories in the Bible have that purpose. Some certainly could have the simpler purpose of recording historical facts for posterity. All we have to ask is "What did the authors mean?"

Millions of faithful Christians have believed that the Gospel authors meant to say that the Son of God came down from heaven, died for our sins, and rose from the dead in proof of his claims. Other millions of people have not believed, never heard the story, or, having heard it, did not want to be bothered with it.

But the question of faith was independent of written Gospel in the first years of Christianity. There wasn't any New Testament yet. Now, as then, people may find the means of salvation without being experts in Biblical literary forms, without having the original or perfectly corrected texts. Our faith is contained in the Bible and practically, I suppose, the Church without it would have had a much more difficult time preserving the original faith. But we need not shiver and shake in the fear that scholars will prove parts, or all of the Bible false. They can prove at most that we may have misread the meaning of the authors, but not that we have misread the meaning of the Author. The ultimate fear — that the enemies of the Bible may disprove its historical validity — can never by ours. It is part of our faith that that can never be done.

So after all, Kathy, I may have answered your question in my first two paragraphs. There are various forms of literature in the Bible: parables, poems, and myths, but there is no reason to exclude honest history. In the Catholic view, the more knowledge we acquire about the myths, the surer we can be of the history. In God's ancient providence, the myths were written to uphold the history.

Interfaith Communion

THE LETTER:

I recently met a young Catholic student (age 20) who told me this touching story. She and a group of non-Catholics attended a week-end retreat. During subsequent months, a close relationship developed in this group which included a desire by non-Catholics to attend Mass.

Several of the non-Catholics asked their Catholic friend if they could receive Communion. The young girl's love for her friends was such, that, after telling them she didn't think it was possible, she became so sad she began to cry and had to leave the service.

My question: Is there any way these beautiful youngsters can receive Communion without formally embracing the Catholic faith? What would Jesus have done if He saw this yearning?

J.M., M.D.

THE ANSWER:

Doctor, I dislike any suggestion of repartee in connection with a question that involves the Holy Name, but I think the Lord would have told them to go and take instruction, join the Catholic Church, and make their First Communion according to standard operating procedure.

A good deal of the interest in intercommunion, meaning the reception of the Eucharist in one denomination by members of another, comes, as it seems to me your question comes, from an excess of sentiment, as distinguished from sound Eucharistic devotion. I frankly confess, that I (long ago and far away) in preparing children for First Communion did my best to instill sentimental piety. I still do not think it an entirely misbegotten emotion. If it is instilled before the age of adolescent skepticism, it stays with a person an incredibly long time.

I know this because my wearing of the Roman collar on trains and planes used to attract many apparently lonesome fellow travelers who sometimes boozily, but often just dreamily, would confide that the day of their First Communion had been the happiest of their lives. Often their stories went on into details of rather sordid lives and too often their First Communions were among a total of very few Communions. But to each of them the memory of First Communion came like an incense-bearing breeze from Heaven.

How could it be otherwise? *Communion,* the word itself, is a synonym for *love,* the most blessed of all emotions. But love, sentiment, and sentimentality shade into one another so subtly that the question "Which is which?" arises in the discussion of nearly every act of devotion toward God, including Holy Communion.

Religious thought, like religious writing, extends from the aridities of theological footnotes to the sopping-wet sentimentalities of the amateur hymn writer. Some of the divisions in the Christian faith have arisen over the question of which end of this wick should be clipped off. Ronald Knox quotes an example of the wet end, telling us how among the members of the Church of the Brethren (1746 A.D.) the wound in our Lord's heart came to be described as "the dearest little opening of the sacred, precious and thousand times beautiful little side." And I suppose Teilhard de Chardin could represent the dry end: ". . . in the cosmos system there would appear to be no structural reason for localizing and delimiting within the whole sphere of existence and action of each individual center considered on its own." In solving the difficulties of intercommunion, truth and reason are found between the extremes of loveless abstraction and brainless pietisms.

Of intercommunion, whether motivated by brain power or love power, I think the official Roman Catholic Church is unready to approve, though the truth is that under certain very specific conditions she does allow the reception of Communion by persons who have not gone through the ceremony of

"formally embracing the Catholic faith." This permission is
found not in any formal, clearly infallible pronouncement
addressed to the whole world by the Holy Father, but only in
an "Instruction on who may be permitted to Eucharistic
Communion" issued by the Secretariat Promoting Christian
Unity, the members of which, understandably, are in favor of
stirring up a little action. But even they insist that the outsider:
1) believe the same things about the sacrament that the
Catholic Church does; 2) be in a state of "urgent necessity"; 3)
be unable to have recourse to his own minister; 4) ask for the
sacrament spontaneously, not at the prompting of a Catholic.

Personally, I can't bring to mind any such combination of
person and circumstances in all my wide experience. It would
seem to me this person would on these terms be on the brink of
converting to the Catholic faith anyway. The proposed
recipient would have to be a baptized person, well-instructed in
the Catholic faith, ready to obey the Catholic bishop, in
physical or spiritual danger, cut off from his co-religionists,
and in possession of an extraordinary actual grace.

Obviously, Doctor, this concoction of legalisms would not
permit your friendly young representatives of a non-Catholic
faith to receive Communion at a Catholic Mass. The young
Catholic girl of your letter was right in her judgment, if a little
sentimental in her reaction.

It would even seem that the commission members were
trying to prevent, rather than promote, intercommunion. Of
course, other denominations are openly opposed to it. The
Church Council of the American Lutheran Church, in a
statement in 1971, said that no Lutheran should receive
Communion in a Catholic church even if he is invited by the
priest in charge. The statement points out the implications of
such Communion, including that of submission to the local
Catholic bishop and the Pope.

I suppose that a detached atheist would say that the
spokesmen in both Churches were probably jealous of their
own authority. But if he were logical as well as detached, he
could see that both authorities were, paradoxically, promoting

unity. The disobedient (those that receive Communion in another denomination with no one's permission) make up a kind of third force and surely there is less unity in a division into three parties than there is into two.

You see, Doctor, the Eucharist has always been a symbol of unity not only in love but also in belief and discipline. I don't mean to parallel the following situation with the one you described, but let me tell you about the worst violation of this principle I can remember.

I was Sunday assistant in a parish that was unhappily to witness the defection of all three co-pastors. Among the outrages they perpetrated before leaving their posts was a Sunday evening Mass with music by a hired all-Baptist combo: trumpet, drums, and piano in the sanctuary.

Good feeling ran high and at Communion time the celebrant went first to the musicians, who were in the midst of a selection. Of course, this celebrant expected them to break off their tune only momentarily to receive the Eucharist. But he was, nevertheless, foiled in his intentions when they pursed their mouths and shook their heads like babies refusing food, with him like an anxious mother trying to force acceptance, even pushing the trumpet from the trumpeter's lips. It might have been that the musicians just felt too busy at the moment, but I like to think that as good Baptists they understood the symbolism of the Eucharist, unity of love, *belief,* and *discipline,* better than the celebrant.

So, Doctor, while I take no exception at all to your feelings in what is really a delicate religious matter, I do think that this conception of the Eucharist as a symbol of unity of belief and discipline, as well as of love, is important. When you use the Eucharist to promote unity of belief rather than to symbolize, by restricting participation, a unity already achieved, you are abusing the symbolism. As for unity of discipline, the Lutheran 1971 statement only echoes what the Secretariat Promoting Christian Unity said. Reception of Communion in the Catholic Church means identifying yourself with a group bound to obedience to the Catholic bishop named in the Eucharistic prayer.

The proclamation of this symbolism goes back to the early centuries when the Church was converting the Roman world. The Eucharist was only for the baptised, who had been instructed in its meanings. The catechumens, those under instruction, were allowed to attend only the first part of the Eucharistic assembly. They heard the Liturgy of the word, and were then dismissed. Only the confirmed faithful could stay for the offering of the Sacrifice and reception of the Body and Blood of Christ.

There were, of course, practical as well as symbolic reasons for this exclusion. In the days of the persecutions, each catechumen had to have a sponsor, not only for future guidance in the Faith, as babies now have a sponsor at their Baptisms, but to exclude spies seeking the secrets which underground Christians needed to keep for survival in that hostile society. Only after a trial period were converts admitted to the Eucharistic celebration, the core and substance of the Christian faith and life.

It seems clear that well-intentioned Christians should not offer the Catholic Church their allegiance in the Eucharistic sign of unity and obedience, since they do not believe as we do, not want to obey the same authorities that we do. The Church is not denying them anything, only insisting on rational behavior.

Doctor, in these popular-level articles, I can really give only the gist of the documents covering this matter of intercommunion. To fill in, one should read the Vatican II *Constitution on the Sacred Liturgy* (1964), the *Decree on Ecumenism* (1965) and the Papal encyclical, *Mysterium Fidei* (1965). For 1975 material, read page 584 of the Seabury edition of the *Common Cathechism,* the work of an international team of about 40 equally represented Protestant and Catholic theologians: "... numerous Christians in both Churches regard any form of intercommunion or concelebration as dishonest, while the leadership of both Churches continue up to the present to repudiate every experiment in this direction ...."

On the Catholic side the higher powers leave the local bishop with authority only to apply the four points made above. He cannot interpret them, for instance, to see in a golden wedding anniversary or in an interfaith marriage, the "urgent necessity" required by the Instruction for the giving of the Catholic Eucharist to a person who has not "formally embraced" the Catholic faith.

Doctor, after my writing all this, I can see you reading it and, at this point, leaning back, stroking your chin, and protesting. You quite possibly know as much about all this legislation as I do, and look on me as one who has missed your point. You are not overly sentimental, you are simply interested in increasing the love of people for each other and for the Blessed Sacrament, and in a general increase of understanding. Your point, you might reiterate, was to be done with all this petty legislation and get on with the fuller message of the Gospel.

Well, I still cannot go along with you. But I have just had an insight that might bear on the whole question. You are thinking of the Eucharist as the sacrament of love, the one in which God expressed his love for us and we our love for Him. This I agree with, but in the Gospel of John, chapter 6, our Lord has promised the Eucharist, and some of the disciples found the saying hard and walked no more with Him. Jesus did not call them back.

This would seem to mean that though the sacrament was to be one of love, it was not necessarily for everyone. This is the foundation of all the bothersome legislation of the Church upon the Eucharist.

The sacrament of universal invitation for which you seem to be groping is not the Eucharist, but Baptism. That is not only open to all who believe, but can even be administered validly by those who do not believe. Again the legalist puts in his point that the pagan, Mohammedan, Jew, or even atheist who baptizes must intend to do what the Church intends. But despite this restriction on the minister, Baptism is the most ecumenical of the sacraments and the symbol of God's universal invitation.

People understand this. I remember an apostate priest who

appeared on a TV talk program some years ago who had a
hearty chuckle about what people were doing to his children.
Many of his still-Catholic lay friends of former years would
visit him, and in the course of the visit somehow entice the pre-
kindergarten kids into the kitchen, hold their heads under the
running faucet, and pronounce the holy words of Baptism. The
apostate said so many people did this that the kids got used to it
and didn't even try to squirm away. The good lay people were, I
suppose, somewhat misguided. The story about them affords
only tempered amusement, but it illustrates their belief that
God's love and grace should be thrust on people be they
unknowing or even unwilling.

I go unhorrified at this bestowal of Baptism, because the
people were acting out its symbolism of universal invitation. I
remain horrified at the priest who tried to force Communion
on the unwilling Baptists because he was not acting out the full
symbolism of unity of love, belief, and discipline.

But let me try to get back, Doctor, to the tone of your really
tender and sincere letter. To be even argumentative when
talking about the love of God is a kind of contradiction. Let me
say that as I read your letter, the weeping Margaret of the
Hopkins poem came to mind. Little Margaret, as you remember, wept at the sight of the falling leaves and the passing
of summer. She is told in the last two lines of the poem:

> It is a blight man was born for
> It is Margaret you mourn for

In other words, there was some question as to what she was
really crying about. Could it be that the girl in your letter wept
not only because her dear friends could not receive the
Eucharist she herself loved, but also because there was between
her and them no perfect union of love and belief?